THE NORWEGIAN-AMERICAN HISTORICAL ASSOCIATION

LAWRENCE O. HAUGE, *President*

NORWEGIAN-
AMERICAN
STUDIES

Volume 30

1985

The Norwegian-American Historical Association

NORTHFIELD · MINNESOTA

Printed in the United States of America
at the Colwell/North Central inc.,
St. Paul, Minnesota

To the Memory of Peter A. Munch

Preface

THE SCENERY of Alaska and the west coast of the mainland United States is strongly reminiscent of the coastal districts of Norway. Many Norwegians were attracted to these parts of the continent; the landscape, as well as familiar modes of livelihood in lumbering and fishing, added to the region's appeal. Some Norwegians moved there from their settlements in the Midwest and others migrated to the area directly from Norway. It might be claimed that they transferred a Norwegian coastal culture to the Pacific coast. This volume of *Norwegian-American Studies*, the thirtieth in the series, makes evident the rich opportunity for scholarly research that Norwegian settlement in the Far West provides; six of the nine articles in the collection are devoted to this topic.

In her essay, Patsy Adams Hegstad identifies the motivating forces for Scandinavian migration to Seattle and the Puget Sound area in general. These included topographical and climatic conditions, employment possibilities, and active recruitment by economic interests. But also important were family connections and the emergence of immigrant social and cultural institutions. Rangvald Kvelstad reveals similar pull factors in his sympathetic account of Norwegian pioneers in western Washington: a Norwegian community grew up on the Kitsap peninsula with the little town of Poulsbo as its natural center.

There is a sense of adventure in Kenneth O. Bjork's colorful essay on Norwegians in Alaska. They worked, to be sure, to develop bountiful forest and fishing resources. Their wandering northward in large numbers was, however, associated with the discovery of gold and the prospects of easy riches in the gold fields of Alaska and the Klondike. Interwoven in this intriguing tale is an attempt marred by greed and scandal to introduce domestic reindeer from Norway into Alaska. Sverre Arestad surveys Norwegian fishing enterprise on the Pacific coast, a major branch of the economy in which Norwegians from around the turn of the century constituted a dominant element. Arestad, however, moderates the common view of their role in the founding years.

The lead article by Lloyd Hustvedt profiles the shifting fortunes of a Norwegian-American labor leader, O.A. Tveitmoe. Tveitmoe was a product of radical reform currents at the close of the last century; he pursued his socialist ideology and political ambition in California. The article is highly suggestive of the volatile situation in which organized labor strove to gain a voice. World War I and the victory for Bolshevism in Russia adversely affected the entire American left, the progressive camp as well as the socialist. Many earlier progressives became avidly anti-radical. In this connection, Terje I. Leiren discusses the political career of Seattle mayor Ole Hanson, who began as a progressive but in 1919 joined the crusade against the Reds. Taking into account Hanson's Norwegian immigrant background, Leiren analyzes his change of allegiance.

Larry Emil Scott's contribution on the poetry of Agnes Mathilde Wergeland might properly be considered together with the articles on the Far West. She was a professor of history at the state university in Laramie, Wyoming. But the author's interest is primarily in Wergeland's inner life as reflected in her sensitive and revealing verse, and he thinks of her as among the finest of the Norwegian-American poets. James S. Hamre presents the educational philosophies of three prominent Norwegian-American defenders of the academies — secondary schools — established by Norwegian Lutheran churches. Hamre concludes that the views of these men represented a minority position within the immigrant community, a fact that contributed to the demise of the academy movement. Claire Selkurt investigates the material culture of Luther Valley, a pioneer Norwegian settlement in southern Wisconsin, and shows the persistence of certain Norwegian traditions in architecture and in furniture-making. Simultaneously there was a broader movement toward adopting prevailing American styles in both forms and materials.

C.A. Clausen continues his listing of recent publications in the field of immigration, assisted for Norwegian titles by Johanna Barstad, librarian in the university library in Oslo. Charlotte Jacobson describes new acquisitions in the Association's archives. In preparing this volume, I have enjoyed the gracious assistance of our board member Terje I. Leiren, who initially helped to plan the volume and solicited articles from west-coast authors. It remains to acknowledge with thankful appreciation the kindly services of Mary R. Hove, my competent and dedicated assistant in the editorial process. Her professional skills and genial cooperation are constant resources.

ODD S. LOVOLL

St. Olaf College

Contents

NORWEGIAN-AMERICAN STUDIES

Volume 30

by LLOYD HUSTVEDT

1   *O. A. Tveitmoe: Labor Leader*

THE FUTURE looked grim for Olaf Anders Tveitmoe on April 16, 1894, as he stood in the courtroom in Red Wing, Minnesota, and heard the district judge, W. C. Williston, sentence him to eighteen months of hard labor at the Stillwater State Prison. He appeared alone and no one spoke on his behalf. He was twenty-eight years old, intelligent, idealistic, married and the father of two children. He was six feet tall, had sandy hair and slate blue eyes, and despite his powerful-looking frame he weighed only one hundred fifty-five pounds.[1]

Born in Valdres, Norway, December 7, 1865, Tveitmoe came in 1882 to the Holden community in Goodhue county, Minnesota, where he worked as a farmhand.[2] Because he had received some secondary education in Vestre Slidre, Valdres, he was placed in the second year of a three-year preparatory program when he entered St. Olaf's School (later St. Olaf College) in the fall of 1886. Following the classical line of study he did fairly well, with average scores of 92 and 89 respectively for his two years of academy work. He attended only thirty weeks of a thirty-six-week term as a college freshman, which perhaps explains why his

3

average dropped to 77. This concluded Tveitmoe's formal education.[3]

Tveitmoe may have helped to found the *Manitou Messenger*, the St. Olaf College student newspaper, in 1887. In all events he functioned as its first business manager and later became exchange editor, which involved selecting excerpts from many sources. He revealed a wide range of reading. Only one article in the *Messenger, Den norske bonde* (The Norwegian Farmer) is known to have been written by Tveitmoe. For an academy student it is ably written, in Norwegian, with a certain poetic flair. Assisted by hindsight, one can see that his main points have importance: The Norwegian rural folk owed their cultural progress, first, to their adoption of Christianity; second, to their sustained struggle for independence; and third, to their gradual acceptance of enlightenment. Much, however, remained to be accomplished in the last-mentioned category.[4]

After leaving St. Olaf's School in the spring of 1889, Tveitmoe married Ingeborg Ødegaard, who had also emigrated from Valdres in 1882. A son, the first of six children, was born on May 25, 1891.[5] Life remained unsettled. He continued doing farm work, taught in a Norwegian religion school, and served a brief stint as postmaster at Sogn, a small country store in Warsaw township, Goodhue county. More important, he turned his energies to the Farmers' Alliance movement, and for the better part of a year served as county lecturer for that cause. Late in September, 1892, he bought from Peter M. Ringdal, a Populist political aspirant, a share in the *Tribune*, a Farmers' Alliance newspaper in Crookston, Minnesota.[6] Tveitmoe had little or no money, but Ringdal agreed to accept notes if backed by collateral. Either as total or partial payment, Tveitmoe gave Ringdal a promissory note for $200, dated October 1, 1892, due one year later, at eight percent interest. The note was countersigned by K. K. Hougo, a Leon township farmer of moderate means and an acquaintance if not a friend of Tveitmoe. Tveitmoe became editor and secretary of the Tribune Publishing Company, a position for which he was hardly ready. His English was crude, his tone harsh and caustic, and his language perhaps even libelous when he went after those he felt had betrayed the party. Then without explanation Tveitmoe's name was removed from the *Tribune*'s masthead for January 31, 1893. After a few months, he began to work for *Normanden*, a Norwegian newspaper in Grand Forks, North Dakota. Later the *Tribune* went over to new owners with promises of better management and a more moderate tone.

Then something unexpected happened. A few months after Ringdal received Tveitmoe's note, he sold it at a discount to the Citizens State Bank in Cannon Falls, Minnesota, the very bank where K. K. Hougo did his banking. When Hougo was informed about this transaction, he denied ever signing the note. Exactly what transpired later is not known, but more than a year passed before Tveitmoe was indicted, on March 15, 1894, for "forgery in the second degree." The Goodhue county sheriff apprehended him a week later. His plea was "not guilty." A jury trial held on March 31, which could not have lasted much over an hour, produced no witnesses for the defense and three witnesses for the prosecution: Hougo, Ringdal, and H. A. Scriver of the Citizens State Bank. J. C. McClure, Red Wing's city attorney, defended Tveitmoe, but there was no defense. The jury found him guilty as charged. A motion for a new trial was denied, but a request for a twenty-day stay was granted. He entered Stillwater Prison on April 20.[7]

Certain that he could redeem the note when the time came, Tveitmoe had acted recklessly. It is strange that

5

O. A. Tveitmoe (1865–1923), ca. 1907.

no one came to his aid. Norwegians in Goodhue county were not always kind to each other, but as a rule they did not let their own go to prison if they could prevent it. Nearby was a solid pocket of settlers from Valdres who could have helped. No mention was made at the trial whether restitution had been or could be made for the note. The fact that Tveitmoe had moved to another state may be an explanation. It is possible that he sought no help. Later in life he declared that since boyhood his credo had been "never to ask for bread from a friend, and never to beg for mercy from an enemy." Ultimately some external support must have entered the picture; Governor Knute Nelson granted him a pardon on December 19, 1894. Tveitmoe returned to his family in Grand Forks.[8]

All was quiet until June 22, 1897. As secretary for a planned cooperative colony, named Ny Hardanger, to be located near Toledo, Oregon, Tveitmoe appealed in *Rodhuggeren* (The Radical), of Fergus Falls, Minnesota, for participants. Using the language of the Populists, he called upon day-slaves, factory drudges, exhausted farmers, and all with will and courage to join the venture. The colony would operate on the utopian principles of John Ruskin; members would be required to invest $500, and an unnamed person had provided a seed fund of $3,000. He closed by asserting that socialism "can work." He anticipated opposition and he was right.

Waldemar Ager, writing for *Reform*, in Eau Claire, Wisconsin, picked up the cudgel. Rather than attacking the cooperative plan, he focused on Tveitmoe's dreary picture of the working man. Ager, who classified himself as a working man, declared that his experiences had been pleasant, and he dismissed Tveitmoe as a "calamity howler." Ager's article unleashed heated responses from many sources both in support and in opposition. Ager, unduly unkind in his polemic, ultimately alluded to Tveitmoe's past. The debate ended when S. Romtvedt from Windom, Minnesota, president of the proposed colony, stepped in with a sober article, declaring that such cooperative enterprises had enough problems without adding newspaper feuds. Tveitmoe, he stated, had been asked to step down as secretary until an investigation could be made.[9] At this time or shortly thereafter, Tveitmoe moved to Toledo with his family, which had grown to three children. A fourth child, a daughter, was born at Toledo, December 31, 1897. No information is available as to the outcome of Ny Hardanger except that it failed. Some time in 1898, Tveitmoe moved to San Francisco where in a short period of time he rose to power and high position in the labor movement.

San Francisco was rapidly becoming the most unionized city in the nation when Tveitmoe arrived in 1898. The total number of union members in California in 1902 was listed at 67,500, and 45,000 of these were in San Francisco alone. Los Angeles, for example, had fewer than 5,000. The depression of the early 1890s had given way to a much improved economy because of the war in the Philippines, the gold rush in Alaska, increased trade with the Orient, development of California oil, and irrigation in the Imperial Valley. Ironically enough the earthquake disaster of 1906 proved to be a blessing for labor, making necessary the rebuilding of large sections of the city. San Francisco's remoteness from other large urban centers also favored the unions in their rise to power. There was no nearby supply of labor from the outside in the event of industrial disputes.[10]

There were three central labor bodies in San Francisco in 1898: the San Francisco Waterfront Federation, the San Francisco Labor Council, and the San Francisco Building Trades Council. The Labor Council, formed in 1892, replaced two earlier clashing councils which had voluntarily disbanded to clear the way for one organization. The need for a separate federation for the building trades continued to be felt, however, and in February,

1896, a permanent organization was effected by seven unions — carpenters, painters, decorators, and others — representing 4,000 members. By the summer of 1901 the Council had grown to thirty-six component unions with 15,000 members. In theory the Building Trades Council was at its inception a subordinate body of the Labor Council. In fact some building trades unions held membership in both organizations. In practice, however, the Building Trades Council became increasingly independent and ultimately one of the most powerful central bodies of its kind in the country. Two men helped to make it so: Patrick Henry McCarthy and Olaf Tveitmoe.

P. H. McCarthy had helped to organize the Building Trades Council in 1896, but did not become its president until July, 1898. At this time Tveitmoe was working as a cement worker's helper. The cement workers were organized in June, 1899. Tveitmoe became this union's first secretary and later its president. The new union enjoyed astonishing success. Within three months it had more than 200 members and had succeeded in increasing wages from $2.50 to $4 per day and reducing hours from ten and twelve to eight.[11] Tveitmoe's precise role in this success is not known, but in light of what followed it must have attracted the attention of McCarthy and other leaders. When the Building Trades Council started its own newspaper, *Organized Labor*, first issued on February 3, 1900, Tveitmoe became its editor. The following July he was elected recording and corresponding secretary of the Council. Because the proceedings of the weekly Council meetings were carried in *Organized Labor*, his election to this office may have had a practical side, yet it further concentrated power into the hands of these two men. McCarthy and Tveitmoe then took the major initiative in forming the state Building Trades Council in 1901, which in time built to an affiliation of nineteen local councils organized on the county level. McCarthy became president of this state federation and Tveitmoe became its general secretary, positions they both held until 1922. They ruled, then, not only over the strongest of the local councils but over everything called building trades in California.

P. H. McCarthy, referred to unflatteringly in some circles as Pin Head McCarthy, was born in Ireland, March 17, 1861. Having learned the carpenter's trade he, like Tveitmoe, came to the United States at the age of seventeen. He helped organize the National Brotherhood of Carpenters and Joiners in Chicago before going to San Francisco in 1886. In a short time he became president of the Carpenters Union, Local 22, the largest in San Francisco. Much interested in local government, he helped to draft a new charter for San Francisco in 1900, and later served on the city Civil Service Commission. He was elected mayor of San Francisco in 1909, but was defeated in 1911, and again in 1915. Rumor had it that he aspired to become governor.

McCarthy and Tveitmoe complemented each other in beneficial ways. McCarthy was more of a public figure, but within the rank and file of labor itself Tveitmoe was equally conspicuous. The boundaries between personal ambition and dedication to the cause could sometimes be blurred in the case of McCarthy; with some justice it was thought that he aimed to "rule or ruin." On the other hand, Tveitmoe, if he did not exactly shun the limelight, never actively sought it. McCarthy may have been the more practical of the two in matters of labor organization and strategy, but also the narrower in vision in that he focused to a selfish degree on the interests of the building trades. Tveitmoe, much more the philosopher, had a global concern for working men, skilled and unskilled alike. As far as labor leaders go, however, they were both conservative in practice. They headed the elite unions where pride in skilled workmanship was an honored tradition.

How could Tveitmoe, new to the ranks of labor, attain high office overnight among the most skilled of workers? A number of reasons can be cited. The higher echelons of expanding labor needed men with education and an ability to write. Later scattered references indicate that some may have had an exaggerated picture of Tveitmoe in this respect: He had come from a wealthy and prominent family in Norway; he had received higher education both in his homeland and in this country; and he had taught school and owned a newspaper in Minnesota. Without further information, such credentials seem impressive.

He possessed advantageous physical and personal traits. He was tall for that time and exuded physical strength, but this was combined with a certain scholarly and aristocratic bearing. While he gave many speeches, he was more a quiet persuader than an orator, and this built trust. He was deeply loyal to cause and friends, generous and kind to a degree which generated loyalty in return. Although he might be the last to call for a strike, he would give all for its success once under way, and when it was over, he was the first to forget. Louis Adamic called Tveitmoe "a dark Scandinavian . . . a 'gorilla'." [12] He may have been a "dark Scandinavian," but a "gorilla" he was not. He was an intellectual and a would-be philosopher, tormented by carping unions on the one hand and industrial greed on the other.

The ideology of the Farmers' Alliance to which he had adhered transferred with ease to the cause of labor. In 1892, the Omaha Platform of the People's Party of America, a third-party movement of disaffected farmer and labor organizations, declared that the people were demoralized, that workers were denied the right to organize, that the toil of millions was boldly stolen to build colossal fortunes for a few, and that the Pinkerton system was a menace to liberty. In addition, the platform called for the restriction of Asian contract labor and other "undesirable" immigration, and for the nationalization of railroads, telegraph, and telephone. Throughout most of his life Tveitmoe clung to the belief that the world hovered between utopia and catastrophe. The Omaha Platform, in its preamble, predicted that the alternatives to the needed reforms were "social convulsions, the destruction of civilization, or the establishment of an absolute despotism." He also found comfort in the Farmers' Alliance doctrine that "the cranks win." Because they are progressive thinkers in advance of their time, "cranks" are always in the minority. All reformers from Galileo to John Brown must run the gantlet of ridicule and abuse. But, fortunately, abuse is followed by a degree of toleration, which is succeeded by a hearing, which in turn gives way to public support. Henrik Ibsen's plays, which Tveitmoe read with care and understanding, provided additional support for such thinking.[13]

Ignatius Donnelly, prominent Minnesota Populist and author, was a decided influence. Since Donnelly lived in nearby Hastings, Minnesota, they must have met when Tveitmoe stumped in Goodhue county for the Farmers' Alliance. Donnelly was much interested in Norse mythology, specially in the concept of *Ragnarok*, according to which world cataclysm is followed by an age where "all ills grow better." In all events, Tveitmoe read Donnelly's novels, and *Caesar's Column* (1890) remained especially vivid in his mind. In this novel the final struggle between capitalism and a tortured and maddened working class was commemorated by a huge column of bodies encased in concrete.

Tveitmoe came to San Francisco with a fair founda-

12

tion in the classics as well. He must have been alone among the labor bosses in being able to drop an occasional Latin quotation. His reading in Norwegian literature may not have gone far beyond Norse mythology, Bjørnstjerne Bjørnson, and Henrik Ibsen. When Bjørnson was on his deathbed late in 1909, Tveitmoe carried a long article on him in *Organized Labor*, including a translation of the first chapter of Bjørnson's novel *Arne*. He regarded Ibsen as the greatest revolutionary of them all and used effectively for the cause of labor the title of Ibsen's last play, *When We Dead Awaken*. While Tveitmoe was hardly a pious man, he knew the fundamentals of Lutheran theology and was much attracted to the Sermon on the Mount. He unsuccessfully promoted a plan to attach a chaplain to each of the local councils.[14]

In all likelihood his reading of Charles Darwin, Herbert Spencer, Georges Sorel, and Thorstein Veblen took place after he came to San Francisco. Veblen, a second-generation compatriot from Valdres, Norway, taught at nearby Stanford University from 1906 to 1910. Tveitmoe's earlier efforts to found a cooperative colony in Oregon emerged later in new form. For many years he unsuccessfully promoted a plan that the Council and its affiliated unions should buy a large tract of California land as a refuge for working families hurt by strikes, lockouts, or general unemployment. During temporary idleness the vast skills found in the building trades could be used for building for themselves. The cost, claimed Tveitmoe, would not exceed what otherwise had to be raised by way of defense funds and strike pensions. He watched painfully as the land he had in mind rose in price from eight dollars an acre to one hundred.[15]

As an instant influence on Tveitmoe when he came to San Francisco, Burnette G. Haskell (1857–1907) merits

13

Lloyd Hustvedt

mention. More brilliant and better educated but more erratic than Tveitmoe, Haskell in 1882 had founded in San Francisco the International Workingmen's Association, a secret card-carrying socialistic organization which reached its peak of popularity ten years before Tveitmoe arrived. The organization began to dissolve when Haskell turned his energies to the founding of an ill-fated communistic colony near Visalia, California. Many of his disciples, however, inspired by the Communist dictum, "Workers of the World, Unite! — You have nothing to lose but your chains — You have a world to win," had become leaders in various San Francisco unions. Tveitmoe clearly reappears in Haskell's appeal, "Educate, organize, agitate, unite." He either shared or adopted Haskell's vision of labor libraries, labor temples, lyceums, and a stronger labor press, together with a hope for universal brotherhood and global interdependence of workers. Along with his emphasis on education, Haskell drifted toward violence: "War to the palace, peace to the cottage, death to luxurious idleness . . . Arm, I say, to death! for Revolution is upon you." To the contrary, Tveitmoe wrote against violence, not only for moral reasons but as the worst possible political tactic. It invited public wrath and played into the hands of the employers who could at times destroy their own property in such ways that the unions would get the blame.[16]

A positive and perhaps stabilizing influence on Tveitmoe for the years to come was a fellow countryman, Andrew Furuseth, without question the most respected labor leader in San Francisco. Both were members of the San Francisco Norwegian Club and they saw each other frequently. Save for one instance when he scolded Furuseth for what he felt was meddling in labor matters outside his domain, Tveitmoe wrote about him with respect and affection.[17]

14

Organized Labor, with offices at 429 Montgomery Street, was an eight-page, five-column weekly which came out on Saturdays. It was governed by a board of directors representing stockholders who owned 50,000 one-dollar shares. As a rule the affiliated unions subscribed on behalf of their members and Tveitmoe was thereby spared the financial problems of many editors. While circulation figures were not made public, the newspaper seemingly never lacked for either subscribers or advertisers. The directors declared a 20 percent dividend at the end of the first year, but the subscription rate of $1.50 may have been slightly higher than was common for other weeklies.[18] When the state council was organized in 1901, *Organized Labor* became a statewide newspaper.

Nearly from the beginning the front cover made up the editorial page, often characterized by daring headlines, followed by text which used bold print and much enlarged letters for slogans, epigrams, and phrases deserving emphasis. Dashes and exclamation marks were used liberally. Most of the inside pages were given over to routine business, like local union news, reports and proceedings of the weekly council meetings, including the minutes of the Labor Council, with whom relations, more often than not, were strained. The newspaper kept a watchful eye on labor news across the country; listed California firms declared "unfair" but spoke well of them when they had corrected their errors; listed the names of members who had transgressed union rules, and chastised recalcitrant unions without mercy. There was a section "For the Ladies" which for a time was written by one Mary Field, an outspoken advocate of women's rights.[19] When space permitted, articles of general interest were added, including the curious choice of Cole Younger's version of Jesse James's Northfield bank robbery.[20] The normal pattern could be interrupted to make room for the proceedings of the annual convention of the state council, or for the issues surrounding Labor Day, which was met with enthusiasm. But by 1913, Tveitmoe declared that Labor Day parades had served their purpose. He advised his readers to "commune with nature or your inner self. But do not walk when it leads nowhere. Labor has walked too long."[21]

In the first issue the editor promised a newspaper of which no union member would be ashamed. The paper would at all times advance the interests of labor and seek to harmonize differences between existing unions. He declared that the cause of labor went far beyond shorter hours and increased wages; it included educated children, happy homes, prosperous communities, good government, and the development of a higher esteem for the working class. Arrogant wealth had been and would remain an enemy, but equally destructive were the passions, selfishness, and prejudices found within the ranks of labor itself. If increased wages, claimed the editor, meant only more beer and not increased comfort and recreation, all was lost. The editor extolled productive labor, but decried drudgery. A system of labor which sapped health, shortened life, and starved the intellect had to be abolished. He closed by asserting that "all education is of no avil, if the idea of justice is not uppermost."[22]

A thorough treatment of Tveitmoe's twenty-two-year career as journalist would require a separate article. Basically he lived up to the promises made in the first issue. *Organized Labor* urged an end to child labor, supported woman suffrage and welcomed women as political candidates, but drew the line when women took over men's work at lower wages. It opposed the war in the Philippines, capital punishment, conscription, and potential American intervention in the revolution in Mexico. A special target was the power of judges to issue court injunctions and administer punishment for contempt of court. Because both could be used as fearful weapons against labor, California judges were watched with care. Sun Yat Sen was regarded as one of history's foremost revolutionaries. Tom Mann, England's pacifistic labor leader, with whom Tveitmoe corresponded, received attention. He liked George Bernard Shaw's directive that the soldiers should shoot the generals and go home, but feared that the generals would be quickly replaced. Beginning around 1910, one can detect a drift toward broader concerns of labor. Unskilled workers, he wrote, had been neglected, as had farmhands and migrant workers. Tveitmoe ultimately showed sympathy for the Industrial Workers of the World (IWW), and he dared to present a long and objective but also friendly description of syndicalism. If *Organized Labor* had ever been a parochial newspaper, this became less and less true. Tveitmoe anticipated World War I years in advance and saw its coming as the feared cataclysm.[23] In 1912 he still had hope: "Neither prison bars nor grim gallows can seal the sighs for liberty or stem the pen that writes the hopes that cheer. Let the workers of the world clasp hands over the oceans which divide them, both mentally and physically, from Peking to London. Let them fight by ceasing to work for the drones, and the final battle is done." But later he could only despair as the workers of Europe turned nationalistic when the war broke out.[24] However, *Organized Labor* remained patriotic when the United States entered the war and there were no strikes within the building trades unions in California during that time.

Although he had the medium to do so, Tveitmoe never placed himself in the foreground. In fact, he warned against those who would pose as heroes. The labor movement was not built on "noise, bombastic

17

phrases, and honeyed words." The real hero is not the object of worship. On the contrary he is more often subjected to the "vilest vituperation and denunciation." "This maudlin, nauseating hero worship which infests the labor movement is disgusting to all who have the least spark of manhood in them." This did not mean, of course, that personalities like Samuel Gompers, Clarence Darrow, Mother Jones, and P. H. McCarthy were neglected. But in keeping with this view, *Organized Labor* carried only one article on Joe Hill (Joseph Hillstrom) and his death sentence in Salt Lake City. Although the article was long, no mention was made of his poetry and labor songs and there was no later article about his execution.[25]

Tveitmoe's style varied with the occasion. He could publish what amounted to written lectures in a clear, logical, and sober fashion. When ideas became bigger than his language could carry, he drifted into slogans and epigrams. While he often pleaded for temperate language, especially in negotiations, he did not hesitate to call names when reconciliation was impossible or unwanted. He assessed the *Petaluma Daily Courier* as follows: "One of the most bitter and densely ignorant, stupid, irascible, anarchistic, anti-union-labor country sheets that has ever mutilated grammar, spoiled rhetoric, or disgraced a venerable but dilapidated printing press." His affinity for alliteration could go to lengths like "Its [the trusts'] clammy claws clutch the whole world." To the publisher-editor of the *Los Angeles Times* he wrote: "Pass, brutal bully, into the oblivion you have merited." He described Los Angeles as follows: "There she stands the queen of the southland, with her hand outstretched for the tourists' gold and her heel upon the neck of the wage worker. The mistress of Huntington's all-devouring industrial system, bowing in servile obedience to a band of putrid pirates, whose carcasses were so rotten and decayed they could neither be saved nor purified by all the salt and water in the Pacific Ocean." Rarely in labor history have secretary's reports included poetic pieces like the following: "When the earth was young and warm and moist, storing up treasures and wealth for the life, comfort, happiness, and wellbeing of its future inhabitants, there was no 'Big Business' and no children of Big Business." Tveitmoe rarely used humor. He could be ironic when he converted MM&E (Manufacturers, Merchants, and Employers Association) to "Money, Misery, and Exploitation." When William Randolph Hearst turned against labor he was dubbed "Willie Worst." Tveitmoe was perhaps at his best when confusion and comedy set in at the time the San Francisco hackmen were being organized. Union drivers refused to take part in the same funeral procession with non-union hackmen. Each party therefore took a separate route to the cemetery, but ultimately had to meet in a ugly mood at the grave site. Tveitmoe's conclusion was that "A non-union corpse is nearly as bad as a living scab."[26]

Test and triumph came early for the new secretary of the Building Trades Council of San Francisco. The millworkers, still on a ten-hour day, wanted a reduction to eight. *Organized Labor* took a moderate and conciliatory tone, hoping for successful negotiations. Before any strikes were called, the millowners declared a lockout on August 11, 1900. Building contractors ran out of materials and unions throughout the building trades were threatened with work stoppages. The Building Trades Council established its own mill which ran around the clock, supplying the contractors with the needed materials and thereby frustrating the millowners' plan to enforce support from the building contractors. The millowners had to yield, but they argued that now they could not compete with outside mills having longer hours and lower wages. The Council came to the rescue. It promised that their unions would work only with materials prepared by union mills where working conditions equalled or surpassed those for which they had bargained, establishing not only a closed shop but a closed market as well. It would be difficult to overstate what this victory meant to the Building Trades Council in terms of future power. From 1901 to 1905 it controlled not only its labor body but the entire industry. When S. H. Kent, president of the Builders Exchange, was asked in the East about labor problems in San Francisco, his abrupt answer was, "We have no labor troubles, we give the men what they want." In 1905, Tveitmoe could weep with Alexander the Great, "There is nothing more to organize in the building industry in San Francisco." The Labor Council, which regarded the Building Trades Council as its subordinate, claimed credit for the victory. Tveitmoe was magnanimous. He denied the truth of this, but pointed out that goals were more important than who received the credit. All of labor had gained.[27]

In fact there were hardly any strikes within the building trades in San Francisco for the next twenty years. The electrical workers wanted a strike in 1907, but the Council refused to endorse it. When this union refused to obey, it was expelled and the Council created a new union, made up of members loyal to the central body. The most serious strike came in 1910. Because they had to prepare their material, hod carriers began work fifteen minutes early, morning and noon, making an eight-and-one-half-hour day. They wanted an eight-hour day. The strike put the bricklayers out of work, which in turn put others out of work. After more fuss than the issue warranted, the strike was settled. The hod carriers continued to work the additional half-hour but received extra pay. By 1914 the employers had banded together into the Building Trades Employers Association. The Council waited for the day it could put an end to this threat. This happened when the house-smiths wanted an eight-hour day. Fifty firms agreed but ten companies locked out their workers. The Employers Association demanded return to work under the old conditions. The Council responded that these workers had been locked out and that they had found other work. The lockout ended in 1917 and the Employers Association disbanded.

The beginning of the end of the McCarthy-Tveitmoe regime can be traced back to 1916. The longshoremen's strike of that year, which had nothing to do with the Building Trades Council, aroused San Francisco employers. The Chamber of Commerce created a law and order committee which became the Industrial Relations Committee of the Chamber of Commerce when the United States entered World War I. Its main objective was to make San Francisco an open-shop city. The war did much to demoralize the building industry. Perhaps half of the workers went to the shipyards. Prices rose faster than wages, yet there were no strikes. The attitude grew that San Francisco was backward, that Los Angeles, with its open-shop policy, was thriving, that the unions prevented initiative on the part of the employers, that the closed-shop system prevented the normal flow of capital into construction, and that union rules were oppressive and added to costs.

Confrontation took place in 1920 when seventeen of the building crafts unions asked for an increase in wages. Their case was just. Based on 1914 index figures, the cost of living stood at 200 while wages registered 170. The Builders Exchange, the employers' association in the building trades, now a strong body of contractors and suppliers, ordered the employers to refuse all increases. Negotiations broke down and the Exchange

21

Lloyd Hustvedt

threatened a lockout for October 7, 1920. The Industrial Relations Committee of the Chamber of Commerce held the balance of power. The Building Trades Council agreed to arbitrate. While the arbitrators were in session prices began to fall at an astonishing rate and when the award was made the arbitration board announced a seven-and-one-half percent reduction in wages. The Building Trades Council refused to accept the award, arguing that the issue was only whether wages should be increased. The Builders Exchange declared a lockout for May 9, 1921. The Industrial Relations Committee obtained the support of bankers, suppliers, and other local employers. Union employers could obtain neither materials nor loans. The Building Trades Council tried, as it had done in 1900, to provide the needed supplies, but the materials field was too broad. Against a background of earlier successes, it tried litigation but failed. The Building Trades Council voted to accept the award on June 10. But there was more humiliation. The employers notified their employees that they could return to work only under open-shop conditions. A general strike followed, but it was soon lost, marking a complete overthrow of the closed-shop system which had dominated San Francisco building trades for more than twenty years. Tveitmoe, now a sick man, was spared much of the hostility that came P. H. McCarthy's way. McCarthy resigned as president of the San Francisco Building Trades Council in January, 1922, and shortly thereafter as president of the state council. Tveitmoe as secretary did likewise, but continued as editor of *Organized Labor*. Against a background of beneficial labor legislation which had been passed in California after 1910, the defeat was not as crushing as it would appear on the surface.

How did McCarthy and Tveitmoe transform a fledgling central labor body into a machine that for twenty years dominated the building industry in San Francisco, if not in the entire state of California? The answer is centralization of power, discipline, and conservative prudence. From the beginning the Council isolated its component unions by not allowing them, at the cost of expulsion, to ally themselves with any other federation. Believing that solidarity was more important than numbers, care was exercised as to what unions were admitted, and unruly ones were expelled. The Council had, in fact, the awesome power to unseat delegates regarded as detrimental to the interests of the Council, and could therefore crush any seeds of strife that could grow into civil wars. This power went so far that several delegates were fined in 1914 for taking President McCarthy's name in vain. Another source of power was that only the Council could issue quarterly working cards, without which no union man could work. In some cases unions were kept in line through heavy assessments which created debt obligations. At no time was there any hint that the officers of the Council were corrupt in financial matters, but there were frequent mutterings that they intervened in local union elections, and that the election laws were loose enough to permit manipulation.

Whatever the truth may be, McCarthy's and Tveitmoe's positions were secure as long as they had the support of the Council delegates. It was a sore point for many that a general referendum was not used between 1904 and 1921. In fact, the rules did not even require majority support of the individual unions, only that of the larger ones. Unions with 100 or fewer members seated three delegates. Larger unions added one delegate for each 100 additional members. For example, the Carpenters Union, Local 22, of which McCarthy was also president, had twenty delegates, ten percent of the entire Council. This practice was in direct violation of

23

American Federation of Labor (AFL) regulations which did not permit representation from any one union to exceed ten. So confident was the Council that it did not affiliate with the AFL until 1908, when the AFL granted flexibility on some of its rules.[28]

If the methods of the Council were not at all times democratic, the blessings that flowed from it were many. It brought about much needed uniformity of practice within the building trades. Independent strikes became virtually impossible. Without the support of the Council, strikes would lead to certain failure and expulsion. Control over the business agents prevented any "private arrangements" between union and employer and eliminated graft like "strike insurance." The Council brought into line unions which exacted too high initiation fees, imposed exorbitant fines, or gave unduly severe examinations. In fact, the Council functioned as a court of appeals and could reverse decisions made by local unions. If the unions at times chafed at their loss of former independence, the San Francisco employers were pleased. So carefully did the Council monitor the economic climate that it informed its unions in 1903 that it would endorse no demands for higher wages until times became more prosperous. When the earthquake struck San Francisco in 1906, the Council suspended its working regulations and did not exploit the disaster to labor's advantage. The same cannot be said for many other segments of the San Francisco business world.[29]

Contributing to the success of the Council and to the building of a trust base with San Francisco employers was Tveitmoe's patience and "pragmatic conservatism." Organized labor, he pointed out, was as susceptible to arrogance of power as any other group, and periods following successful strikes were specially dangerous. He urged that the unions be loyal to their

employers, that they live up to the letter of their contracts, that the business agents be candid and open in
their negotiations and never resort to "diplomatic trick-
ery." He went so far as to support fines for shoddy
workmanship. Tveitmoe, to be sure, was never gentle
with external agencies that threatened organized labor,
but he was no less firm when he went after unions for
petty quibbling, for feuding, for incessant jurisdictional
disputes, and for their too frequent attention to immediate goals at the expense of long-range ones. While
Tveitmoe defended to the end labor's right to strike, he
saw it as a last resort — as an industrial war where the
losses on both sides were heavy. He believed that seventy-five percent of past strikes could have been prevented, and that the ideal union was the one that
reached its goals with the fewest strikes. But, if a strike
could not be averted, careful preparation was a prereq-
uisite: educational meetings, increase in dues, acquisi-
tion of good lawyers, sympathy of at least one or two
daily newspapers, and finally the patience to wait for
the right moment.[30]

Tveitmoe's "go slowly" thinking, which prevailed
throughout his lifetime, emerged as early as 1901. When
the Labor Council took in a rash of newly-created
unions, hastily put together by an eastern organizer who
did not remain to watch over the children he had fos-
tered, Tveitmoe became worried. "A group of men with
union cards," he wrote, "is no more a union than a pile
of bricks is a house." It was sad, he continued, "to behold the embryo union tumble out of the cradle and en-
deavor to carry away the earth and the planets on top of
it." Borrowing imagery from Hans Christian Anderson,
he noted that the Labor Council had "gathered under its
wings a varied collection of eggs and hatched some
curious ducklings and labeled them trade unions." Unskilled labor had done what skilled labor never dreamt

of doing, namely, "Organize today! Strike tomorrow!"[31] When one shaves away the bombastic Populist-Labor rhetoric that Tveitmoe could and often did use, a responsible citizen emerges.

More through fickle fate than through personal wish or design, Tveitmoe became involved in San Francisco politics. The background for this is highly complicated, but a simplified explanation must suffice. The teamster strike in San Francisco in 1901 was bitter and violent. When the teamsters were defeated, they, and many unions with them, felt that the city administration had favored the employers. This led to the formation of the Union Labor party, which considered Andrew Furuseth as a candidate for mayor. He not only refused to be a candidate, he rejected the entire concept of the party, calling it "class politics," a party rising more out of resentment than common sense. Furuseth reversed his position later when a San Francisco grand jury failed to indict men involved in violence against the unions. We already have class politics, he concluded.[32]

Tveitmoe, speaking for his Council, opposed the idea of a labor party, claiming that a municipality was best served when public servants were selected from the broader community without regard to class. What was worse, he added, working men ceased to be working men when they became politicians.[33] Undaunted by such rebuffs from high places, the party found a candidate for mayor in Eugene E. Schmitz, president of the Musicians Union, an orchestra conductor and a composer of modest talents. Astonishingly enough the young, handsome, affable, but politically inexperienced Schmitz blossomed into a successful campaigner, and to the consternation of the "better people" won the 1901 election. *Organized Labor*, which had supported the Democratic candidate, proved to be a gracious loser and

Tveitmoe wrote kindly about Schmitz as a person. But when Schmitz ran for reelection in 1903, Tveitmoe was far from gracious: "The prattling parasite who preaches class hatred and scares away investors from this great city is a public enemy."[34] In this election *Organized Labor* supported the Republican candidate, but Schmitz won handily.

When the next election came up, in 1905, new developments had taken place which led Tveitmoe's newspaper to support the Union Labor party as strongly as it had formerly opposed it. Many were puzzled, claiming opportunism as a motive. Whatever motives may have been involved, the surface arguments were convincing enough. The San Francisco Citizens' Alliance, an avowed enemy of labor, had been formed in 1904. *Organized Labor* believed that the Alliance was behind the move which fused the Democrats and Republicans on a common ticket for the sole purpose of defeating the Union Labor party. The alternative to supporting the Union Labor party, the argument went, was to back the Citizens' Alliance, an unthinkable position. The Building Trades Council could not have chosen a worse time to shift position. Schmitz and his administration were embroiled in multiple but as yet unproven charges of graft and corruption. Later, word had it that when the Union Labor party was swept into office in the fall of 1905, all the burglar alarms in San Francisco went off on their own initiative.[35]

Dating back to the election of 1901, Abraham Ruef, a brilliant attorney and a genius in campaign strategy, had step-by-step entrenched himself as "city boss." He had visions of becoming a United States senator, and was more interested in power than in money, though he did not shun the latter. He had taught Schmitz all he needed to know to be mayor and proved to be an able counselor in both good deeds and bad. Sketched in bold lines, the

27

picture was as follows: If business establishments both small and large were in doubt as to the outcome of franchises, licenses, contracts, and proposed ordinances, they could "retain" Ruef as their attorney; he in turn would exert influence on Schmitz and his eighteen-member Board of Supervisors. The largest of the "attorney fees" that Ruef received was $200,000 from Patrick Calhoun's United Railroads of San Francisco. Ruef passed on some of his disguised bribe money to Schmitz and the supervisors.

Some of the leading citizens of San Francisco had become suspicious as early as 1902. Among them were Fremont Older, the crusading editor of the *San Francisco Bulletin*, and Rudolph Spreckels, the multimillionaire owner of the San Francisco Gas and Electric Company. They wanted to "get Ruef" and "clean up" the city. President Theodore Roosevelt assisted. He released to their services Francis J. Heney, a government special prosecutor, and William J. Burns, a competent and relentless detective who worried little about the ethics or legality of his methods. In this arrangement, Spreckels paid the bills and Older provided the publicity.

The famous San Francisco graft prosecution, however, was not formally inaugurated until October 20, 1906. For five months the state labored to build a case on slender evidence. Then in March, 1907, Older, Spreckels, Heney, and Burns forced one Golden M. Roy, under threat of exposure for a forgery in Oklahoma, to participate in a trap which led to the successful bribing of several supervisors. This trap in turn led to confessions from sixteen supervisors that they had accepted bribes. They were granted immunity for the evidence they provided against Ruef and the mayor. Based on a promise of immunity for all but one indictment, Ruef confessed on May 15, 1907, and changed his plea to guilty. The "Immunity Contract" was, however, later voided and Ruef was tried again, found guilty, and sentenced to San Quentin penitentiary for fourteen years. In a separate trial, Schmitz was found guilty on June 13, 1907. The judge ordered him jailed immediately and on July 8 sentenced him to San Quentin for five years. The district court of appeals later reversed this decision and was upheld by the state supreme court.[36]

On January 17, 1907, Schmitz appointed Tveitmoe and J. J. O'Neil, editor of the *Labor Clarion*, the Labor Council's newspaper, to fill two vacancies on the Board of Supervisors, and they were inducted into office January 21, 1907. As matters turned out, they were the only two supervisors not involved in the graft scandal. When the mayor was absent, Tveitmoe found himself in the unique position of presiding over a board made up of self-confessed felons, men whom Tveitmoe had labeled as lacking even "the honesty to stay bought." The reason that these men continued to serve on the board for more than three months after their confession was that they had become Rudolph Spreckels' puppets. Had they resigned immediately, then an indicted but yet not convicted mayor would have had to appoint their replacements. When the mayor was sentenced on July 8, his office had to be declared vacant. A likely course of events would have been that the supervisors would elect Tveitmoe or O'Neil as mayor. The supervisors would then resign from office, leaving their vacancies to be filled by the new mayor. Nothing of the sort happened. Instead, the supervisors, at the behest of Spreckels, chose Charles Boxton, a fellow grafter, as mayor. This gave the prosecutors time to produce a "candidate" from outside the board. A week later the "boodle board," as it had come to be known, elected Edward R. Taylor their mayor. His first order of business in that office was to accept the resignations of those who had voted for him. Tveitmoe declared that he would not sit on the new board until a court had ruled on the legality of this election. When the court found the methods valid, Tveitmoe returned to fill out his term.[37]

"We are intent on redeeming the city and vindicating Union Labor," wrote Tveitmoe to his wife and his son Angelo, who were visiting relatives in Norway. In the coming election he hoped for a ticket "made up of the best, ablest and cleanest men in the city."[38] This was more than a dream. By 1905 the Union Labor party had become rather a name than a reality, and a rehabilitated Union Labor party had high potential for success. In addition, public opinion was turning against the prosecution, which many felt had promised more than it had delivered. True, they had succeeded in convicting two men for receiving bribes, but progress was slow in prosecuting the sources of bribes higher up. By August, 1907, Tveitmoe was freqently mentioned as the likely candidate for mayor on the Union Labor ticket; in fact, he was the only one mentioned. Tveitmoe made no formal announcement, but played an "I am in the hands of friends" role, letting, as it were, the office seek him rather than he it.[39]

Meanwhile Burns, the detective, sent his son Raymond to Minnesota, and on September 24 the San Francisco *Bulletin* carried a front-page spread under the headline, "Supervisor O. A. Tveitmoe Proves to Be Ex-Convict." The cruelty went even farther. It carried the mug shots (front and side view) of Tveitmoe with shaven head, in prison uniform bearing the number 3920. The *Bulletin* justified its action by pointing out that Tveitmoe had visited the convicted Schmitz at the Ingleside jail, thereby identifying himself with the "Schmitz-Ruef reign of thievery and bribery." It continued, "In a crisis where this man is a LEADER striving to persuade good citizens to follow him in ways he knows to be bad, it becomes the sacred obligation to aid those citizens to see him for what he is, that they may not place him in any greater trust than his qualities deserve."[40] The Bulletin not only wanted to "get" the grafters, it was after the entire Union Labor party. With Tveitmoe out of consideration, the candidacy went to P. H. McCarthy. The appointed-incumbent Taylor won the election; but in 1909, he refused to run, and against weaker candidates McCarthy won the election by a plurality of 10,000 votes. His administration was a "clean" but a weak one. Tveitmoe wrote many of McCarthy's speeches.

More trouble lay ahead for Tveitmoe. Early in 1910 San Francisco employers informed labor leaders that they could no longer compete with Portland, Seattle, and particularly Los Angeles, where wages were thirty percent lower and working hours longer. Both employers and union labor would benefit, they said, if San Francisco and Los Angeles were "equalized." Strengthening union labor in Los Angeles would be difficult, largely because of General Harrison Gray Otis, publisher-editor of the *Los Angeles Times* and president of the Merchants' and Manufacturers' Association, an organization of industrialists aimed at destroying labor unions. Having discovered Nietzsche, Otis believed in aristocracy, superiority, and the exercise of might. He was so vain, pompous, unfair, and vicious that even many of his supporters disliked him. Hiram Johnson, later governor of California, outdid even Tveitmoe in describing Otis: "He sits there in senile dementia with gangrened heart and rotting brain, grimacing at every reform, chattering impotently at all things that are decent, frothing, fuming, violently gibbering, going down to his grave in snarling infamy."[41]

31

Together with representatives from other trades, Tveitmoe, Andrew Gallagher, and Anton Johannsen from the Building Trades Council "invaded" Los Angeles. Tveitmoe left San Francisco with the title "President of the General Campaign Strike Committee for the Unionizing of Los Angeles." Johannsen, a Chicago carpenter, had come to San Francisco as organizer for the state Building Trades Council. He was young, handsome, fearless to a swashbuckling degree, and dispassionate. Although intelligent, his labor philosophy was simple enough: "In the absence of power all our declarations for justice are so much wind." [42] A deep, almost fraternal, friendship developed between Tveitmoe and Johannsen. In Los Angeles the strike committee was joined by Job Harriman, a prominent socialist leader who served as attorney for the struggling Los Angeles unions and was destined to be a candidate for mayor in 1911.

Because the iron workers were the toughest fighters, had a strong national organization behind them, and had the greatest grievances, the San Francisco leaders used them to spearhead the attack. They asked for a higher wage scale. When this was refused, the iron workers throughout Los Angeles struck. Strikebreakers came in from the Midwest and were met with strong-arm squads from San Francisco; deputies beat up the strikers, and the strikers beat up non-union workers; a city ordinance banning picketing was enacted, and in a short time 470 workers were arrested who in turn demanded jury trials, enough to clog the courts for many years. General Otis dashed about the city with a cannon mounted on his automobile. In his newspaper he appealed to all decent peoples to drive out the "San Francisco gorillas." On September 3, he called for drastic action. "The danger of tolerating them is great and immediate. . . . Their instincts are criminal, they are ready for arson, riot, robbery, and murder." During this time, through assessment and appeals, Tveitmoe raised $334,000 in aid money for the strikers.[43]

On October 1, 1910, at 1:07 a.m., there was an explosion in Ink Alley behind the Times Building, a medieval fortress of a structure. Within minutes the building was filled with gas and flames. Twenty-one persons lost their lives and the building was wrecked. Because Otis had an auxiliary plant ready, the *Times* came out only a few hours late. Otis screamed "anarchic scum" and "leeches upon honest labor," and invited the readers' attention to the "wails of poor widows and the cries of fatherless children."[44] From the labor side came the observation that employees had for several weeks been sickened by gas fumes and that no major officials or editors had been present at the time of the explosion; it was suggested that Otis himself had either been negligent or had planted dynamite in order to blame labor and collect insurance.

On occasion historical reality can seem more contrived than fiction. Present in Los Angeles at the time of the explosion was detective William Burns. He had been hired by the National Erectors' Association to find and arrest men behind dynamiting that had been taking place sporadically, mostly in the East, since 1905. The mayor of San Francisco engaged him to investigate the explosion in the Times building. Burns had a suspect, James B. McNamara, a printer by trade. His brother John J. McNamara was the secretary of the International Association of Bridge and Structural Workers, with headquarters in Indianapolis, Indiana. Another person Burns had under surveillance was one Ortie McManigal. Six months later, on April 14, 1911, McManigal and James B. McNamara were arrested in Detroit, and John J. McNamara was arrested later in Indianapolis. Burns extracted what was purported to be a full confession from McManigal, who claimed responsibility for a string of explosions, including the Christmas Day, 1910, explosion at the Llewellyn Iron Works, the only other case where dynamite was used in Los Angeles after the Times building was destroyed. Fearing complications with extradition, Burns kidnapped the McNamaras and brought them to Los Angeles, where they were promptly indicted.

After much hesitation Clarence Darrow agreed to defend the McNamaras. The case assumed extraordinary proportions. All of sudden the issues that had divided capital and labor for many years met for a showdown in a Los Angeles courtroom. The *Times* and other anti-labor factions convicted the McNamaras at once, while labor supporters throughout the country claimed that they had been framed. Samuel Gompers believed in their innocence and appealed for contributions to their defense fund. Before their arrest, Tveitmoe had announced a $7,500 reward for the apprehension of those responsible. *Organized Labor* never claimed that the McNamaras were innocent, only that they deserved a fair trial and able defense. Tveitmoe must have known that the evidence against the McNamaras was strong because he worked closely with Darrow in preparing for the trial. When Darrow's team was infiltrated by prosecution spies, Tveitmoe helped to develop a code, keyed to an English dictionary, to prevent further leaks.[45]

Los Angeles leaders had their own private stake in the trial which began October 11, 1910. The primary election of October 30 made it clear that Job Harriman, the socialist, would be elected mayor unless unforeseen events intervened. The McNamara case had united the socialists and the workers. Darrow's own explanation of what happened is briefly as follows: Convinced that the trial would end with conviction and execution, he bargained for more lenient sentences if the McNamaras confessed. The prosecution together with men like Otis agreed to a life sentence for James B. and a ten-year sentence for Joseph J.[46] A confession, in fact, served their purposes better. It would embarrass Harriman and diminish the power of labor. The McNamaras confessed on December 1, 1911, a few days before the election. Harriman was defeated. Theodore Roosevelt wired congratulations to detective Burns.

Labor suffered a blow from which it would only slowly recover. Millions had believed in the innocence of the McNamaras and would have continued to do so even if they had gone to the gallows. Tveitmoe learned of the McNamaras' confession either in New York or on his way to New York from Atlanta where he had attended the AFL national convention. In all events, he was with Samuel Gompers when he wept, during a news conference, as he said "It won't do labor any good." Tveitmoe sent a telegram dated December 2 to his own newspaper urging everyone "to keep cool heads." On December 9, he acknowledged that "every union man and woman is justly indignant. They realize now that, not only have they been grievously imposed upon, but that the cause so dear to their hearts has received a blow from which it will not soon recover." Digging deeper he asked for national soul-searching: "How shallow to go about bellowing for their death. . . . How imbecile to think that any deep-lying causes of this most significant chapter of history will be in the least affected if you put these men to death or a hundred of them!" If we as a nation had no more power of reflection than this, he argued, "Then . . . we have other things to reform besides labor unions." At the annual convention of the state Building Trades Council he declared in his report that save for a few religious denominations the building trades practiced the principle of non-violence more than any other group. Then came his long-remembered words: "If Labor should invoke as law AN EYE FOR AN EYE AND A TOOTH FOR A TOOTH, the world would have a deluge of human blood, without a saving Ark or a Mount Ararat, but with numberless Caesar's Columns to mark the final landings."[47]

When Tveitmoe spoke the words above, he, along with Johannsen, Eugene A. Clancy, business manager for the iron workers in San Francisco, and J. E. Muncey, an iron-worker leader from Salt Lake City, had already been indicted in Los Angeles for conspiracy. On December 31, 1911, the *San Francisco Examiner* carried as a headline: "Tveitmoe and Associates Indicted in Dynamite Case: San Franciscan Said to Be Head of *Times* Blast." Tveitmoe's leadership in the Los Angeles strife had made him a marked man. Detective Burns, with no evidence, had named Tveitmoe on the eve of the explosion as a prime suspect. Ortie McManigal's confession had come under Burns' tutelage, and it must be left to guess what may have been manipulated. According to the confession, James B. McNamara had told him that when he left for San Francisco, his brother John had instructed him to seek out Clancy, who would introduce him to "the bunch" and "the Old Man," meaning Tveitmoe. The contention was that Tveitmoe had provided James B. McNamara with two assistants, M. A. Schmidt and David Caplan, who had in fact helped McNamara to acquire dynamite. Caplan and Schmidt disappeared after the explosion. Tveitmoe acknowledged that he knew Caplan but had met Schmidt only once. In all events, indictments presented on February 6, 1912, in the United States District Court of Indiana soon replaced the Los Angeles charges. Astonishingly enough, Johannsen was not indicted in Indiana, so his case remained hanging. But as Tveitmoe pointed out, it would be difficult for even a biased court to try only one man for conspiracy.

The Indiana grand jury indicted fifty-four men on the charge of conspiracy to violate the laws of the United States, with a maximum sentence of two years; there were also twenty-five separate counts of illegally transporting dynamite and nitroglycerin on passenger trains or conspiracy to do the same. The maximum penalty was eighteen months for each offense, making possible a combined sentence of more than thirty-nine years.

Tveitmoe and Clancy, the only California men indicted, were arrested February 19. Jafet Lindeberg, a Norwegian who had made a fortune in the Alaska gold mines, posted Tveitmoe's bond for $5,000. The celebrated trial, which produced 549 witnesses and 25,000 pages of records, began October 1, 1912, exactly two years after the *Los Angeles Times* explosion. Judge Albert B. Anderson presided, and district attorney C. W. Miller was the chief prosecutor. John Worth Kern and William N. Harding were the main defense attorneys. A remarkable feature was that Kern was at that time a highly respected United States senator (1911–1917) from Indiana. Clarence Darrow, indicted for attempted bribery of a jury member in the McNamara case, was tied up in Los Angeles.

As was true for the McNamara case, the trial rested heavily on McManigal's confession. Here, too, the trial operated on two levels. First was the valid prosecution of alleged criminals. Second was the attempt of capital, especially the steel industry, to administer a crushing blow to labor by convicting important labor leaders. When Tveitmoe was indicted in Los Angeles, he claimed the prosecution there had promised him immunity if he would implicate Samuel Gompers.[48] It is impossible to unravel the Indianapolis trial with any degree of clarity. The main thread is that McManigal,

37

using what he called an "infernal machine" — a clock — to time the explosion, had done a number of bombings under the direction of one Herbert Hockin of the International Bridge and Structural Workers, who was a subordinate of Joseph J. McNamara, who in turn was responsible to Frank M. Ryan, the president. It is worth noting that Hiram R. Kline of the carpenters union, from Chicago, and Tveitmoe were the only two men indicted outside of the iron workers. Conspiracy trials are elusive affairs; the indicted are tried both as a group and as a collection of individuals. Competent evidence against one person can, in the mind of a jury member, spill over to another because of association.

Because the evidence against Tveitmoe was slender, the prosecution resorted to libel and innuendo. Much was made of his role as strike leader in Los Angeles. He had raised $330,000 from "honest workers" to create a "reign of terror" in Los Angeles which culminated in the Times bombing. "You cannot allow brainy men like Tveitmoe who have the ability to raise hundreds of thousands of dollars . . . to put all the responsibility on the McNamaras." Tveitmoe was said to have told John J. McNamara to "send out the wreckers." When McManigal came to San Francisco after planting explosives in the Llewellyn Ironworks on December 25, he was said to have left a note in Clancy's office to the effect, "Tell Tveitmoe that his Christmas present has been delivered." This was linked to a letter Tveitmoe wrote to John J. McNamara on December 19, 1910, which concluded: "Trusting Santa Claus will be as kind and generous to you with surprises and presents of the season as he has been to us in the Golden State . . ." Save for this Christmas greeting, the other allegations were not substantiated. It was true that James B. McNamara lived for a time in San Francisco before going to Los Angeles and that he picked up the assistance of Schmidt and

Caplan, who later disappeared. No evidence was produced that linked Tveitmoe to these men, save for a foolish stunt he and Johannsen pulled during the McNamara trial. Mrs. David Caplan, under constant surveillance by Burns detectives, was about to be given a subpoena. Tveitmoe and Johannsen, in the best mystery-novel style, arranged for her escape, first by taxi to Reno, Nevada, and then by train to Chicago. Tveitmoe and Johannsen claimed that their act was a humanitarian one. She had been harassed by the detectives to the point of mental breakdown. Moreover, they argued, a wife could not testify against her husband. The fact that they had accomplished this under the very nose of detective Burns only heightened Burns's intense dislike if not hatred of Tveitmoe. Burns, capable as he was, never developed professional detachment. The men he suspected and pursued were personal enemies.[49]

Much was made of a $1,000 check that John J. McNamara sent to Tveitmoe in August, 1910. But this was a clear response to an earlier letter from Tveitmoe, dated July 26, appealing for financial support for the Los Angeles strikers. Detective Burns, when he testified, cleverly managed to bring the Minnesota incident into the picture, and suggested that Tveitmoe had been behind a plot "to blow him up." Otherwise, the prosecution referred to him as the "bomber on the West Coast" and a "fat parasite" on labor, and insisted that if proper justice had been done he would be in San Quentin with the McNamaras rather than in Indianapolis. "If I were prosecuting officer of Los Angeles county," said attorney Miller in summary, "Tveitmoe would be prosecuted for murder."[50] The newspapers picked up the more dramatic charges against Tveitmoe, and out of context they were damaging.

Tveitmoe never took the witness stand, but he became one of the more conspicuous defendants. When testimony was relevant, he took careful notes, but when the hearing became dull, he lost himself in a book, which proved to be *The Rubaiyat of Omar Khayyam* in Latin, a parting gift from Johannsen — rather incongruous reading for "labor bombers." He was reprimanded for smiling when a witness was examined: "I will not permit any demonstrations, whether by smiling or otherwise," said Judge Anderson. Mary Field was permanently excluded from the courtroom because of "anarchistic" statements in an article in *Bridgeman's Magazine* of October, 1911. The court also noted that she had talked much to Tveitmoe, who also had been overheard to drop "anarchistic" remarks. Apparently the court never learned that she was a correspondent for *Organized Labor*. Tveitmoe twirled his hat on his cane as he waited for the verdict of the jury, which came on December 28 after forty-one hours of deliberation. Thirty-eight men were convicted and sentencing took place on December 31. Frank M. Ryan, president of the Iron Workers International, received the longest sentence, seven years. Eight men, including Tveitmoe and Clancy, were given six years. Six were given suspended sentences, and the remainder received sentences ranging from one to four years.[51]

So sure had the prosecution been of conviction that the train, dubbed the "Dynamite Special," which would transport the convicts to the Leavenworth federal penitentiary had been ordered a month in advance. After the sentencing the convicted men were marched five blocks to jail in single file, handcuffed to a deputy on both sides, before a large crowd. In an effort to rise above the humiliation, they broke into song: "Where is Your Wandering Boy Tonight?"[52]

Normally the convicted men could have been released on bail pending appeal, but these proceedings were delayed. Tveitmoe wrote from Leavenworth on

January 3, 1913, praising the institution: The place was spotlessly clean, the food was good, the warden and his officers treated them like men. Had it not been for family, friends, and cause, "I might relinquish the world for my New Year's home." Later Tveitmoe elaborated on how tolerable prison life could be, if one's inner life was in order.[53]

The state building trades annual convention took place late in January, but without Tveitmoe. He was unanimously reelected general secretary. Job Harriman and Clarence Darrow were guest speakers. Behind Harriman, when he rose to speak, were two American flags. When these were drawn back, a large picture of Tveitmoe appeared. The audience arose as one in long applause. Tveitmoe, who was opposed to making heroes of labor leaders, had, for a day at least, become one.[54]

Released on bail pending appeal, Tveitmoe and Clancy returned to San Francisco on March 8. They were met by a crowd estimated at more than 2,000, and a band led a parade up Market Street, which ended with speechmaking. Tveitmoe was in fine fettle: There was no reason why labor men should not be put in prisons, if they were foolish enough to build them. Persecution, he said, had ceased the moment the "conspirators" entered prison. He harbored no particular bitterness toward the court, for it was only part of a larger system. The Sunday issue of the *San Francisco Call* covered the event as a feature story. The pictures were flattering and the language sympathetic.[55]

In January, 1914, the United States Court of Appeals for the Seventh District, Chicago, upheld the sentences for twenty-four of the convicted men, including Tveitmoe's friend Clancy. The decision in the case of Tveitmoe was reversed and a new trial was ordered. The court ruled that the evidence against Tveitmoe was incompetent. It did not follow, because he had been a strike leader, that he had any connection with West Coast bombings. Directing special attention to Tveitmoe's Christmas greetings to McNamara, which the court must have found to be the most incriminating piece of evidence, it commented as follows: "Neither content thereof nor circumstances in evidence are indicative of reference to explosions." Proceedings for a new trial began in June, 1914, but no additional evidence againt Tveitmoe had been acquired and early in July the case against him was *nolle prossed*, meaning that the prosecution would proceed no further.[56]

Burns detectives found M. A. Schmidt and David Caplan in February, 1915. Tveitmoe and Johannsen raised money for their defense. Schmidt was given a life sentence and paroled after twenty-two years. Caplan, a Russian Jew and a Tolstoy disciple, served two-thirds of a ten-year sentence. McManigal, the arch-bomber of them all, went free. He changed his identity and it was rumored that he later worked in the sheriff's department in Los Angeles. Schmidt quoted Guy Biddinger, a Burns detective, as follows: "They don't want you [Schmidt], nor do they want Caplan — they want to hang Tveitmoe and Johannsen and you can help them and then you will be free." If Schmidt can be relied upon, Burns's unpaid four-year pursuit of Schmidt and Caplan may have been motivated by a continuing hope to "get" Tveitmoe.[57]

How far Tveitmoe was involved in the Los Angeles bombings must be left to conjecture. In his favor is his longtime emphasis on "civilized, twentieth-century strikes." The building trades unions in California have no history of setting explosions. The iron workers, however, had since 1905 made it costly for resisting employers by destroying cranes and other expensive equipment. The Iron Workers International had its own network of men across the country and hardly needed Tveitmoe's help. Even if they trusted him, risks would be compounded if they included men outside their own unions. Whether involved or not, he became a "victim of the times." The fact that Johannsen — on the surface, at least, as implicated as Tveitmoe — was indicted in Los Angeles but not in Indianapolis may be attributed to a belief that his lower office was not worth the bother. The prosecution must have regarded the possible conviction of Tveitmoe as a special prize — a powerful West Coast leader, a representative of the conservative unions, and one who stood close to Samuel Gompers. Not to be overlooked is the special animosity that detective Burns felt toward Tveitmoe. It can be safely assumed that all evidence that could be procured against Tveitmoe came to light. Burns, who had an army of detectives, had Tveitmoe under constant surveillance and had named him a suspect from the start. Burns had clearly coached McManigal's confession. McManigal, nearly illiterate, had come to regard his captor as a friend, and may have agreed to include details detrimental to Tveitmoe, some of which seem to lie beyond normal recall. It should also be kept in mind that whatever McManigal had to say about Tveitmoe consisted of his remembering what James B. McNamara had told him as they hid out together in Wisconsin.[58]

In all likelihood, however, Tveitmoe knew or came to know much more than he ever revealed. He was close to Eugene Clancy, whose conviction was upheld. The explosion, caused by sixteen sticks of dynamite planted outside the building near some ink barrels, was never intended to kill anyone. The secondary ignition of ink and gas did that. A biased labor supporter could therefore readily see it more as an unfortunate accident than as murder. Given the class-war mentality that prevailed

43

on both sides, the only thing that can be said here with certainty is that Tveitmoe would never have testified against a fellow union member, even to clear himself, and that in the face of imminent defeat his posture would be to save what could be saved.

Ira B. Cross, California's labor historian, claimed that Tveitmoe's influence declined after the Indianapolis "dynamite" trial: "Although his usefulness was at an end, he retained his official connection with the building trades movement . . . until 1922."[59] Cross's assessment need not be argued against, but it does merit elaboration. Tveitmoe suffered no apparent loss of leadership within his own unions. He took a prominent role in the Stockton, California, strikes in 1914–1915, where the strikers' own agents uncovered a clumsy plot on the part of company detectives to implicate Tveitmoe by planting dynamite in his suitcase. Despite competent evidence and later confessions, little came of this in the courts.[60] In 1911 Tveitmoe was national vice president of the Cement Workers Union and third vice president of the Building Trades Department of the AFL. If he had ever been destined for higher position on the national level, nothing came of it. The lengthy litigation process not only drained his energy, but, for long periods of time, drew him outside the mainstream of his duties. In the area of labor politics, his image had already been damaged by the *Bulletin* story in 1907. The fact that the appeals court had overturned the decision against him attracted only minor attention in the newspapers. Louis Adamic, as late as 1931, wrote as if Tveitmoe had been convicted and had served his six-year sentence.[61]

More to the point perhaps is the fact that, in addition to his personal decline, Tveitmoe suffered the general fate of "conservative" labor. Against a background of respectability, the AFL had reached a peak of militancy in 1911, threatening even to support the Socialist party. Oppressed by the guilt of the McNamaras and the later convictions in Indianapolis, the AFL lost its momentum, leaving the field open to more radical unions who said "To hell with Gompers' polite trade unionism." Inspired by the success of industrial leaders in Los Angeles and by the tactics of General Otis, San Francisco employers began to mobilize to bring about an open-shop city. They were quite successful in gaining the support of the "moral folk" who never bothered about distinguishing between conservative and radical unions. Tveitmoe's earlier stance of "fair play" and community concern, once a source of strength, could now be interpreted as hypocrisy by the right wing and as weakness by those on the left. The Union Labor party began to lose influence in San Francisco in 1912, and ceased to be an organized force altogether when legislation ruled out party designation for candidates running for municipal offices. More with hope than with assurance, Tveitmoe wrote: "If this war [World War I] is fought to make the world safe for democracy, labor must come out a clear winner."[62] In fact, President Wilson's promise of a "reward" for labor's loyalty in World War I never materialized. Instead the war brought falling prices and unemployment as well as thousands of new millionaires who strengthened the anti-labor forces.

In light of what has been mentioned above, it becomes more understandable why Tveitmoe, as he watched the rise of labor opposition in his own backyard, cast some longing glances in the direction of the IWW — why he flirted a bit with syndicalism, why he sought hope in a dream of international worker solidarity, and why he came to believe that every labor body, no matter how strong or independent, needed the back-

45

ing of a group of sympathetic unions, be they moderate or radical. This may also explain why a secretary of a successful but isolated building trades union turned his attention to the vast areas untouched by organized labor, like farmhands and migrant workers. In thought Tveitmoe seems to have skirted if not crossed the boundaries of socialism more than he made public. On the other hand, for reasons perhaps as much prudent as sincere, he denounced Bolshevism as a significant threat to this country during the postwar years. The antidote to it, however, was not force, but fair dealings with labor in general.[63]

Tveitmoe served for a number of years as president of The Japanese and Korean Exclusion League, which was organized in San Francisco on May 14, 1905, and renamed The Asiatic Exclusion League in 1908; his role here was, in his own time and even more in retrospect, an unattractive one. The Exclusion League can be best explained as a continuation of years of agitation against the Chinese which had led to their exclusion in 1882. When Japan relaxed its emigration restrictions, the Japanese replaced the Chinese as "cheap labor." On the whole, the Japanese were more industrious than the Chinese, more prone to organize and to protest oppression. They also bought or rented small parcels of land and turned them into prosperous fruit or truck farms. In the cities they were successful in business, and unlike the Chinese they did not form the equivalents of Chinatowns.[64] Union labor to the last man, Andrew Furuseth included, looked upon the Chinese and the Japanese as a weapon in the hands of industry to bring down wages and destroy the unions. The opposition, however, went beyond labor. Farmers and small business men discovered that their "cheap labor" could turn into dangerous competitors and unwanted neighbors. Others were out-and-out racists who wanted to preserve the West Coast for people of European background.

46

To a degree The Exclusion League was a paper organization. In no year did its income from dues or other sources exceed $5,000. The only person to receive a salary — $12 per week — was a clerk-secretary. Yet the League is not so easily dismissed. The league centralized, sustained, and in all likelihood intensified anti-Japanese sentiments that were already there. It sought to carry out a three-point program. It lobbied for legislation that would restrict the entry of Japanese equal to that of the Chinese; it called for the boycotting of Japanese business establishments; and it pursued a propaganda campaign to inform the public about the "Yellow Peril." The first two measures were largely unsuccessful. The effectiveness of the propaganda campaign is more difficult to measure. In all events, the League had free ready-made voices in the labor newspapers, in many San Francisco dailies, and particularly in *Organized Labor*, which had even before the formation of the League campaigned for exclusion of Orientals.[65]

According to the propaganda message, the Japanese were not only a tool of the capitalists, but a social menace as well. The main arguments advanced by *Organized Labor* were that the Japanese could not be assimilated without injury to the larger culture; that they had such distinct racial, social, and religious prejudices that future friction was inevitable; and that it was impossible to compete with their low wages and standard of living. In a Labor Day speech, Tveitmoe declared that labor should "guard the gateway of the Occidental civilization against Oriental invasion." Despite preliminary remarks of respect for the Chinese and Japanese civilizations, he could write, "Any Caucasian who patronizes the yellow or brown is not a good citizen, not true to his race, not loyal to his ancestry, not faithful to his God and country." Tveitmoe never changed his position with regard to exclusion, but by 1910 he called for toleration and disclaimed any racial bias, though he retained the

47

thought that Asians will "bring down our standard of living."[66]

Tveitmoe was president of the Norwegian Club in San Francisco in 1906, the year of the earthquake and the year that the famed explorer Roald Amundsen arrived with his ship *Gjøa* after sailing through the Northwest Passage. In the civic festivities that followed, Tveitmoe, speaking in Norwegian, joined other speakers like the mayor and Benjamin Ide Wheeler, president of the University of California. Functioning as toastmaster at a banquet given by the Norwegian Club, he proposed that *Gjøa* be turned over to the United States government and that it be the first ship to pass through the Panama Canal.[67]

The early years for the Tveitmoes in San Francisco were economically modest at best. A daughter, Rose Anna, died in 1901, at the age of nine months. Around 1902 they moved into a home of their own at 119 Prospect Avenue. Later they bought a house in Santa Cruz, California. Investigating charges that Tveitmoe lived there in a "palatial residence or mansion," the *Santa Cruz Sentinel* found on Almar Avenue a "neat, attractive but unpretentious cottage," which was about to see a $300 addition.[68] When time permitted on weekends, Tveitmoe could be found sitting by the ocean with a book and his pipe. He also bought a section of land in the Mohave Desert, perhaps with the hope of finding oil, but nothing came of it. Edith Blanche, born in Toledo, Oregon, was the last of the Tveitmoe children to die, in 1976. Angelo, the oldest and the only son, worked for the Internal Revenue Service and was an excellent violinist. He met his future wife, whose name like his mother's was Ingeborg, when he visited Norway in 1907. All of the living grandchildren were born

after Tveitmoe died, but they remember their grand-
mother, who died in 1935.[69]

Tveitmoe suffered a stroke on his birthday, December 7, 1917, which impaired his left side. But as
Cress Gannon, business manager for *Organized Labor*,
stated, "He knew not what it was to give in." There was
much discussion preceding the annual convention of
the state council in 1922 as to whether Tveitmoe would
resign as secretary. Linked as he had been to P.H.
McCarthy, now unpopular because of the reversal of
fortunes for the building trades unions in 1921, he
chose to resign rather than risk losing an election. In a
short, unsentimental resignation speech, he confessed
that his assistant A. G. Gilson, who succeeded him as
secretary, had for the past five years handled most of the
routine work. He stayed on, however, as editor. At the
following annual convention, held at San Bernardino,
California, the new president, Frank C. McDonald, announced that their former secretary had died at his
home in Santa Cruz on March 19, 1923, at the age of
fifty-eight.[70]

It is customary to speak well of the dead. Among the
many tributes to Tveitmoe, some strike a chord of inner
sincerity. Cress Gannon, an intelligent Australian immigrant who had worked close to Tveitmoe since 1900
and who succeeded him as editor of *Organized Labor*,
wrote, "To all the world he appeared to be the man
nothing in the world could disturb or ruffle. His easy-
going manner was assumed." Gannon then went on to
make sense of his strange headline, "Poor Tveitmoe is
Dead." He explained that Tveitmoe had quietly suffered much, both physically and mentally, and that he
had been a victim of "injustice and cruel wrong." A
close friend, Ed Gammon, called him the "friendly philosopher whom no defeat could embitter nor victory
spoil . . . a genial spirit who consoled in adversity and

49

enthused in our joys." He never spared himself in a battle but when the fight was over he was the first to reconcile, claimed Gammon, and "when victory came he modestly disclaimed all credit." Gammon concluded: "The kindest, gentlest friend I have ever known is dead." There may be something in Gammon's estimate. Among Tveitmoe's papers were found a large number of old and uncollected promissory notes and I.O.U.s. Anton Johannsen, who had moved back to Chicago, saw Tveitmoe as "California's Labor Sage." The legendary Mother Jones, in a telegram to Ingeborg, called him "labor's greatest soldier."[71]

It was, then, Tveitmoe's lot in life to leave a provincial rural environment in Norway and enter a setting in America where people from all of Europe and other parts of the world became, as it were, his associates and friends or opponents. Driven by a vision of a better day, he lived out his life on the cutting edge where the less privileged met the more powerful with their claim to a greater share in America's resources and a larger voice in planning its future. Given modest changes in circumstances, especially during his Minnesota years, he might have become a lawyer, a congressman, a professor of philosophy, or even a college president. In 1919, at the state council's annual convention and in a pessimistic mood which was unlike him, he reflected on the notion that "we cannot control what happens to us." He questioned whether the world, contrary to his earlier hopes, was getting much better despite "progressive and prodigious wisdom." It was even possible that "man's temporal abode" was getting worse. Finally he found consolation in a conclusion that might appropriately serve as his epitaph: "Therefore in blessings as well as in the ills of life, less depends upon what befalls us than upon the way it is met."[72] It was perhaps with more insight than they realized that other labor leaders called him "The Old Man."

NOTES

[1] The State of Minnesota *vs.* O. A. Tveitmoe, County of Goodhue. District Court. First Judicial District. Case 423. Register of Criminal Action, Volume B, 347. A certified transcript of the proceedings of the trial taken in shorthand by the court reporter was carried in the *San Francisco Bulletin*, September 24, 1907.

[2] *Minneapolis Tidende*, December 9, 1912. Olaf was born out of wedlock to Ingebjørg Anfinnsdatter Berge (1832–1899) of Vang in Valdres and Anders O. Sløte from Nord Aurdal in Valdres. In 1872, she married Anders Olsen Tveitmoen, born Ristebrøtin in Vestre Slidre in Valdres. He ran the Tveitmoen farm from 1869 until his death. Olaf had two half-brothers, Anders (1873–1888) and Ola. The latter took over the farm after his mother's death, but later emigrated to San Francisco, perhaps around 1908.

[3] St. Olaf College, Record of Students, Volume 1, 32–33.

[4] *Den norske bonde. Tale af O. Tveitmoe, Manitou Messenger*, June, 1888. The *Manitou Messenger* began publication as a monthly in January, 1887.

[5] The Tveitmoes had six children: Angelo Zacharius Ingeman (1891–1955); Evangeline Ingeborg (1892–1932); Clara Elizabeth (1895–1958); Edith Blanche (1897–1976); Rose Anna (1900–1901); and May Rose Anna (1903–1964). See San Francisco Census Records, 1900.

[6] P. M. Ringdal (1861–1934) later rose to prominence in Minnesota politics. He was the unsuccessful Democratic candidate for governor in 1912.

[7] State of Minnesota *vs.* O. A. Tveitmoe.

[8] *San Francisco Examiner*, January 1, 1912. Governor. Executive Journal, Volume J, 277, at Minnesota Historical Society.

[9] *Reform* (Eau Claire, Wisconsin), July 6, August 24, September 7, October 12, 1897, and December 9, 1912.

[10] For general information on California labor history the author has relied heavily on Ira B. Cross, *A History of the Labor Movement in California* (Berkeley, 1935), and Frederick L. Ryan, *Industrial Relations in San Francisco Building Trades* (Norman, Oklahoma, 1936).

[11] Cross, *Labor Movement*, note 20, 338.

[12] Louis Adamic, *Dynamite: The Story of Class Violence in America* (New York, 1958), 201.

[13] John D. Hicks, *The Populist Revolt: A History of the Farmers' Alliance and the People's Party* (Minneapolis, 1931), 439–444; *Farmers' Alliance* (Lincoln, Nebraska), February 5, 1890; *Organized Labor*, January 1, 1910.

[14] *Organized Labor*, December 25, 1909, November 21, 1914, and February 10, 1917.

[15] *Organized Labor*, February 18, 1905, September 26, 1908, and September 20, 1913. According to Tveitmoe the unions had a six-month option to purchase 32,000 acres of land in 1901.

[16] Cross, *Labor Movement*, 156–165; *Truth* (Haskell's newspaper), November 17, 1883; *Organized Labor*, March 23, 1901.

[17] *Organized Labor*, August 3, 8, 1903, and April 24, 1915.

[18] *Organized Labor*, November 24, 1900.

[19] Mary Field began writing for *Organized Labor* in the issue of March 9, 1912. She vowed to take women "out of the kitchen and into the streets and into the world".

[20] *Organized Labor*, July 27, 1901. Tveitmoe had undoubtedly become acquainted with Cole Younger at the Stillwater penitentiary in 1894.

[21] *Organized Labor*, July 19, 1913.

[22] *Organized Labor*, February 3, 1900.

[23] For selected references, see *Organized Labor*, March 10, 1900, and May 31, 1902 (child labor); May 11, September 28, 1912, January 10, June 27, 1914, and November 16, 1918 (women); March 2 and September 28, 1912 (Mexico); June 22, 1912 (courts and judges); April 20, 1912, and March 15, 1913 (Sun Yat Sen); March 30, June 8, 1912, September 27, 1913, and July 10, 1915 (Tom Mann); November 21, 1914 (Shaw); December 18, 1909, April 20, 27, 1912, and March 13, 1913 (unskilled workers and IWW); February 20, 1904, March 30, April 6, 13, 20, 27, May 11, 25, 1912, April 25, May 2, September 5 and 28, 1914 (World War I).

[24] *Organized Labor*, March 30, 1912, and November 21, 1914.

[25] *Organized Labor*, September 20, 1902, and October 2, 1915.

[26] *Organized Labor*, April 4, 1903, May 2, 1914, December 26, 1903. Description of Los Angeles was quoted by Anton Johannsen in *New Majority* (Chicago), March 31, 1923; January 20, 1912; January 19, 1901.

[27] *Organized Labor*, May 1, 1901, January 28 and March 11, 1905.

[28] *Constitution and By-laws of the Building Trades Council of San Francisco*. *Organized Labor*, March 11, 1905, and April 25, 1914.

[29] *Organized Labor*, June 6, 1903, April 21 and 28, 1906.

[30] For representative references see *Organized Labor*, February 24, August 11, October 20, 1900, March 30, 1901, March 4, 1905, January 16, 1909, January 29, 1910, December 5, 1914, and March 20, 1918.

[31] *Organized Labor*, June 22, 1901. In July, 1900, the Labor Council had a membership of thirty-four unions. Fifteen months later it had ninety-eight. On May 2, 1901, Tveitmoe observed that "San Francisco is experiencing a union Pentecost breeze. It passes; the air is charged with electricity, but beware of the storm."

[32] *San Francisco Bulletin*, August 25, 1901; *San Francisco Examiner*, October 28, 1901.

[33] *Organized Labor*, October 19 and 24, 1901.

[34] *San Francisco Call*, November 1, 1903.

[35] On November 5, 1904, *Organized Labor* still contended that unions should not enter politics, but on September 23, 1905, it regretted that it had no choice. For a more complete statement on the Union Labor party, see Edward Joseph Powell, "The Union Labor Party of San Francisco, 1901–1911" (Ph.D. dissertation, University of California, Berkeley, 1937), and Walter Bean, *Boss Ruef's San Francisco* (Berkeley, 1967).

[36] The conviction of Schmitz for extortion was overruled on a technicality. Extortion meant obtaining money by means of threat to do *unlawful* injury. The mayor had a right to withhold or threaten to withhold, for example, a liquor license. The court of appeals acknowledged that obtaining money by threatening to do a *legal* act was unethical, but it was not punishable by law.

[37] *Journal of Proceedings: Board of Supervisors* (published annually by The City of San Francisco), January 21, 1907; *San Francisco Examiner*, March 24, 1907 (Jay Gould is said to have defined an honest man as one who stayed bought); *Proceedings*, May 6, June 17, 24, July 8, 15, and 29, 1907.

[38] O. A. Tveitmoe to his wife and son, July 13, 1907.

[39] "Tveitmoe Enters Mayoralty Race," *San Francisco Examiner*, August 16, 1907.

[40] The *San Francisco Bulletin* may have held the story in order to release it just before the Union Labor party held its nominating convention.

[41] Cited in Irving Stone, *Clarence Darrow for the Defense* (New York, 1941), 270.

[42] *Industrial Relations: Final Report and Testimony Submitted to Congress*, August 23, 1912, 5:4799.

[43] O. A. Tveitmoe, *Final Report of the General Campaign Strike Committee*, September 1, 1912. The brewers in Los Angeles struck first on May 19, 1910, and won a favorable settlement on August 11. By June 1, every metal-trade plant had been locked out or struck, involving 1,200 workers. They returned to work, defeated, in February, 1911. The anti-picketing ordinance was enacted July 16. Court injunctions were also used. For a complete statement, see Grace Heilman Stimson, *Rise of the Labor Movement in Los Angeles* (Berkeley, 1955).

[44] *Los Angeles Times*, October 2, 1910.

[45] *Organized Labor*, July 29 and October 21, 1911; *New York Times*, January 3, 1912; Stone, *Clarence Darrow*, 273.

[46] Clarence Darrow, *The Story of My Life* (New York, 1932), 180–186.

[47] *Organized Labor*, January 20, 1912. One puzzled journalist who covered the convention changed "Caesar's Columns," a reference to Ignatius Donnelly's novel (see above, p. 00), to "Caesar's impalation poles."

[48] *San Francisco Examiner*, January 16, 1912; *New York Times*, January 16, 1912.

[49] All the major daily newspapers and news magazines covered the Indianapolis trial, which lasted from October 1, 1912, to the end of that year. The author has relied on the *New York Times* for general coverage and on the *San Francisco Examiner*, which had a special interest in Tveitmoe and Clancy. A. Bergh and Mary Field, sympathetic to the unions, reported for *Organized Labor*. For selected references, see *New York Times*, January 2, 3, 16, February 7, 19, October 5, and December 31, 1912; *San Francisco Examiner*, December 31, 1911, January 1, 16, 21, February 20, October 2, 5, 9, 10, 25, November 1, 8, 12, 19, 24, 27, December 1, 19, 28, and 29, 1912; *Organized Labor*, January 6, October 5, October 26, November 2, 9, 23, December 7, 1912, January 4, 11, and 18, 1913.

[50] *San Francisco Examiner*, December 1, 19, 25, 27, and 29, 1912; *New York Times*, December 31, 1912.

[51] *San Francisco Examiner*, November 24, 27, and December 1, 1912; *New York Times*, December 31, 1912. Hiram Kline received a suspended sentence, leaving Tveitmoe the only person outside of the iron workers to be sentenced.

[52] *San Francisco Examiner*, December 29, 1912. The "Conspiracy Case" was reviewed in *Organized Labor*, March 14, 1914.

[53] *Organized Labor*, January 18, 1913.

[54] *Organized Labor*, January 25, 1913.

[55] *San Francisco Call*, March 9, 1913.

[56] *San Francisco Examiner*, June 4 and July 4, 1914; *Organized Labor* printed the court of appeals decision, January 10, 1914.

[57] *Organized Labor*, January 15, 1916; Stimson, *Labor Movement in Los Angeles*, 45. Biographical sketches of Schmidt and Caplan by Pauline Jacobsen appeared in *Organized Labor*, April 10 and 17, 1916.

[58] Clearly with the help of detective Burns, McManigal published his confession under the title *Ortie McManigal's Own Story of the National Dynamite Plot* (Los Angeles, 1913). A picture of Burns appears in the front ma-

terial. In his book *Masked War* (New York, 1913), Burns writes as if Tveitmoe was the ringleader of the Los Angeles explosions and the others were his puppets. The book was written before the court of appeals overruled Tveitmoe's conviction.

[59] Cross, *Labor Movement*, 284.

[60] *Organized Labor*, October 3, 17, and November 14, 1914.

[61] Adamic, *Dynamite*, 264.

[62] *Organized Labor*, March 20, 1918.

[63] *San Francisco Call*, March 18, 1919.

[64] Cross, *Labor Movement*, 262–267. 127,000 Japanese came to the United States between 1901 and 1908. Even after the "Gentlemen's Agreement" between the United States and Japan in 1907, by which the latter agreed not to issue passports to either skilled or unskilled workers, 118,000 Japanese entered from 1909 to 1924. For a more complete statement, see Roger Daniels, *The Politics of Prejudice: The Anti-Japanese Movement in California and the Struggle for Japanese Exclusion* (New York, 1969).

[65] *Organized Labor* regularly carried the reports and proceedings of The Exclusion League.

[66] *Organized Labor*, September 7, 1907, December 26, 1908, and January 29, 1910.

[67] Ralph Enger, *The History of the Norwegian Club of San Francisco* (San Francisco, 1947).

[68] *Santa Cruz Sentinel*, June 19, 1913.

[69] Neale Tveitmoe, of Walnut Creek, California, a son of Angelo, provided much information on family matters.

[70] *San Francisco Examiner*, December 8, 1917; *San Francisco Chronicle*, March 25, 1922; *Organized Labor*, April 1, 1922; *San Francisco Chronicle*, March 20, 1923; *San Francisco Examiner*, March 20, 1923; *San Francisco Bulletin*, March 21, 1923.

[71] *Organized Labor*, March 24, 1923; *New Majority* (Chicago), March 31, 1923; Jones to Ingeborg Tveitmoe, March 25, 1923.

[72] *Organized Labor*, March 22, 1919.

by PATSY ADAMS HEGSTAD

2 *Scandinavian Settlement in Seattle, "Queen City of the Puget Sound"**

FOUNDED IN 1851 on the wooded southeastern shore of Puget Sound, Seattle was acquiring by the turn of the century the Scandinavian flavor which still remains a feature of the city. Until the latter 1880s Scandinavians had comprised a relatively insignificant proportion of the city's population, but by 1890 they constituted fully one-fourth of Seattle's foreign-born. After that, the number of Seattle residents native to the Nordic countries increased steadily, exceeding 5,000 in 1900 and expanding to nearly four times that by 1910. In the latter year no less than eight percent of the city's inhabitants, or one person in twelve, had been born in Denmark, Finland, Norway, or Sweden. The actual number of first-generation Scandinavians in Seattle reached its zenith in 1920, peaking at 23,856. Throughout the entire period 1890–1960, however, as Table 1 shows, Nordic immigrants comprised a sizeable fraction of Seattle's population and between one-fourth and

*This article is based upon the writer's doctoral dissertation, "Naturalization Propensity and Voter Registration of Nordic Immigrants in Seattle, 1892–1900," at the University of Washington.

one-third of its foreign-born. The "queen city of the Puget Sound" had become one of the important places of settlement for Scandinavians in the Pacific Northwest and had earned the reputation of being a center of Scandinavian culture in the Far West.[1]

That the Nordic population moved from relative numerical unimportance among the foreign-born of Seattle before 1890 to such numbers as to become one of the city's distinctive features involves a variety of factors. In addition to geographical and physical characteristics of the Puget Sound area, economic opportunities, and the general movement west, there was also active recruitment of Scandinavian immigrants by the state, by business, and by private individuals. Although the precise relationships among these and other factors have not been documented and perhaps cannot be, their importance is suggested by specific cases and studies.[2]

Descriptions of Puget Sound written by Scandinavians repeatedly emphasized its similarities to regions in Norway, Sweden, or Finland. Thos. Ostenson Stine's glowing descriptions of Puget Sound and Seattle included the observation that "When you throw your eye upon Puget Sound, and behold the fleet of fish barges, rolling upon her briny breast, a reminiscence of the coast of Norway steals into your soul." Ernst Skarstedt likened the climate and landscape of Washington generally to that of Norrland, noting that they shared "mountains, dark evergreen forests, and rushing rivers." Ingrid Semmingsen quotes an early immigrant's description of Puget Sound as being "as like Hardanger as any place can be." Semmingsen herself continues in a similar vein, describing the landscape with its "sounds and islands, fjords and mountains" as reminiscent of Vestlandet. The cartographer G. E. Kastengren, who settled in Seattle, went so far as to com-

56

Table 1: Seattle's Nordic population, 1870–1970

Date	Total Population	Total Foreign-born	Foreign-born as percent of Total Population	Danish-born	Finnish-born	Icelandic-born	Norwegian-born	Swedish-born	Combined Nordics	Nordics as percent of Total Population	Nordics as percent of Foreign-born
1870	1,605[b]	515	32.1	NA	NA	NA		51[c]	51	3.2	9.9
1880	6,910[b]	1,981	28.7	NA	NA	NA	190[e]		190	2.7	9.6
1890	42,837	13,656	31.9	457	NA	NA	1,353	1,525	3,335	7.8	24.4
1900	80,671	22,003	27.3	641	424	NA	1,642	2,379	5,086	6.3	23.1
1910[d]	237,194	60,835	25.6	1,879	1,298	NA	7,191	8,678	19,046	8.0	31.3
1920	315,312	80,976	25.7	2,228	2,256	NA	9,119	10,253	23,856	7.6	29.4
1930	365,583	73,029	20.0	1,987	1,950	NA	9,745	9,634	23,316	6.4	31.9
1940	368,302	59,612	16.2	1,514	1,740	NA	8,436	7,670	19,360	5.3	32.4
1950	467,591	77,445	16.6	1,970	2,199	NA	10,447	8,559	23,175	5.0	29.9
1960	557,087	89,967	16.1	1,651	1,981	124	11,065	6,938	21,759	3.9	24.2
1970	530,860	48,423	9.1	670	520	97	4,721	2,430	8,438	1.6	17.4

a Figures are taken from United States Census reports: 1870–1970.

b These figures are for King county rather than for Seattle. Prior to 1890, because of the community's small population, the census compendia did not tabulate separately the foreign-born inhabitants of Seattle. Seattle had 250 residents in 1860, 1,107 in 1870, and 3,533 in 1880.

c The census tabulations combined Norwegians and Swedes in these years.

d Only the figures for 1910 and later include Ballard, which was first settled in 1855, incorporated in 1888, and annexed to Seattle in 1907.

pare the maps of Scandinavia and the Seattle area in detail, finding remarkable similarities between the Baltic Sea and Lake Washington and between Swedish, Norwegian, and Finnish towns and bays and those of southeastern Puget Sound. In addition to topographical similarities, Kastengren noted physical and climatic ones as well. "The summer also is reminiscent of summer in Scandinavia and the Baltic area, although the winters are milder on Puget Sound. Swedes and Norwegians find here majestic mountains, which remind them of their own magnificent mountain chains, clad in the same dark green and covered with the same glistening snow. Settlers from Finland can likewise find here scenery to satisfy their longing for the land of the thousand lakes."[3]

It was Kastengren's avowed belief and the usual inference of others such as Stine and Semmingsen that the topographical, physical, and climatic similarities between areas of the Nordic countries and the Puget Sound region were among the reasons that so many Scandinavians were drawn to the Seattle area. The Swedish geographer Helge Nelson likewise suggested a causative relationship between geographic similarities and settlement patterns, writing that "the migration of the Swedes to different areas is . . . determined in a high degree by the natural conditions of the country whence they hail. . . . Thus, it is not accidental that . . . so many North Swedes from Värmland, Dalecarlia and Norrland are to be found in the forests and the sawmills of the Pacific coast."[4] In linking natural physical conditions with occupations such as forest and sawmill work, Nelson also referred to a second factor related to settlement patterns — economic opportunity.

Seattle, Puget Sound, and Washington as a whole in the 1890s offered economic incentives to those in more established parts of the country as well as to foreigners arriving directly from abroad. The arrival of the Scandinavians in large numbers coincided with that of other peoples, largely of North European stock, who participated in the American movement westward. While the attractions of the West served to pull migrants and the expanding railroad network offered an accessible means of transportation, conditions in the Midwest, such as the depletion of prime lands, drought, and economic depressions, pushed them toward the West. Augmenting the number of potential Scandinavian migrants to western destinations like Seattle were those emigrating directly from the Nordic countries during this era. Three-fourths of the total emigration from Scandinavia took place in the thirty-five-year span from 1881 through 1915, the Norwegian, Swedish, Icelandic, and Danish exodus being primarily before 1900 with only the Finnish occurring largely after the turn of the century.[5]

Springing from the general movement westward, the rapid growth of Seattle yielded a variety of opportunities. A reputation for economic "good times" and full employment brought many Scandinavians to Seattle in the late 1880s, particularly following the fire of 1889. Attracted by high wages, people flocked to get work rebuilding the city; unskilled laborers earned a daily wage of $2.00 to $2.30, skilled workers $4.00 to $6.00, while some positions paid as much as $8.00 per day. These figures seem generous indeed when viewed against the national average earnings paid unskilled workers for a six-day week of $8.88 in 1892 and $8.94 in 1900, or even of $17.61 per week in 1892 and $18.06 in 1900 for skilled workers in the building trades.[6] Seattle's "good times," however, were interrupted by the depression of 1892–1893, which caused a decline in wages, an increase in unemployment, and a slowing of population growth. Oskari Tokoi, an immigrant who

59

later returned to Finland and became premier, left a poignant personal account of life in Seattle at this time in his memoirs, depicting the winter of 1894 as "this winter of terrible unemployment."[7]

Prosperity was not to return fully until the beginning of the Alaska-Yukon gold rush in 1897, and then it came in abundance. As the outfitting and transportation center supplying participants in the gold rush, Seattle was transformed from a frontier town into a bustling city. Outlying communities, as well as Seattle itself, were also affected. For example, in the mills and logging camps around Ballard, which was not annexed to Seattle until 1907, wages had been only 7½¢ to 15¢ per hour for ten-hour days and the impact of Alaska gold brought welcome raises. People poured into Seattle, and by 1900 the city had grown to a population of 80,671 as compared to 56,842 in 1897. In addition to the brisk trade with Alaska, turn-of-the-century Seattle was greatly expanding its Asian trade. The city's commercial and banking importance was well established, laying the foundation for its dominance of the banking business in the state after 1900. Manufacturing played a lesser role at this time in Seattle's economy, which was dependent in 1900 on lumbering, fishing, and mining. Shipbuilding came to be of importance especially after 1897, both in Seattle and in Ballard. Ballard more than Seattle was the center for lumber and shingle mills, and in 1900 it boasted of producing more shingles than any other city in the world.[8]

That the economy was tied largely to trade, lumbering, fishing, and mining meant that the occupational structures of Seattle and Ballard offered Nordic immigrants jobs with which they were familiar. Of course, many immigrants took different occupations in the United States than they had had in Scandinavia, in some cases making relatively frequent changes.[9] Still, there seems to be a positive relationship between the occupational structure of the place of settlement and that of the place of emigration. The modern research of Hans Norman and Lars-Göran Tedebrand lends support to this principle, which has a long tradition in earlier literature.[10] Thus, it is hardly surprising to find Nordic immigrants attracted by the possibilities for employment which the Seattle area offered.

At the turn of the century most Scandinavian men in Seattle and Ballard found employment in the industrial and crafts sector, with trade and commerce increasing in importance for them by 1900. Especially in 1892, as Table 2 indicates, an extremely large number of the Nordic immigrants were common laborers. Fully 86.9 percent of the sizeable Icelandic colony resident in Seattle's fourth ward in that year worked as laborers. By 1900 most of the Icelanders had left Seattle, possibly victims of the depression of 1892–1893. While their case is the extreme, nonetheless substantial numbers of all the Scandinavians occupied this low socioeconomic niche: 49.3 percent of the Finns in 1892, though just 6.6 percent of them in 1900; 37.8 percent of the Swedes, compared to 23.3 percent of them in 1900; 33.9 percent of the Norwegians, and 20.7 percent of them in 1900; and 30.2 percent of the Danes, and 20.6 percent of them in 1900. Building and construction were another major source of jobs for Scandinavian men, as well as one which was traditional for them; 17.5 percent of the Swedes in 1892 and 13.7 percent of them in 1900, 17.3 percent of the Danes in 1892 and 13.7 percent in 1900, and 14.9 percent of the Norwegians in 1892 and 15.4 percent in 1900 worked in these occupations. Wood and mill work provided some employment for Scandinavians, particularly for Swedes and Norwegians, although this was not really a major factor in their em-

61

Table 2: Occupations of Nordic-born men living in Seattle and Ballard in 1892 and 1900

Occupations	Danes 1892	Danes 1900	Finns 1892	Finns 1900	Icelanders 1892	Icelanders 1900	Norwegians 1892	Norwegians 1900	Swedes 1892	Swedes 1900
Agriculture	7 (2.1%)	21 (4.5%)	3 (4.5%)	7 (1.7%)	0 (0.0%)	0 (0.0%)	25 (2.4%)	31 (2.4%)	31 (2.9%)	55 (3.1%)
Farming	4	6	0	0			15	6	18	11
Dairying	2	5	1	0			0	9	4	6
Agricultural Labor	0	0	0	0			2	1	3	1
Horticulture	1	5	0	0			1	3	4	5
Forest Work	0	5	0	7			7	11	2	32
Other	0	0	2	0			0	1	0	0
Public Service & Liberal Professions	6 (1.8%)	18 (3.9%)	0 (0.0%)	2 (0.5%)	0 (0.0%)	0 (0.0%)	30 (2.9%)	44 (3.4%)	28 (2.6%)	34 (1.9%)
Administration	1	7					6	7	2	4
Education & Church	1	1					6	8	5	12
Medicine	2	0					4	8	2	4
Artistic Activities	2	1		1			2	1	1	3
Engineering, Architecture	0	6		1			6	13	12	9
Law, Journalism	0	3		0			6	7	6	2
Industry & Crafts	202 (60.5%)	258 (55.4%)	47 (70.1%)	230 (56.5%)	298 (89.0%)	37 (78.7%)	652 (63.4%)	811 (62.3%)	733 (68.0%)	1,034 (57.3%)
Metal	7	18	0	4	0	0	18	33	24	52
Various Technical	1	5	0	0	0	0	3	5	0	8
Wood & Millwork	11	10	0	11	1	4	46	70	33	84
Paper & Printing	5	1	0	0	0	0	18	9	5	5
Food & Tobacco	8	9	0	0	1	1	4	15	8	11
Textile	5	15	2	4	1	0	21	35	41	36
Leather	2	6	0	0	1	0	8	7	6	10
Building & Construction	58	64	9	26	3	8	153	201	189	247
Mining	0	24	2	147	0	0	4	53	6	113
Fishing	0	3	1	10	1	10	12	99	1	21
Unskilled Labor	101	96	33	27	291	14	348	270	408	420
Unspecified	4	7	0	1	0	0	17	14	12	27
Trade & Commerce	77 (23.1%)	152 (32.6%)	13 (19.4%)	162 (39.8%)	7 (2.1%)	7 (14.9%)	186 (18.1%)	355 (27.3%)	214 (19.9%)	606 (33.6%)
Commerce	22	35	1	5	3	4	83	73	71	84
Hotel & Restaurant	23	23	4	9	3	1	32	41	62	86
Transportation	32	94	8	148	1	2	71	241	81	436
Domestic Work	3 (0.9%)	3 (0.6%)	0 (0.0%)	0 (0.0%)	0 (0.0%)	0 (0.0%)	5 (0.5%)	8 (0.6%)	8 (0.7%)	20 (1.1%)
Servants	1	1					1	0	2	7
Laundry	2	2					4	8	6	13
Unemployed	23 (6.9%)	5 (1.1%)	3 (4.5%)	4 (1.0%)	4 (1.2%)	1 (2.1%)	93 (9.0%)	28 (2.2%)	37 (.4%)	25 (1.4%)
Unknown	16 (4.8%)	8 (1.9%)	1 (1.5%)	2 (0.5%)	26 (7.8%)	2 (4.3%)	37 (3.6%)	25 (1.9%)	27 (2.5%)	29 (1.6%)
Totals	334(100.0%)	466(100.0%)	67(100.0%)	407(100.0%)	305(100.0%)	44(100.0%)	1,028(100.0%)	1,302(100.0%)	1,086(100.0%)	1,803(100.0%)

Sources: Tabulated individually from King county assessor census manuscripts for Seattle and King county, Washington, 1892, in Archives and Manuscripts Divi-

ployment, at least at this early period. Mining likewise provided jobs for Nordic immigrants, becoming by 1900 an important employer of Finns (36.1 percent of whom were miners) and bearing witness to the pull of the coal mines in King county. Fishing was of little importance to Seattle and Ballard Nordics in 1892, but by 1900 it came to employ 7.6 percent of the Norwegians.

In this decade, however, the real growth of Scandinavian employment was in trade and commerce. Although hotels, restaurants, saloons, and general commerce employed a fair number of the Nordic immigrants, the most significant increase resulted from the arrival by 1900 of many Scandinavian seamen. Like the mines of King county, the port of Seattle and its developing network of trade lines exerted an increasing pull. Whereas relatively few Scandinavians had worked there in 1892, in 1900 35.9 percent of the Finns, 19.9 percent of the Swedes, 16.0 percent of the Norwegians, and 15.7 percent of the Danes were seamen.

Sectors outside industry and crafts, on the one hand, and trade and commerce, on the other, were not important numerically as employers of Nordics in Seattle and Ballard. Agricultural occupations, including lumbering, accounted for a small percentage of the Scandinavian immigrants, as might be expected in a generally urban area. While a good many of the influential persons within the Scandinavian communities were in public service and the liberal professions (as well as in trade and commerce as businessmen), their numbers were nevertheless small. Very few of the Nordic men worked as domestic laborers, a province in which their female counterparts were well represented.

Scandinavian immigrant women were largely housewives and servants, as Table 3 shows. Approaching at least 50 percent for each of the nationalities in 1892, housewifery by 1900 had become the occupation of well over half of the Scandinavian women. The largest proportion was among the Danes, no less than 70.3 percent of whom were housewives in the later year. In 1892 servants accounted for about one-third of the Icelandic and Swedish women, one-fourth of the Finns and Norwegians, and one-fifth of the Danes. While the proportion of servants in 1900 declined to 18.3 percent of the Swedes, 18 percent of the Norwegians, 13.9 percent of the Icelanders, and only 7.2 percent of the Danes, the number of Finnish maids rose to 35.9 percent. These women usually lived in the homes of their employers, often prominent citizens in the city's fourth or fifth wards. Laundry work employed other Nordic women, especially Norwegians and Swedes.

The women represented in industry and crafts were concentrated in textiles as seamstresses and milliners, although by 1900 a few Norwegian and Swedish women were employed in paper and printing, food and tobacco, and general labor. The slightly fewer women in trade and commercial occupations than in industrial and craft jobs were mostly boardinghouse and hotel proprietors, waitresses, and clerks. There was an occasional merchant among the Norwegians and Swedes. Scandinavian women were even less involved in public service and the liberal professions than were the men; no Finnish or Icelandic women were found in this category. While the men were distributed throughout this sector, the women were virtually all teachers or nurses. One Swedish woman, however, was a "doctress." Agriculture employed few Scandinavians of either sex in Seattle and Ballard, and only one woman was thus employed. She was a Norwegian-born farmer residing in Ballard in 1900.

The means by which immigrants learned of the physical and occupational attractions of Washington and

Table 3: Occupations of Nordic-born women living in Seattle and Ballard in 1892 and 1900

Occupations	Danes 1892	Danes 1900	Finns 1892	Finns 1900	Icelanders 1892	Icelanders 1900	Norwegians 1892	Norwegians 1900	Swedes 1892	Swedes 1900
Agriculture Farming	0 (0.0%)	0 (0.0%)	0 (0.0%)	0 (0.0%)	0 (0.0%)	0 (0.0%)	0 (0.0%)	0 (0.1%)	0 (0.0%)	0 (0.0%)
Public Service & Liberal Professions	3 (1.7%)	2 (1.0%)	0 (0.0%)	0 (0.0%)	0 (0.0%)	0 (0.0%)	6 (0.9%)	7 (1.0%)	4 (0.5%)	3 (0.4%)
Education & Church	0	0					0	4	0	0
Medicine	3	2					5	3	4	3
Artistic Activities	0	0					1	0	0	0
Industry & Crafts	9 (5.1%)	8 (4.1%)	0 (0.0%)	1 (1.3%)	1 (1.1%)	4 (1.1%)	26 (3.8%)	31 (4.5%)	23 (3.0%)	24 (2.8%)
Paper & Printing	0	1	0	0	0	0	1	2	0	1
Food & Tobacco	0	0	0	0	0	0	0	1	0	0
Textile	9	5	0	1	1	4	25	23	23	21
Unskilled Labor	0	2	0	0	0	0	0	5	0	2
Trade & Commerce	7 (4.0%)	4 (2.1%)	0 (0.0%)	1 (1.3%)	0 (0.0%)	1 (2.8%)	15 (2.2%)	20 (2.9%)	17 (2.2%)	28 (3.3%)
Commerce	3	1	0	0	0	1	1	10	4	4
Hotel & Restaurant	4	3		1		0	14	10	13	24
Domestic Work	30 (17.0%)	14 (7.2%)	8 (25.8%)	28 (35.9%)	32 (34.0%)	5 (13.9%)	155 (22.8%)	125 (18.0%)	243 (31.4%)	157 (18.3%)
Servants	29	13	8	28	28	3	141	107	225	142
Laundry	1	1	0	0	4	2	14	18	18	15
Housewives	103 (58.5%)	137 (70.3%)	18 (58.1%)	43 (55.1%)	44 (46.8%)	10 (55.6%)	388 (57.1%)	417 (60.0%)	377 (48.7%)	521 (60.8%)
Unemployed	19 (10.8%)	8 (4.1%)	4 (12.9%)	4 (5.1%)	16 (17.0%)	1 (2.8%)	63 (9.3%)	28 (4.0%)	52 (6.7%)	27 (3.2%)
Unknown	5 (2.8%)	22 (11.3%)	1 (3.2%)	1 (1.3%)	1 (1.1%)	5 (13.9%)	27 (4.0%)	66 (9.5%)	58 (7.4%)	97 (11.3%)
Totals	176 (100.0%)	195 (100.0%)	31 (100.0%)	78 (100.0%)	94 (100.0%)	26 (100.0%)	680 (100.0%)	695 (100.0%)	774 (100.0%)	857 (100.0%)

Sources: Tabulated individually from King county assessor, census manuscripts for Seattle and King county, Washington, 1892, in Archives and Manuscripts Division, Suzzallo Library, University of Washington, Seattle; and U.S. Census Office, manuscript federal population census schedules, 1900.

more specifically of Seattle were varied, ranging from recruitment activities of state and local officials or business interests to informal contacts with friends and relatives living or traveling in the area. While officials and businessmen did not direct their activities specifically toward any one group, though at times they opposed the settlement of given nationalities, the established American community in general seems to have seen Scandinavians as desirable. Thus, in May, 1891, *The Seattle Press-Times* chose to reprint an article from the *New York Sun* entitled "Scandinavian Emigrants; Healthy and Spirited Emigrants Bound for the West," which lavishly praised the qualities of these people. By way of contrast it derided those from Eastern Europe, saying that "if all other immigrants from Europe, including those from Poland, Hungary, and Russia, were as spirited as these Scandinavians, and would follow their example, how much better it would be for them." [11] Similarly, an editorial appearing on November 8, 1892, endorsed a plan to restrict immigration by requiring that immigrants pay a sizeable deposit at entry, which the writer said would not prevent "tens of thousands of thrifty Swedes, Norwegians, Germans and men of other nationalities coming hither at their own expense" while stopping "the wholesale manufacture of European emigration." [12] The Swedish-American journalist Ernst Skarstedt wrote of the *Seattle Post-Intelligencer*'s receptiveness to immigrants, especially to Scandinavians, and observed that Scandinavians had won "a certain prestige" in Washington state. [13]

That the efforts of state officials in fact reached Scandinavians is exemplified through the writings of both Skarstedt and the Norwegian O. B. Iverson. By the time of Skarstedt's arrival on Puget Sound, state officials as well as private citizens had a well-established role in immigrant recruitment. The territorial governors took an active part in attracting settlers, with Watson Squire, who was governor from 1884 to 1887, being particularly noted for his efforts. Skarstedt termed his annual report of 1884 "a real masterpiece," and one suspects that it was a factor in Skarstedt's own decision to travel to Washington in 1885. Intertwined with the promotional work of the governors and local officials, and later the state immigration agent, were the activities of private citizens. Indeed, it was a group of volunteer women who in the 1870s formed the Emigration Society, which became a quasi-official board of immigration complete with legislative funding. O. B. Iverson, reminiscing of his arrival in Washington in 1874 as a potential settler, describes his contacts with Governor Elisha P. Ferry and his subsequent visit with Mrs. A. H. H. Stuart, then "acting immigration commissioner." With the work of the Emigration Society continuing into the 1880s, the Washington state constitution formally established under the secretary of state a bureau of statistics, agriculture, and immigration. D. B. Ward, who became the state immigration agent and served from 1896 to 1901, was by occupation a real-estate agent, embodying the collaboration of official and business interests in attracting settlers to the state. His greatest activity was in sending pamphlets and circulars extolling the virtues of Washington to the Midwest and the East.[14]

At the local level, businessmen were of greater importance in promotional activities than officeholders. City directories, which in the case of Seattle first appeared in 1876, were one means by which business interests attempted to provide information to potential settlers. The Seattle Chamber of Commerce, organized in 1882, also published a number of laudatory tracts designed to attract immigrants. In this purpose it met rivalry from the Tacoma Chamber of Commerce, and after 1890 pamphlet production by both bodies increased.

Newspaper editors cooperated in the recruitment efforts by printing "progress editions," which were sent anywhere in the United States without charge. Individual businesses, as for example the real-estate firm of Eshelman, Llewellyn Co., also were important promoters of Seattle and published literature of their own.[15]

Nordic immigrants already resident in the Puget Sound area were also involved in organized efforts to recruit Scandinavian emigrants. As early as 1876 a Scandinavian Immigration and Aid Society had been founded in Seattle with Andrew Chilberg, later to become a prominent local figure, as president. The stated purpose of the society was to "encourage immigration," and to give potential emigrants "such information as shall be to their benefit, such as where good farming lands can be found. It is also the desire of the society when they become able to build an emmigrant [*sic*] house in Seattle, for the reception and temporary occupancy of their countrymen coming here, as immigrants. They also desire the establishment of a land office in Seattle, for the spread of information descriptive of the Territory. The society is also prepared to furnish tickets to parties wishing to make a trip to any part of Europe, and for those desiring to send for friends drafts are issued on the principal cities of Europe. The society desires to correspond with their countrymen in any part of the country."[16]

Like their American counterparts, Scandinavian businessmen participated in immigrant recruitment. For example, H. C. Wahlberg, a Norwegian-born attorney and real-estate agent, wrote an article in the *Washington Magazine* of November, 1889, aimed at both declaring the worth of Scandinavian settlers to the United States and attracting them to Puget Sound, which he described as "preeminently calculated to delight the heart of every Scandinavian."[17] The previously mentioned Andrew Chilberg, who in 1879 became the first Swedish-Norwegian consul in Seattle, promoted Scandinavian settlement not only in that capacity but also as the Northern Pacific Railroad's agent in Seattle and later through his own Chilberg Agency.[18] Another who sought to attract his countrymen to Seattle was the Norwegian attorney and businessman Frank Oleson, who used the newspaper *Washington Posten* as one vehicle.[19] Businessmen in the Midwest also had a role in attracting Scandinavians to Puget Sound. Kenneth Bjork cites the firm of A. E. Johnson and Company, headquartered in Chicago and St. Paul, as important land and ticket agents for immigrants. By the 1880s the firm had a network on both sides of the Atlantic, including branch offices in both Seattle and Tacoma.[20]

The Norwegian and Swedish newspapers of Seattle and Tacoma were additional agents of recruitment, providing much practical information about the Puget Sound area. This ranged from physical descriptions to explanations of Washington's constitution. News of individual Scandinavians and of ethnic institutions such as the churches and societies was regularly featured. Rosters of prominent Nordic immigrants and their accomplishments were also published from time to time, suggesting that the community was a place where Scandinavians could prosper.[21] In the press as well as among private businessmen, midwestern sources also played a part in the westward movement of the Scandinavians. Travel accounts, letters, and news articles from Puget Sound appeared in midwestern Scandinavian newspapers as early as the 1870s, becoming increasingly frequent by the late 1880s.[22]

Guidebooks addressed to Nordic immigrants offered yet another source of information to potential settlers. The earliest of these was Skarstedt's *Oregon och Washington* in 1890. It was published in response to the many inquiries received daily from Scandinavians by the immigration bureau in Portland as well as by newspapers and individuals.[23] Skarstedt went on to write a separate guidebook about Washington, published in 1908 under the title *Washington och dess svenska befolkning*. Living for more than twenty-five years on Puget Sound and writing prolifically, Skarstedt was a factor in attracting Scandinavians, particularly Swedes, to the area. Thos. Ostenson Stine, a Norwegian American who was editor of the *Seattle Daily Times*'s Scandinavian department, wrote a somewhat less influential guidebook in English in 1900 entitled *Scandinavians on the Pacific Puget Sound*. Although overly laudatory in its evaluations, it like the Skarstedt volumes contained much descriptive information on the area and its Scandinavian settlers.[24]

Scores of more general guidebooks and travel accounts by Nordic writers also included descriptions of Seattle and the Puget Sound country, as well as observations about the numbers and conditions of Scandinavians resident there. For example, Carl Sundbeck in 1900 wrote of the rapid growth of Seattle and its large number of Scandinavians and expressed the view that western Washington would become an even more important center of Swedish and Norwegian population.[25] A few years later he described Seattle as "one of America's most interesting and fastest growing cities," a place of natural beauty where "Scandinavians are strongly represented, almost dominant."[26] Thoralv Klaveness likewise saw the attractiveness of Seattle's setting and spoke of the large Norwegian-born population, while K. Zilliacus in 1893 predicted that Seattle had a great future and noted that "lots of Nordics" (*hopar af nordbor*) had settled there.[27]

The very presence of "lots of Nordics" in Seattle suggests a motivation for further Scandinavian settlement as people came to join friends and relatives.[28] It seems hardly a coincidence that so many sources of information not only described the topographical and climatic conditions of Seattle and its economic opportunities but also mentioned something of the circumstances and institutions of the many Scandinavians already settled there.

NOTES

[1] The queen city's growth as a place of Scandinavian settlement is evidenced in its share of the Nordic immigrants living in Idaho, Oregon, and Washington: In 1890 just 4.2 percent of them were in Seattle, in 1900 the figure increased to 11.0 percent, by 1910 it was 17.8 percent, and by 1920 19.3 percent.

[2] For a not altogether successful attempt at developing a model to explain the settlement patterns of immigrants, see Richard K. Vedder and Lowell E. Galloway, "The Settlement Preferences of Scandinavian Emigrants to the United States, 1850–1960," in *Scandinavian Economic History Review*, 18 (1970), 159–176. Jorgen Dahlie and Arthur John Brown have made pioneering efforts toward describing immigrant recruitment into Washington. See Dahlie, "A Social History of Scandinavian Immigration, Washington State, 1895–1910" (Ph.D. dissertation, Washington State University, 1967), chapter 1, and Brown, "Means of Promoting Immigration to the Northwest and Washington to 1910" (M.A. thesis, University of Washington, 1942).

[3] Thos. Ostenson Stine, *Scandinavians on the Pacific Puget Sound* (Seattle, 1900), 33; Ernst Skarstedt, "Svenskt nybyggareliv i Amerika," in Karl Hildebrand and Axel Fredenholm, eds., *Svenskarna i Amerika, populär historisk skildring i ord och bild av svenskarnas liv och underbara öden i Förenta Staterna och Canada*, 1 (Stockholm, 1924), 327; Ingrid Semmingsen, *Utvandringen og det utflyttede Norge*, vol. 1 of *Nordmanns-Forbundets Småskriftserie* (Oslo, 1952), 39–40; the information on Kastengren is found in Ernst Skarstedt, *Svensk-Amerikanska folket i helg och söcken. Strödda blad ur svensk-amerikanernas historia, deras öden och bedrifter, nederlag och segrar, livsintressen och förströelser jämte biografiska uppgifter om ett antal märkesmän* (Stockholm, 1917), 327–328.

[4] Helge Nelson, *The Swedes and the Swedish Settlements in North America*, 1 (Lund, 1943), 54. At the same time it should be noted, as Skarstedt did, that Scandinavians settled also in areas quite unlike those to which they were accustomed. He used Swedish settlements in California to exemplify the point. See Skarstedt, "Svenskt nybyggareliv i Amerika," 327.

[5] Emigration figures for the Nordic countries are conveniently summarized in comparative fashion in Andres A. Svalestuen, "Nordisk emigrasjon. En komparativ oversikt," in *Emigrationen fra Norden indtil I. verdenskrig* (Copenhagen, 1971), 12, along with Bjarni Vilhjalmsson, "Tillæg. Udvandringen fra Island. En oversigt," in the same volume, 161–163.

[6] See John Nordeen, *Svenska klubbens historia 1892–1944* (Seattle, 1944), 28–29, or sample the classified advertising in the local press of the era, as, for example, *The Seattle Post-Intelligencer* of February 15, 1892, where a team-

71

Patsy Adams Hegstad

ster seeking "ten men to buck ties" offered $2.50 per day. The figures for wages paid nationally are found in Paul H. Douglas, *Real Wages in the United States, 1890–1926*, vol. 9 of *Publications of the Pollack Foundation for Economic Research* (Boston, 1930), 137, 175. Unfortunately, Douglas gives no regional comparisons of wages. Kenneth O. Bjork, however, observes in *West of the Great Divide, Norwegian Migration to the Pacific Coast, 1847–1893* (Northfield, Minnesota, 1958), 12–13, that the westward movement of Norwegians was due in part to the expectation of higher wages in the West.

[7] Oskari Tokoi, *Sisu*, "*Even Through a Stone Wall*," in *Makers of History Series* (New York, 1957), 56–57.

[8] Standard histories of Seattle which cover this period are Clarence B. Bagley, *History of Seattle from the Earliest Settlement to the Present Times*, 3 vols. and supplement (Chicago, 1916); Frederic James Grant, ed., *History of Seattle, Washington* (New York, 1891); and C. H. Hanford, ed., *Seattle and Environs, 1852–1924*, 3 vols. (Chicago, 1924), as well as Thomas W. Prosch, "A Chronological History of Seattle, 1850–1897," unpublished typescript, 1901, Northwest Collection, Suzzallo Library, University of Washington, Seattle. Neil Clifford Kimmons, "The Historical Development of Seattle as a Metropolitan Area" (M.A. thesis, University of Washington, 1942); Alexander Norbet MacDonald, "Seattle's Economic Development, 1880–1910" (PhD. dissertation, University of Washington, 1959); and the city directories of Corbett and Co. and of Polk's Seattle Directory Co. also provide insights into the city's development. Margaret I. Wandrey lists mill and logging camp wages in *Four Bridges to Seattle. Old Ballard, 1853–1907* (Seattle, 1975).

[9] To date no documented study of the degree of occupational change has appeared, though references to the phenomenon are numerous. See, for example, Skarstedt, *Svensk-amerikanska folket*, 329; Agnes M. Larson, "The Editorial Policy of *Skandinaven*, 1900–1903," in *Norwegian-American Studies and Records*, 8 (Northfield, Minnesota, 1934), 115–116; and Anders Myhrman, "Finlandssvenskarna i Amerika," in *Emigrationen och dess bakgrund*, vol. 5 of *Svenska Kulturfondens skrifter* (Ekenäs, Finland, 1971), 48–49.

[10] Hans Norman, *Från Bergslagen till Nordamerika. Studier i migrationsmönster, social rörlighet och demografisk struktur med utgångspunkt från Örebro län 1851–1915*, vol. 62 of *Studia Historica Upsaliensia* (Uppsala, 1974), 215–230; Lars-Göran Tedebrand, *Västernorrland och Nordamerika 1875–1913. Utvandring och återinvandring*, vol. 42 of *Studia Historica Upsaliensia* (Uppsala, 1972), 207–213.

[11] *Seattle Press-Times*, May 7, 1891, 4.

[12] *Seattle Press-Times*, November 8, 1892, 3.

[13] Ernst Skarstedt, *Oregon och Washington. Dessa staters historia, natur, resurser, folklif m.m. samt deras skandinaviska inbyggare. En handbok för dem, som önska kännedom om nordvestkustens förhållanden* (Portland, Oregon, 1890), 187, 211–212.

[14] See Ernst Skarstedt, *Washington och dess svenska befolkning* (Seattle, 1908), 31, and O. B. Iverson, "From the Prairie to the Puget Sound," ed. by Sverre Arestad, in *Norwegian-American Studies and Records*, 16 (Northfield, Minnesota, 1950), 94, 98–99. Iverson was an early settler in Stanwood and was the first Norwegian elected to the Washington legislature, serving in the territorial body in 1876–1877. D. B. Ward's work is represented in Washington, State Immigration Agent. *Report, 1899–1900* (Seattle, 1900).

[15] For fuller discussions of these promotional activities, see Brown, "Means of Promoting Immigration," 34–84, and Dahlie, "A Social History of Scandinavian Immigration," 9–22. Also instructive are the individual Seattle city directories and publications of the Seattle Chamber of Commerce, exemplified by A. S. Allen, comp., *The City of Seattle, 1900* (Seattle, 1900).

[16] "Scandinavian Immigration and Aid Society," *The Northern Star*, February 5, 1876, in Morse Eldridge Scrapbook, 3: 4, Northwest Collection, Suzzallo Library, University of Washington, Seattle.

[17] H. C. Wahlberg, "Scandinavians as American Citizens," in *Washington Magazine*, 1 (November, 1889), 23–24.

[18] Chilberg advertised in Skarstedt's *Oregon och Washington*, 325, and in virtually every issue of *Washington Posten* and *Westra Posten*, as well as in the English-language press. He was president of the Scandinavian-American Bank, which he helped to found in 1892, and one of Seattle's leading financiers.

[19] Of Oleson's efforts, Clarence B. Bagley in his *History of Seattle*, 3: 540, wrote that "probably there is no citizen of the entire northwest who has done more to encourage the immigration of the Norwegian people to this part of America than Mr. Oleson, nor is there any who had done more to advance their interests as American citizens."

[20] Bjork, *West of the Great Divide*, 392–401.

[21] A particularly glowing description is found in *Tacoma Tribunen*, January 23, 1896. The attorney L. Hulsether wrote an explanation of the state constitution in the December 24, 1891, issue of *Washington Posten*. *Westra Posten* of November 1, 1895, contains a prime example of biographical treatment of prominent Nordic immigrants in Seattle. See also Dahlie, "A Social History of Scandinavian Immigration," 26–38, for the role of the ethnic press in immigrant recruitment. Like Dahlie, Brown, "Means of Promoting Immigration," 84, emphasized the importance of the ethnic press in making the area known among the foreign-born, specifically mentioning the role of *Westra Posten* among the Scandinavians.

[22] Carlton C. Qualey, *Norwegian Settlement in the United States* (Northfield, Minnesota, 1938), 190–191, noted that *Washington Posten* and *Tacoma Tidende* enjoyed a "considerable circulation" in the Norwegian settlements east of the Rockies and in Norway; he along with Bjork, *West of the Great Divide*, 429–430, and Nora O. Solum, "Oregon and Washington Territory in the 1870's as Seen Through the Eyes of a Pioneer Pastor," in *Norwegian-American Studies and Records*, 16 (Northfield, Minnesota, 1950), 64–90, document the appearance of Puget Sound items in the midwestern ethnic press.

[23] In "Förord," iii–iv, Skarstedt explains that one of the reasons for writing the book was to provide a source of information in a Scandinavian language for those who did not know English. For Skartstedt's role in recruiting Scandinavians, see Gilbert Brown, "Swedish Journalist and Author Aided in Northwest Movement," *Seattle Star*, October 8, 1937, in Du Buar Scrapbook, 79:26, Northwest Collection, Suzzallo Library, University of Washington, Seattle.

[24] See Carl Sundbeck, *Svensk-amerikanerna, deras materiella och andliga strävanden. Anteckningar från en resa i Amerika* (Rock Island, Illinois, 1904), 434–435.

[25] Carl Sundbeck, *Svenskarna i Amerika, deras land, antal och kolonier.*

Patsy Adams Hegstad

En kort öfversikt till tjänst för emigranter och för våra svensk-amerikanska kolonier intresserade (Stockholm, 1900), 37–39.

[26] Sundbeck, *Svensk-amerikanerna*, 432.

[27] Thoralv Klaveness, *Det norske Amerika, blandt udvandrede nordmænd. Vore landsmænds liv og vilkaar i den nye verden* (Kristiania, 1904), 94; K. Zilliacus, *Amerika-Boken. Hjälpreda för utvandrare* (Stockholm, 1893), 133.

[28] The pull of friends and relatives is exemplified in the memoirs of John W. Nordstrom, co-founder in 1900 of a little shoestore which has evolved into the sizeable Nordstrom software chain. He came to Seattle in 1889 because he had a sister and a cousin living in Tacoma. See John W. Nordstrom, *The Immigrant in 1887* ([Seattle], 1950), especially 20, 22, 43.

by TERJE I. LEIREN

3   *Ole and the Reds: The
"Americanism" of
Seattle Mayor Ole
Hanson*

O
N JANUARY 21, 1919, a wage dispute in Seattle's
shipbuilding industry resulted in a strike by
the Metal Trades Union. Two days later, the Central
Labor Council of Seattle voted overwhelmingly in favor
of a sympathetic general strike by its 130-union membership. On the morning of February 6, the city of Seattle came to a virtual standstill.[1] Politicians in the Pacific
Northwest and throughout the nation saw the action as
the harbinger of a Bolshevik revolution. Newspapers
and periodicals echoed their fear, accusing revolutionary elements in the labor movement, especially the International Workers of the World (IWW), of spreading
treason and sedition. The "Red Scare," which the strike
helped to fuel, also gained impetus from the success of
the revolution in Russia in November, 1917, and the
new government's perceived international misbe-
havior. Their separate peace with Germany and an ag-
gressive revolutionary posture, further exaggerated by
American radical activity, helped to frighten and
bewilder segments of the American public. Immigrants

were often the target of neo-nativist hostility: in the words of one Seattle newspaper, the strike was started by "this riffraff from Europe."[2] Ironically, the man who emerged as a genuine national figure through his actions in defeating the strike was Ole Hanson, mayor of Seattle and himself the son of Norwegian immigrants.

A now-and-then politician, Hanson was a real-estate developer in Seattle whose political position changed from being a supporter of the Progressive Republicanism of Theodore Roosevelt to becoming one of the earliest and most visible opponents of Bolshevism and the Red Revolution. For much of his career Hanson appeared to fit into Jon Wefald's view in his 1971 study, *A Voice of Protest*, of Norwegians in America as "consistently progressive, often radical" and generally found to be standing left of center in their support for reform.[3] Whereas Wefald contends that Norwegian immigrants brought class antagonisms with them and translated those into political expression in the Middle West, Hanson's reform philosophy emphasized class cooperation, but was more firmly founded in a strict moral code. American involvement in World War I crystallized his philosophy, but also carried the seeds of a remarkable shift when, as mayor during the General Strike, he became an advocate of limiting immigration while establishing himself as an outspoken proponent of "Americanism."

It is the purpose of this essay, therefore, to examine the career of Ole Hanson by focusing on his political views as expressed in the public record. How did this son of immigrant Norwegian parents come to be acclaimed as "the melting pot's vindication" and "America's first after-the-war civilian hero"? The *Seattle Post-Intelligencer* noted that although "a native born son of immigrant parents, there is no hyphen attached to this Seattle Mayor's title of American."[4] In his 1964

study of the Seattle General Strike, Robert L. Friedheim claimed that the strike gave Ole Hanson "delusions of grandeur" which eventually led him to declare
his candidacy for the presidential nomination in 1920.
The validity of Friedheim's assertion will be examined,
although there is no doubt that Hanson's battle against
the Reds raised him from obscurity to the status of a ce-
lebrity featured in publications across the United
States. In 1920 he published a compilation of his views
in a book titled *Americanism versus Bolshevism*.[5]

Ole Hanson was born January 6, 1874, to parents who
had emigrated from Gudbrandsdalen and settled in
Union Grove, Wisconsin. As a young man he was interested in the law, but it was business which seemed to
hold the greatest attraction for him. He discovered that
he had a talent as a salesman; after he married in 1895,
he was frequently on the road selling drug supplies.[6]
His legs badly injured in a train wreck which killed one
of his children in 1900, Hanson rehabilitated himself
largely through his own will after doctors had told him
he would likely be permanently paralyzed. Following
the example of his hero, Theodore Roosevelt, Hanson
later told a friend: "I had the feeling that if I could get
out there in the open, with the prairie for a pillow and
nothing but the sky above my head, I could beat the
doctors and bring back my health."[7]

In 1902, this drive brought Hanson with his growing
family to the shores of Puget Sound in the state of
Washington. His first night in Seattle he pitched his tent
on Beacon Hill, an unsettled, wooded height overlooking the young city. He purchased a grocery store but,
dissatisfied, sold it after seven months. He tried selling
life insurance until a building boom in Seattle attracted
him to real estate. Soon display advertisements for Ole
Hanson & Co. became a regular feature in the Seattle
press.

Terje I. Leiren

Ole Hanson (1874–1940).

In the fall of 1908, with the support of the *Seattle Star* and its editor, Kenneth Beaton, Hanson ran for the Washington state legislature from the forty-third district, which included Beacon Hill where he had by that time established his home. Hanson's platform focused on the abolition of racetrack betting in the state, but overall, his campaign issues echoed those of other Progressive Republican politicians. *The Manual of the Eleventh Session of the Washington State Legislature* noted: "Mr. Hanson became a prominent figure in the House at the very opening of the session through his advocacy of the passage of a bill to prohibit the wagering of bets on horse racing. His bill was the first measure introduced in the 1909 Legislature. He is an able speaker and has taken an active part in the floor work of the House."[8]

There is no record of what impact Robert LaFollette, from Hanson's native state of Wisconsin, may have had on the thirty-four-year-old legislator; if LaFollette, or anyone in the Norwegian-American community of his youth, influenced his political views, Hanson never directly acknowledged the debt. On May 17, 1909, however, Hanson, speaking at the 17th of May celebration in Seattle, showed that he was not totally unaware of his Norwegian background: "I am proud to say that my parents were born in Norway, and that I have never had cause to regret my Norwegian ancestry or hang my head in shame at the acts of any of my countrymen." That he had also romanticized his heritage was evident when he told his Norwegian-American audience: "In the forefront of all human progress the sturdy pioneer blazes the way and in the very vanguard of the pioneers will always be found the sturdy, honest men of Norway accompanied by their handsome fair-haired wives." More important was the moral code which Hanson stressed. It would later be his guiding philosophy as

79

mayor, but he had already defined it as a legislator: "There shall be no compromise with wrong and no man shall be allowed to rise in the land proclaiming himself a representative Norwegian unless he at the same time represents all which is best in our American government."[9]

Hanson's remarkable activity as a freshman representative extended to a wide variety of issues before the legislature, including support for an eight-hour day for women, a minimum wage bill, a direct primary, state industrial insurance, local option for alcohol, and collective bargaining. He achieved something of a reputation for his attacks on the Seattle city government for tolerating the brothels south of Yesler Street in downtown Seattle. He received several endorsements from organized labor for his work on the House Labor Committee.[10]

After serving a single term in the legislature, Hanson did not seek reelection, choosing rather to return to his real-estate office. By 1912, however, he was back in politics working in the campaign of Theodore Roosevelt against William Howard Taft and Woodrow Wilson for the presidency of the United States. His friend Kenneth Beaton, secretary of Roosevelt's State Central Committee, said Hanson was "our most forceful orator." Beaton noted that Hanson went through a remarkable metamorphosis in front of an audience. One-on-one he was less than inspiring: an audience, however, was "just what an accelerator is to a gas-engine. It speeds him up."[11] With Wilson's election, Hanson returned to his real-estate interests. He was deeply involved in a major development on the north shore of Lake Washington, where he had earlier bought 2,000 acres of land and was building the city of Forest Lake Park. A financial success, Lake Forest Park was his first venture into developing waterfront property, an experience which a dec-

80

ade later would lead to his development of the California coastal community of San Clemente.[12]

Still infected by the political virus, however, Hanson ran for the United States Senate in 1914. Defeated in his bid, he returned once again to the swivel chair in his real-estate office. By then the World War had begun in Europe and new forces served to revive the off-and-on political career of the realtor-politician.

The tensions surrounding American participation in the war did not escape the Pacific Northwest. Perhaps because of Washington's history of militant unionism, it attracted anti-war advocates and IWW organizers. The prospect of jobs was itself an attraction, as the work force in the shipbuilding industry increased phenomenally from a few hundred prior to the war to more than 20,000 in 1917.[13] Politically and economically, Seattle was a magnet for militant and non-militant labor alike.

By Christmas, 1917, Ole Hanson was once again drawn into the political arena, this time for the office of mayor. No group asked him to run, but he became convinced that the people of Seattle wanted a "war-mayor" and, as he wrote, had grown "tired of the old campaign issues."[14] The old issues, of course, were moral issues — police corruption and toleration of the red-light district. To these, Hanson added "Americanism." In assessing his chances, he wrote: "The business community, just awakening to the righteousness of the measures for which I had fought, still regarded me as somewhat unsafe. The labor forces had never had any fault to find with my record, and I felt that the 'Reds' and the anti-war faction would just as surely be against me. My hope for election, apparently, depended on the great middle class who had no axes to grind, wanted no special privileges, but simply desired a fair, square, business administration, 100 percent loyal."[15] Loyalty was probably the fundamental issue in Hanson's cam-

81

paign. He certainly missed no opportunity to emphasize
it. In his rallies throughout the city, he issued a card on
which was printed: "I stand for construction . . . more
factories . . . a square deal for labor as well as capital
. . . for a loyal, united Seattle . . . free from tur-
moil, treason, and IWW control."[16] His appearances
throughout the city assembled the largest crowds of any
of the candidates and, with his undeniable oratorical
skills, seem to have left no doubt that he was an appealing candidate. Perhaps he was too appealing. A not-un-
friendly newspaper, *The Argus*, asked a pointed rhetor-
ical question: "Do we have [a candidate] who claims to
be a Swede when addressing Swedes, a Norwegian
when addressing Norwegians, and an American when
talking to anybody else?"[17]

If there was a target for Hanson's rhetoric, it was the
IWW. The militant labor organization which urged class
warfare and supported non-violent direct action prose-
lytized for the expected revolution. Although representatives from both industry and finance saw it as part of a
worldwide conspiracy, the movement was more indige-
nous than Hanson believed. Some contemporaries, like
John Spargo, writer for *The World's Work*, were aware
of the American origins of the IWW, but the most visible
element in the organization was the immigrant worker.
In a remarkable article published in *The World's Work*,
Spargo pointed to the reasons for the success of the
"Wobblies." They were, he contended, a product of the
needs of the American industrial system, the itinerant
lumber industry, and the exploited immigrants. Speaking rhetorically, Spargo asked the question undoubtedly on the lips of many Americans who did not understand why Americans, too, might be attracted to the
IWW: "Why should native-born Americans, taught in
our schools, nurtured under our traditions, be so hostile
to the system we have regarded as nearly ideal, the bul-

wark of personal freedom and the guarantee of equality before the law? Why should men of our soil and our speech, the soil and speech of Lincoln, be so contemptuous of those ideals, usages, and traditions we seek to summarize in the term 'Americanism'?"[18]

It is difficult to generalize, of course, but much of the misunderstanding and fear of the IWW was probably due to an inability on the part of most people to deal with questions such as those posed by Spargo. Ole Hanson was only one of many who shared this inability, even though he proudly proclaimed his support for unions and the working man. Hanson's own immigrant experience may, ironically, give a clue as to this apparent "blind spot." He was a second-generation Norwegian American who undoubtedly grew up hearing his parents tell of the poverty and lack of freedom in Norway. A measure of this attitude toward Norway might be reflected in the Hanson family tradition that they came from "near Oslo" when in fact, according to *Washington Posten*, Ole Hanson's father, Thorsten, came from Vågå in upper Gudbrandsdalen, far from Oslo.[19] Writing in *Americanism versus Bolshevism*, Hanson claimed: "My parents had come to this country from Norway. They came here wanting liberty, freedom, and a greater opportunity for themselves and their children. They found this country to be good, and never tired of telling us, in broken English, what a great country this was and how different from any other land in the world."[20]

Having focused on the IWW, Hanson's campaign took on the characteristics of a crusade. He delivered speeches to the "Wobblies" themselves, even entering into the proverbial lion's den, the Labor Temple. Acting as a crusader on a moral mission, Hanson told his listeners that he came not expecting to win their votes or their support, but to tell them the truth. Of his speech, he later wrote: "In closing I denounced the Reds, the

83

IWW's, and their kind, and said, 'If elected I will clean you up, lock, stock and barrel. You do not belong in this country. Your talk of Revolution has no place where the majority can and does govern. You are fighting the best Government yet conceived by man. I shall close every hall where the overthrow of our Government by force and violence is taught. You shall not parade with the Red Flag; you shall obey the law or you shall go to jail. Neither your leaders nor the Chamber of Commerce shall control the City Government. It shall be run for the benefit of all the people, not a particular class.'"[21]

On March 5, 1918, Ole Hanson was elected mayor of Seattle. In spite of his red-baiting many of his views and policies were progressive and, although they created opposition in conservative circles, they made him a generally effective chief executive. He facilitated the purchase of the Seattle Municipal Street Railway from private interests for $15 million, advocated an end to private utilities, and raised the minimum wage of city workers from $3.50 to $4.00 per day.[22] It was not altogether for altruistic reasons, however, that Hanson concerned himself with worker's wages: "A well paid worker," he reasoned, "is not susceptible to the rainbow-hued promises of the Bolsheviki. I consider it not only good morals, but good business to give men what they are entitled to."[23]

In August, the mayor, wanting "to set a good example," went to work in the shipyards after a full day at City Hall. With his brand new overalls, pea jacket, cloth cap, and dinner pail, Hanson reported for work at the Erikson Shipyards. A *Post-Intelligencer* reporter was overwhelmed by his patriotism, but an editorial in the same paper, though allowing it as "a matter of patriotic emergency," balked at the precedent it set for other civil servants.[24] The newspaper argued that the business of government was too important to allow government workers to hold extra jobs. The editors clearly recognized Hanson's gesture as symbolic, thereby explaining their tolerance of it. Although earning only $4.00 per day, wages Hanson admitted were inadequate, shipyard workers were considered by many in Seattle to be "spoiled." They were among the better paid and, because of their preference for wearing silk shirts on Sundays, they came to be known as "that silk shirt gang." One of them, a young boxer named Jack Dempsey, had come across the Cascades from his Cle Elum, Washington, training camp when the United States entered the war.[25] Though shipyard workers were exempt from the draft, there is no indication that this may have been Dempsey's motive. Hanson himself admitted that motives for working in the shipyards varied: "Men went to work in the shipyards for different reasons — some to earn a living, some to assist Uncle Sam, others to escape the Draft, and a considerable number simply to agitate against the Government and bring about chaos in our country."[26]

Whatever the reasons, by November, 1918, the workers were talking strike. The Macy Shipyard Adjustment Board had set a basic national wage for all workers at $6.40 per day, but workers in the Puget Sound shipyards believed that the higher cost of living on the West Coast required higher pay. The Metal Trades Council asked for $8.00 per day.[27] The impasse brought charges and countercharges that inevitably focused on perceived Bolshevik influences in the labor movement. A radical newspaper, the Seattle *Union Record*, supported by union funds and featuring a young woman writer named Anna Louise Strong, became the media organ for the workers.[28] Strong had been removed from the Seattle School Board on March 5, principally for her outspoken opposition to the draft, and had developed a reputation as a revolutionary radical.[29] As chief editorial writer for the *Union Record*, Strong exercised considerable influence on the Central Labor Council. On February 4, she wrote the editorial outlining union action to be taken during the general strike which had been set for February 6 at 10 a.m. Strong announced that the unions would feed the people from twelve temporary kitchens; they would care for the sick and babies and preserve law and order. When industries reopened, it would be under labor management. Unclear as to where it would all lead, the editorial, nevertheless, concluded by stating that "we are starting on a road that leads — NO ONE KNOWS WHERE!"[30]

To say that the editorial challenged the entire city governmental structure is to understate its impact. Although Hanson had no immediate plan of action, he was convinced that municipal services and utilities had to function under the control of the government. That was a principle he had learned in his years of progressive politics. His support for labor in general, however, was waning.

The eve of the strike found Hanson in his bedroom working on "plans for defense including securing cartridges, shotguns, machine guns, drawing up a map showing the places where the men were to be stationed, and massing our forces at what I considered strategic points."[31] He wired Attorney General Vaugn Tanner and asked for troops to be stationed at nearby Fort Lawton if police were unable to handle the situation. As news of the impending strike spread, there began a rush on stores for oil stoves, candles, lamps, and groceries. Housewives filled their bathtubs, fearing the water might be shut off.[32] At 10 a.m. on February 6 the strike began. Twenty-four hours later, after a day of eerie silence throughout the city, Hanson acted. He issued a proclamation to the people of Seattle guaranteeing protection by civic authorities: "The time has come for every person in Seattle to show his Americanism. Go about your daily duties without fear. We will see to it that you have food, transportation, water, light, gas and all necessities. The anarchists in this community shall not rule its affairs. All persons violating the laws will be dealt with summarily."[33] The proclamation was printed on the front page of the *Seattle Star*, which was distributed free in 100,000 copies. The proclamation, in addition to the fact that the streetcars were running on Second Avenue, effectively undermined the strike. The more conservative labor leaders, like young Dave Beck of the Teamsters, began to speak out against the strike. On February 3, *The Argus* published its fear that "the strike could drag on for weeks," but on the 10th it collapsed. Hanson rode the resulting wave of patriotic hysteria to national prominence.

Around the country, he was lauded for his firmness in dealing with the first general strike in American history: The *Portland Oregonian*, the Salt Lake City *Deseret News*, the *Mobile Register*, and the Lincoln *Nebraska State Journal* were quoted by the *Literary Digest* as examples of American newspapers responding with praise to Hanson's actions.[34] A. B. Calder, general purchasing agent for the Canadian Pacific Railway in Seattle, was in New York and wrote back to *The Argus* on February 10 that the slogan of a noisy, shouting crowd in the lobby of the Pennsylvania Hotel was "Ole Hanson for President."[35] *Washington Posten*, a Norwegian-American newspaper in Seattle, noting that he had become a "landsfigur," also began touting him for the 1920 Republican nomination.[36] *The Town Crier*, a weekly publication of the Seattle Fine Arts Society, and never a supporter of Hanson, featured a family portrait on its February 15 cover, but acknowledged it would not be "aroused to a state of enthusiastic hysteria over

Terje I. Leiren

Vol. XIV. No. 7   FEBRUARY 15, 1919   Price 10 Cents

Mayor Hanson and Nine Reasons Why He Insisted That Seattle Remain an American City

Standing—Nellie, Doris. Seated—Ted, Mrs. Hanson, holding Lloyd, Robert, the mayor, holding Eugene and Marjorie, William. A tenth reason, Ole Hanson, Jr., the mayor's eldest son, is absent from the group.

This photograph of Mayor Ole Hanson and his family was printed in The Town Crier, *a weekly publication in Seattle, on February 15, 1919. The caption bears the message: "Mayor Hanson and nine reasons why he insisted that Seattle remain an American city."*

88

Mayor Hanson."[37] If *The Town Crier* would not join in, another former adversary, Edwin Selvin, editor of the conservative *Business Chronicle*, thought perhaps Hanson had finally joined him: "Ole Hanson, Mayor of Seattle, came through. Why does not matter. He did, that's enough. This newspaper has had occasion several times to speak critically of the mayor. It has called him a trimmer, an opportunist, a political mountebank, a demagogue; and has scathingly pointed out his heretofore dangerous socialistic proclivities. As our criticism was unrestrained, so now is our praise for his Americanism in the crisis. . . . Mayor Hanson and Police Chief Warren saved the city. All honor to them and all credit — and all good feeling in venturing to express the hope that Ole Hanson has at last become a conservative."[38] With fame came offers for speeches. Possessing the business acumen to take advantage of the situation, Hanson resigned as mayor in August, 1919. His resignation allowed him to carry his message to an even broader constituency. The fight begun in Seattle, he believed, was far from over: "the battle between the *decent forces of Labor* and the *one big union — IWW element* — has only just begun."[39]

Probably because the foreign element was perceived as being so prominent in the labor movement, immigrants became increasingly the target of attack. In this, the son of Norwegian immigrants showed the way. It may well be that Hanson was the catalyst for the restrictive immigration quotas established in 1923. It is certain that he focused his criticism increasingly on what he called "unassimilated aliens."[40] It is not clear when Hanson became convinced that unrestricted immigration was the major cause of the unrest and anarchy in the United States, but as early as March 1, 1919, a letter he sent to the American Bankers Association's national meeting at the Waldorf-Astoria in New York demonstrates an already established opinion. Quite likely his views reflected the strong feelings aroused by the General Strike. In impassioned terms, he told the bankers that it was "the duty of every patriotic American citizen" to stop the influx of antagonistic aliens and "to demand passage of a law whereby the aliens now in this country are compelled to register their addresses."[41] By the time he published his *Americanism versus Bolshevism*, he claimed to have studied the problem and arrived at the conclusion that "the portal has been held too widely open for successful assimilation and digestion of the incoming alien."[42]

Because he believed immigrants could be useful to the country, however, Hanson opposed closing the door altogether. Laws would be enacted, he hoped, which would function as a faucet on the stream of immigrants: "Is there no way that immigrants may be allowed to come when we need them and stopped when we do not need them?" he asked rhetorically.[43] Anxious, especially, to limit immigration from eastern and southern Europe, Hanson viewed "with alarm the decrease in the numbers from Great Britain and Scandinavia."[44] Primary among the new immigrants who were failing to become "real Americans," noted Hanson, were single males living in urban centers. According to Hanson, they lived in crowded tenements, read the foreign press almost exclusively, and retained "foreign modes of life and foreign methods of thinking."[45]

In Hanson's view, it was essential that the United States deal effectively with the aliens. His suggestions for Americanizing them would be neither easy nor inexpensive; some of his ideas would even contradict the American principle of freedom of movement. Included among his proposals were advocacy of dictatorial control over where immigrants could live and what occupations they could follow. He did, however, also make some enlightened proposals suggesting social, if not political, liberalism, such as the establishment of a cabinet-level Department of Education and a Department of Public Health as ways of mitigating immigrant misery.

"Americanism," Hanson maintainted, should become a regular subject in America's schools. The educational process would, naturally, take some time, but the "irreconcilable agitating alien," as Hanson called him, was an immediate threat with which the country had to deal. "The American people want no trifling with these men. If there are not sufficient laws quickly and inexpensively to deport these people, Congress should enact them, and any president who would veto such necessary and just measures would and should be impeached. This matter could easily be handled and no further comment is necessary. The alien who has not taken steps to become a citizen should at once be asked what his intentions are, and if he shows no disposition to Americanize himself, he also should be sent back. *Let them either become Americans or go home.*" [46]

A similar opinion is expressed in an article titled "The New Americanism," published in *The American Review of Reviews* in June, 1919. Events of the war, according to the anonymous author, have brought about the disturbing realization that "one-sixth of our population was foreign, in language and ideals"; as a result "the rest of the hundred million began to wonder whether, after all, America was the melting-pot of the world." He points proudly to the forced instruction in English for draftees, and to the fact that those not already citizens had to prove "their spirit of Americanism by becoming citizens." A three-year period in the army, he reasoned, would "teach love of and respect for our flag and our country, its ideals and its institutions." [47]

Rejecting the simplistic analysis in the article in *Re-*

view of Reviews, Glenn Frank, in *The Century,* maintained that "Americanization does not mean getting an immigrant ready for his citizenship papers. It means the continuous fostering of the American spirit of liberty, justice, and equal opportunity in every man and woman and institution and policy." [48]

Hanson's sympathy by 1920 was with the author of the article in *Review of Reviews,* not with Frank. In his lecture tour of America he told his audience what he believed Americanism was. Americanism, he reiterated in his book, meant, among other things, rule of law, democracy, increased production, a strong national government, universal military training, education, morality, and success. [49] The answer for the alien who could not be Americanized was deportation. For those who wished to come to America, it meant a rigorous selection procedure. Businessman that he was, Hanson transferred concepts from his commercial world to the political arena and counted up debits and credits. America was a business enterprise, the people its shareholders. Liabilities were to be cut and losses trimmed. [50]

In the summer of 1920, Hanson appeared on the platform at the Republican National Convention, but his maverick style clashed with the realities of politics in the smoke-filled rooms. Although Hanson may have used his speeches to exaggerate his own role in breaking the strike, Friedheim's assessment of him as suffering "delusions of grandeur" lacks credence because it fails to take into account Hanson's immigrant background with its rigid code of moral behavior which was then refined into his peculiar blend of business and progressive politics. His lack of a political organization, something of which he was so proud when he ran for mayor, stopped him on the national level. The nomination went instead to the less strident Warren G. Harding. [51]

Ole Hanson, the Norwegian immigrant's son who

sought to restrict immigration, left politics after his failure to gain the Republican nomination. He moved to California, where he resumed his real-estate operations. Among his many projects, his favorite and probably his best was the seaside community of San Clemente, which a writer for *Sunset* magazine in 1929 called "a dream city" on the Pacific.[52] In politics he was a Cincinnatus, coming and going. A moralist in business and politics, he combined the two in a way which showed him to be as imaginative as he was opportunistic.

NOTES

[1] "Paul S. Dunbar Scrapbook," no. 74, Northwest Collection, Suzzallo Library, University of Washington, Seattle; *Seattle Post-Intelligencer*, February 3, 1919.

[2] *The Argus* (Seattle), February 8, 1919; *The Outlook*, February 5, 1919; Robert K. Murray, *Red Scare: A Study in National Hysteria, 1919–1920* (Minneapolis, 1955), 11–17.

[3] Jon Wefald, *A Voice of Protest: Norwegians in American Politics, 1890–1917* (Northfield, Minnesota, 1971), 29. Contrary to Wefald's thesis, Hanson's reformist views appear not to have been linked to the immigrant background of class antagonism. On the contrary, he repeatedly emphasized the necessity for class cooperation. His views of reform, in fact, were probably rooted in his firmly held moral convictions. Thus, he opposed gambling, alcohol, and corruption for ethical reasons. That, however, is another tradition the Norwegian immigrants brought with them to America.

[4] Ashman Brown, "Papers in East Praise Mayor Hanson for Firm Stand Taken in Strike," in *Seattle Post-Intelligencer*, February 11, 1919. An excellent discussion of the background of hyphenated Americanism is Carl H. Chrislock, *Ethnicity Challenged: The Upper Midwest Norwegian-American Experience in World War I* (Northfield, Minnesota, 1981), 29–55.

[5] Ole Hanson, *Americanism versus Bolshevism* (Garden City, New York, 1920); Robert L. Friedheim, *The Seattle General Strike* (Seattle, 1964), 3, 20–22, is a generally unsympathetic account of Hanson's role and motives.

[6] Kenneth C. Beaton, "His Honor the Mayor: What I Know About Ole Hanson," in *Hearts*, 36 (1919), 14. See also Dolores Huteson Hughes, "The Impractical Dreamer," unpublished manuscript by Hanson's granddaughter. Copy, given to the author by Hanson's daughter, Doris Denison, of San Clemente, California, is in the Scandinavian Archives, manuscripts division, University of Washington Libraries.

[7] Beaton, "His Honor the Mayor," 14.

[8] *Manual of the Eleventh Session of the Washington State Legislature, 1909: The House of Representatives*, copy in the Northwest Collection, University of Washington Libraries.

[9] Speech by Ole Hanson, May 17, 1909, quoted in *Washington Posten*, May 21, 1909.

[10] See pamphlet, "Unite on Ole Hanson," in Seattle — Politics and Government, N 979.743, in Northwest Collection, University of Washington Libraries.

[11] Beaton, "His Honor the Mayor," 15.

[12] See Homer Banks, *The Story of San Clemente: The Spanish Village* (San Clemente, California, 1930).

[13] *Literary Digest*, 60 (March 8, 1919), 48.

[14] Hanson, *Americanism versus Bolshevism*, 4.

[15] Ole Hanson, "Why and How I Became Mayor of Seattle," in *The World's Work*, 39 (December, 1919), 123.

[16] Hanson, "Why and How I Became Mayor," 125.

[17] *The Argus*, February 23, 1918. See also *Seattle Post-Intelligencer*, February 3, 6, and 7, 1918.

[18] John Spargo, "Why the IWW Flourishes," in *The World's Work*, 39 (January 1920), 244–246. Spargo's ideas for the reform of the American political system "in order to combat Bolshevism and kindred forms of social unrest" are found in his *The Psychology of Bolshevism* (New York, 1919), 137–150.

[19] *Washington Posten*, May 16, 1919. Hanson's daughter, Doris Denison, told the author that she believed her family came from the Oslo region. Personal interview with Doris Denison, December 28, 1981, San Clemente, California.

[20] Hanson, *Americanism versus Bolshevism*, 5.

[21] Hanson, "Why and How I Became Mayor," 126.

[22] Ole Hanson, "Smashing the Soviet in Seattle," in *The World's Work*, 39 (January, 1920), 302; *Seattle Times*, May 6, 1918, and July 7, 1940.

[23] Hanson, "Smashing the Soviet in Seattle," 302.

[24] *Seattle Post-Intelligencer*, August 16, 1918.

[25] Nard Jones, *Seattle* (Garden City, New York, 1972), 166.

[26] Hanson, "Smashing the Soviet in Seattle," 303.

[27] Hanson, "Smashing the Soviet in Seattle," 303; "Dunbar Scrapbook," no. 74, Northwest Collection, University of Washington Libraries.

[28] Jones, *Seattle*, 166.

[29] See *Seattle Post-Intelligencer*, March 6, 1918, and *Seattle Times*, March 6, 1918. Hanson, in "Smashing the Soviet in Seattle," 303, accused Strong of being a "Red revolutionist."

[30] *Seattle Union Record*, February 4, 1919; Ole Hanson, "Seattle's Red Revolution," in *The World's Work*, 39 (February, 1920), 406.

[31] Hanson, "Seattle's Red Revolution," 407.

[32] Hanson, "Seattle's Red Revolution," 408. See also "Dunbar Scrapbook," no. 74, Northwest Collection, University of Washington Libraries.

[33] "Proclamation to the People of Seattle," quoted in Ole Hanson, "The Victory Over Seattle's Reds," in *The World's Work*, 39 (March, 1920), 485.

[34] See *Literary Digest*, 60 (March 1, 1919), 15.

[35] *The Argus*, February 22, 1919.

[36] See, for example, *Washington Posten*, May 16, 1919.

[37] *The Town Crier*, February 15, 1919.

[38] Edwin Selvin, "Seattle, Stay Awake," in *Business Chronicle*, February 15, 1919, reprinted as a paid advertisement in *Seattle Post-Intelligencer*, February 17, 1919.

[39] Hanson, *Americanism versus Bolshevism*, 96.

[40] Hanson, *Americanism versus Bolshevism*, 243, 245.

[41] "The Week," in *The Nation*, March 1, 1919, 31.

[42] Hanson, *Americanism versus Bolshevism*, 244.

[43] Hanson, *Americanism versus Bolshevism*, 245.

[44] Hanson, *Americanism versus Bolshevism*, 246.

[45] Hanson, *Americanism versus Bolshevism*, 250.

[46] Hanson, *Americanism versus Bolshevism*, 247–248.

[47] "The New Americanism," in *The American Review of Reviews*, 59 (June, 1919), 656.

[48] Glenn Frank, "The Tide of Affairs: Comment on the Times," in *The Century*, 100 (June, 1920), 220–221.

[49] See Hanson, *Americanism versus Bolshevism*, 282–286, for a remarkable list of differences between Americanism and Bolshevism.

[50] Hanson, *Americanism versus Bolshevism*, 294–295.

[51] Robert Friedheim implies that the Republicans did not consider Hanson a serious candidate. Clarence Darrow, the well-known attorney, called Hanson "a cheap vaudeville performer" because of his "red-baiting" speeches. It may well be that Harding's nomination was a signal that the strident tone set by Hanson was no longer favored by the Republican party. See Friedheim, *The Seattle General Strike*, 174–176.

[52] Neil Stanley, "A Dream City on the Pacific," in *Sunset*, 62 (May, 1929), 14–15. In addition to San Clemente and Lake Forest Park, Hanson also built extensively in Santa Barbara and along Slauson Boulevard in Los Angeles. He developed the desert community of Twenty-Nine Palms, north of Palm Springs. The home of his partner, Hamilton H. Cotton, in San Clemente became Richard Nixon's western White House.

by SVERRE ARESTAD

4   *Norwegians in the Pacific Coast Fisheries*

FOR MORE than a century Norwegians have participated in many branches of the fishing industry
from California to Alaska. Norwegians have been dory
fishermen, harpooners on whaling vessels, cannery
workers, salmon-trap constructors and attendants, crews
on fishing vessels of all sizes, owners and superintendents of salmon canneries, managers and owners
of shore stations, owners and builders of fishing boats,
ship chandlers, owners and operators of factory processors, and prominent members of international fishery
commissions. The gradual development of Norwegian
participation will be traced in this essay from, so to
speak, infancy to maturity, and some attempt will be
made to moderate certain overstated claims about the
importance of Norwegians in the founding and early
years of the Pacific Coast fisheries.

This study will deal with cannery owners, station
managers, superintendents, and boat owners, as well as
those who performed the grueling physical work. The
treatment of the fishermen themselves leans primarily

on published material, but some of it is based on personal experience.

In January, 1943, the author published in *The Pacific Northwest Quarterly* an article bearing the same title as this one, which covered the first sixty years of Norwegian activity. The article was based on extensive research and on numerous interviews with knowledgeable men in the industry. Most of it has been reproduced in the first part of this study, with several changes and a few additions. The changes include elimination of the footnotes, incorporation of several of the original footnotes into the text, and alteration of tenses where necessary. The original version, heavily documented, is readily available.

A few Norwegians were fishermen on the coast from California north to Washington, on Puget Sound, and in British Columbia as early as the 1860s. The first entrepreneur on Puget Sound was John Brygger, sometimes written Bryggot, who established a salmon saltery at Salmon Bay, six miles north of Olympia, Washington, in 1876. A few other Norwegians were also successful, but their activities were minor in relation to the whole salmon industry in the 1870s.

The salmon industry was established relatively early in the nineteenth century, with stations in California and Oregon, and somewhat later in Washington. It was not, however, until the introduction of the canning process that the salmon industry began to attain a dominant position in the fisheries of the Pacific Coast and Alaska. Americans and Canadians organized the fishing companies, built the canneries, acquired the valuable trap sites, and constructed the traps. While Norwegians were not among the early developers of the salmon fishery, several soon became important figures in the Alaska salmon industry. The most noteworthy of these was Peter Thams Buschmann, who organized several canning concerns and built at least five canneries, and for whom Petersburg was named. Several of Buschmann's five sons, all of whom were born in Norway, were active in the salmon industry before 1900. Egil Buschmann, for example, was general superintendent of the Naknak Packing Corporation. In 1905, L. A. Pederson was manager of the Bristol Bay and Naknak packing companies, and in the same year Sofus Jensen was manager of the Altoona Packing Company. By 1918, Norwegians were even more evident. In that year a man named Hawkinson managed the Carlisle Packing Company, and Martin Lund and Chris Tjosevig were owners of the Eyak River Packing Company, both in the Prince William Sound area. Others of importance were O. C. Mehus, Hans D. Sorvik, Einar Beyer, and his nephew Haakon B. Friele.

Einar Beyer of Bergen, Norway, visited Seattle in 1906 and returned in 1914 to settle there. Haakon B. Friele was born February 3, 1897, in Bergen and completed a course in liberal education at Bergen Katedralskole in 1914. Two years later he received a certificate from the Bergen School of Commerce; he arrived in Seattle in December of the same year. Beyer was the principal organizer and first president of the Wise Packing Company. Friele worked for his uncle until 1918, when the company was sold, and continued to work for two successive owners until he went to Copenhagen in 1920 to open an office for the Great Atlantic and Pacific Tea Company. In the fall of 1921, he returned to Seattle to organize the Nakat Packing Company for the grocery chain, and to serve as its president and general manager. Nakat had six canneries in Alaska with 800 employees, producing 250–300 thousand cases of salmon annually, which were sold through the chain's own stores. Friele was the corporation's buyer for Seattle and the Northwest. He also served as director and vice president of the Association of Pacific Fisheries.

In addition to their activities as fishermen and entrepreneurs, Norwegians were rather early interested members and even officers of various associations of fishermen and of international fish commissions. August Buschmann, H. B. Friele, and Harald Synnestvedt were members of the Association of Pacific Fisheries and the latter two enjoyed the honor of being president of that association.

In the 1920s a Norwegian was operating one of the largest salmon mild-cure stations at Port Alexander on Baranof Island. He was Karl Hansen, from Bø in the Vesterålen Islands, an experienced fisherman but unfortunately prone to seasickness. Seeking relief from the ardors of the sea, Hansen landed at Port Alexander in Southeast Alaska in 1916. When he arrived the place had only one cabin, with a store offering bait, gear, coffee, and snuff, whose proprietor was Per Strømme, also from Bø, who had arrived shortly before.

By 1917 Karl Hansen had opened his mild-cure station. He already had a contact in Seattle, Jorgen Jacobsen, who marketed Hansen's product for lox among Jewish buyers in Chicago, Boston, New York, and Philadelphia. Hansen always competed successfully in that market, largely because he was a perfectionist and had workers who could meet his demands. Jacobsen died in the early 1920s, and afterward Hansen used the brokerage firm of Eriksen and Bye of Seattle as agents. Hansen developed his operation to include a permanent residence, a store, a processing station and warehouse, a dock, a water system, a two-story office building, and living quarters and a dining hall for the workers. He also acquired two boats to transport the finished product — iced down — to shipping centers such as Prince Rupert, British Columbia. Eventually Standard Oil erected a fuel storage tank and a gasoline tank at the station, which served Hansen's needs and those of fishermen far and wide. At the peak of Hansen's productivity — in the late 1920s and early 1930s — 1,000 to 1,200 trollers, with half as many boats, delivered fish to his station. The permanent population increased rapidly over the years.

Originally king salmon provided the product, but no king salmon under fifteen pounds was accepted for mild-cure — the smaller ones were utilized in other ways. When the king salmon harvest dwindled, large silver salmon were successfully substituted. These, too, eventually ceased to be present in sufficient quantity to warrant continuing the operation. In its heyday, Hansen's station processed more than a million pounds of salmon in a season. The trollers were paid the grand sum of 50¢ for a fifteen-pound or larger king salmon but only 25¢ for the smaller ones.

Norwegians have been more important as salmon fishermen than as entrepreneurs, although here, too, their importance has been overstated. A few Norwegians, to be sure, became fishermen in the seventies and even in the sixties, but their numbers were indeed small. An analysis of the figures by nationality for the year 1892 shows that Norwegians then composed but a small percentage of the fishermen in the region. In that year there were 3,458 fishermen in Washington, of whom 287 were Norwegians; in Oregon there were 2,822 fishermen, with only 261 Norwegians, while in California there were 173 Norwegian fishermen out of a total of 4,766. Figures for the nationality of the fishermen in Alaska in 1892 are not available, but the percentage of Norwegians would probably be considerably less than in the state of Washington. In British Columbia there were a few. This would mean that by 1892 fishermen of Norwegian birth participated to the extent of 8.9 percent in the fisheries of Washington, 9.3 percent in Oregon, 3.65 percent in California, possibly 3 or 4 percent in Alaska, and scarcely at all in British Columbia. Except for California, the figures apply almost exclusively to salmon. Later, Norwegians became quite active in the Columbia River salmon fishery.

After 1892, the salmon industry on Puget Sound developed rapidly and, as time went on, the pattern in the industry changed in two striking particulars. The first of these was the evolution of the fish trap, which became the most important source of the canneries' supply of salmon. As a result of this change in the method of catching fish, two national groups came to be dominant as fishermen. At the turn of the century, most of the maritime nations of Europe were represented, but by 1930 the Slovenians had become the principal purse-seine fishermen, while the Norwegians led in trap fishing and won a considerable share of the purse-seine fishing as well. After the traps ceased to be used, the purse seine came into its own again, and the Slovenians became the dominant salmon fishermen on Puget Sound, with Norwegians participating only to a minor extent.

In Alaska the evolution of salmon fishing was much the same as on the Sound. There, too, Norwegians became the most important trap fishermen, they participated to a large extent as gill netters and trollers, but they were only a small factor as purse seiners. It is estimated that 50 percent or more of the trap fishermen and 25 percent of the gill netters were Norwegian in the 1930s. John Dybdal of Bellingham, Washington, served one of the large salmon canneries there for many years as "outside" man, the company representative who oversees the operations at the fishing banks. In 1942 he estimated that at least 75 percent of the trap fishermen on Puget Sound were of Norwegian extraction before the traps were closed in 1934. Of the 705 gill netters registered in 1939 with the Alaska Fishermen's Union in Seattle, 307 were born in Norway. The same proportion held for Portland, Oregon, but San Francisco had mostly Italians with only a few Norwegians. In 1939 there were 2,810 gill-net fishermen in the Bristol Bay area, of whom approximately 700 or 25 percent were of Norwegian extraction. Elsewhere in Alaska they participated to a very minor degree except in a few areas.

As cannery workers Norwegians have never been and are not now important, although some have been employed as machinists, blacksmiths, tallymen, and carpenters in the salmon canneries of Alaska. Available records do not permit an accurate classification of the cannery workers of that region as to nationality, but an estimate would place the Norwegian participation in the 1930s between 5 and 10 percent, with the smaller figure probably more nearly representing the truth.

A branch of the salmon industry in which Norwegians have been heavily engaged, in such areas as Alaska and the Washington coast, is trolling. This fishery is characterized by the fact that the boats and gear are owned and operated by the individual fishermen. Previous to 1905, trolling was done from hand-powered canoes or rowboats and Indians were the principal fishermen. As the mild-cure industry was developed and as the fresh fish markets increased, the demand arose for more king salmon and cohoes. These two species of salmon became more and more scarce within a reasonable distance from the markets, and eventually the salmon fleet of Puget Sound became a deep-sea fleet with stations on the Washington coast and in Neah Bay. The trolling fleet, with headquarters in Seattle, was composed of 750 boats, employing 1,500 fishermen. From late spring until early autumn the trolling fleet caught an average of some six million pounds of salmon annually. After the regular salmon fishing season was over, about 250 of the sturdier boats augmented their crew of two with a third man and went fishing for albacore tuna off the Washington and Oregon coasts. The average annual catch of tuna was about twelve million pounds. When the season was over, some 250 boats of the fleet fished for dogfish and soupfin shark, which were valued for their livers. This provided the fishermen with employment for the months during which they otherwise would have been idle or forced to seek other work.

From the time of World War I up to the mid-1930s, the salmon trollers often complained that they were not given fair consideration by the fresh fish buyers. Prices fluctuated according to the amount of fish on the market; the trollers were often dissatisfied with the grading and with the system of disposing of their fish at the fishing grounds. As a result of these grievances there emerged, in 1935, a Fishermen's Cooperative Association, with offices in the Bell Street Terminal, Seattle. This was an association of the boat owners, but since all boat owners also fished it was a form of fishermen's association as well. The primary purpose of this organization was to act as agent for the fishermen in their dealings with the fresh fish buyers. It maintained three stores, one at Westport, one at Neah Bay, and one at Seattle, which supplied the fishermen with ice, oil, food, and gear.

Arne Antonsen, who was manager of the Fishermen's Cooperative Association when it was founded in 1935, stated that the salmon trolling fishery on the Washington coast was developed principally by Norwegians and was for years dominated almost exclusively by them. He knew most of the fishermen and estimated that about 90 percent were of Norwegian extraction. The figures for the number born in Norway dwindled with time, and many of the later salmon trollers were American-born

Norwegians. William Hecker was agent for the Alaska Fishermen's Union in Seattle in 1941 and knew hundreds of fishermen personally. He estimated that about 35 percent of the Alaska fishermen were of Norwegian extraction. 3,239 fishermen were then registered with the Seattle Union, of whom 762 were born in Norway and perhaps 350 were second-generation Norwegian Americans. This is approximately 34 percent, very close to Hecker's estimate.

Norwegians have been particularly active in the Alaskan cod fishery, both as fishermen and as entrepreneurs. In the early years, cod fishing was carried on by large vessels sent out from San Francisco. Later, vessels were also sent to the fishing grounds from Seattle, Anacortes, and Poulsbo. Some time in the 1870s the first shore station was erected, and after that time, particularly after 1886, numerous shore stations were built. At first the fisherman attached to the shore stations fished from oar-driven dories, but in the 1920s gasoline-driven boats of from two to twelve horsepower came into general use. These boats were usually owned by the fishermen themselves, cod fishing being in that respect much like salmon trolling. Despite these developments, the larger vessels have always been more important to the industry, and have taken the bulk of the fish.

A large percentage of the fishermen at the Alaska stations have been Norwegians. They have also been skippers and owners of vessels, agents at shore stations for the large codfish companies, and founders of shore stations. In 1905, for example, King & Winge, Seattle shipbuilders, were the principal owners of the King & Winge Codfish Co. Winge was a Norwegian. Other Norwegians, like John Einmo and Lars Mikkelson, opened codfish stations in Alaska. Their countrymen also founded the Pacific Codfish Co., a home-curing station, in Poulsbo, Washington, in 1911.

Norway was once the principal whaling nation in the world, but Norwegians in America were never important in the development and growth of that industry here. Whaling was introduced to the Pacific Coast in 1855 with the erection of a kind of shore station by Portuguese fishermen in California. Because of their success, other stations were soon established and in a few years Pacific Coast whaling had risen to the dignity of a real industry. By 1892 there were thirty-six vessels in operation, employing 1,240 men. Of these men, fifty, or only about 4 percent, were Norwegians. In the same year the whaling fleet of New Bedford, Massachusetts, operating in the North Pacific with twenty-one vessels carrying a total crew of 645 men, had but fourteen persons born in Norway — less than one sailor per vessel. Later, however, Norwegians became more important as sailors and even gunners and skippers on these vessels. By the beginning of the twentieth century the Pacific Coast whaling industry had dwindled to practically nothing. After 1905, however, it was revived by thorough modernization and in this Norwegians played a larger part.

Norwegians came to the Pacific Coast in comparatively large numbers at about the same time that the herring and fish oil industries were being developed. So, although not the founders of these industries, they were important as their developers. The herring fishery was established in 1888, the same year that fishing for halibut began, but for a score of years herring was used principally as halibut bait. As late as 1910, only 180 men were employed. After fifteen more years of development, the herring fishery had reached its heyday, with fifty-four salting plants and reduction plants for converting herring into meal and other products, which employed 1,839 persons. By 1935 the number of persons employed in the industry had been reduced by exactly 500, to 1,339.

There are no records which reveal how many of the herring fishermen were Norwegians, although people in the industry are inclined to believe that the percentage was large. For a number of years the Alaska herring fleet was called "The Norwegian Navy," and the term was apparently justified. Edward Weber Allen wrote in *North Pacific* in 1936: "We were a little too early in the season to see what those who would follow in a month or so would find at the Ketchikan waterfront — its pilings, docks and floats fairly alive with cannery tenders, purse-seine boats, tugs, and scows; and the brawny, tough, swearing, but withal good-hearted, honest and self-reliant salmon, herring, and halibut fishermen, mostly Norwegian." The records of the United Fishermen's Union of the Pacific at Seattle show that in the late 1930s the largest number of boats clearing through its office for herring fishing in Alaska were manned by Norwegian fishermen. Peter Thams Buschmann of Petersburg, Alaska, was the first to salt herring in commercial quantities. In 1898 only a few thousand barrels were packed and marketed among the Scandinavians in the Middle West. Other Norwegians followed Buschmann — Storfold & Grondahl Packing Co., of Washington Bay, Baranof Island, and Einar Beyer, in Southeast Alaska, — so that by 1918 100,000 barrels were being packed. Carl Overby and Chris L. Foss were also prominent entrepreneurs in this business.

The sardine industry, founded in 1904 and almost exclusively confined to California, attracted quite a number of Norwegian fishermen. In the late thirties, as many as sixty-three Norwegian-owned boats engaged in the California fishery. After 1934 a small sardine industry operated on the Washington and Oregon coasts and the fishermen engaged in this industry were principally Norwegians. Norwegians were also involved in processing and marketing.

Another of the fish industries on the Pacific Coast in which Norwegians were extremely active was the dogfish and soupfin shark liver fishery. This industry, which increased in importance after the supply of liver oils from European and other areas was cut off as a result of World War I, was a boon to the seasonal fishermen. Most of the fishermen engaged in the liver-oils industry were Norwegian-American halibut fishermen and salmon trollers. Some idea of the importance of the industry to the men who engaged in it can be judged from the following figures. By November 15, 1941, after a month's fishing, over a quarter-million dollars worth of soupfin shark livers and over half a million dollars worth of dogfish livers had been unloaded in Seattle, a tremendous increase over 1940. The largest individual catch came in March, 1942, when the crew of the halibut schooner *Tordenskjold*, whose captain was the Norwegian-American Carl Serwold, landed $60,000 worth of soupfin shark livers from a two-weeks' fishing trip. Each fisherman received a share amounting to $6,000 for that single trip.

Although not the founders of the halibut fishery, Norwegians became its principal developers in the second phase of the evolution of the industry. The uninterrupted development of this industry in the Pacific Northwest dates from 1888, when two vessels from Gloucester, Massachusetts, made catches of halibut on Flattery Bank and in the adjacent region. For several years thereafter, two methods of catching halibut were in use. At first eastern interests, with Pacific Coast headquarters located in Vancouver, British Columbia, took the greater part of the catch in North Pacific waters, using large vessels and steamers. Individual fishermen, however, used small halibut schooners of from five to ten register tons. The large vessels, the steamers, and the small schooners increased in numbers for a period

107

of years, with the large vessels catching the greatest share of the halibut. Small boats increased in importance, however, after the turn of the century, especially after 1905, the year which marks the change to small power-driven schooners. By 1910 the power-driven schooners, which were the property of the fishermen themselves, occupied the most important position in the halibut industry; by the early 1920s they enjoyed full control of the field. As the operations of larger vessels and steamers became unprofitable, the eastern financial interests withdrew from the industry, leaving it one whose capital investments, aside from receiving stations and wholesale departments, were owned by the fishermen themselves.

In this second phase of the industry, Norwegians began to participate actively as halibut fishermen. During the years of transition, they became increasingly important as fishermen and as boat owners, and by the 1920s they had become the dominant group. Concerning the position of Norwegians in the halibut industry in 1940, Harold Lokken, then manager of the Vessel Owners' Association of Seattle, wrote to the author: "At the present time, there are approximately four hundred American vessels engaged in fishing halibut in North Pacific waters. These vessels are manned by from three to eleven fishermen each, making a total in all of approximately three thousand fishermen engaged in catching halibut as a livelihood. . . . At the present time over nine persons in every ten engaged in the [halibut] industry are Norwegians. This average will hardly be exceeded by any other industry in the country. Several years ago, the Norwegians in the industry, with a few exceptions, were all born in Norway, but today, due to immigration restrictions, to the inroads of old age among the old-timers in the industry, and to the lack of better opportunities in other industries for the sons of yesterday's halibut fishermen, the pattern in the industry is being changed by the replacement of the Norwegian-born fishermen by youngsters born of Norwegian parents in this country."

Aside from their activities as fishermen and as entrepreneurs in the Pacific Coast fisheries, Norwegians have been engaged both as workers and as employers in allied industries: as chandlers, boat builders, and inventors of fishing gear and canning machinery. They have been marine architects, fish brokers, and financial backers of fishermen who acquire their own boats and gear. They have been actively interested in all legislation that has affected the fishing industry, and they have aided the work of the halibut and sockeye commissions. They have held important positions in both employers' and workers' organizations, such as the Association of Pacific Fisheries, the halibut vessel owners' associations of Seattle and Ketchikan, the various fishermen's co-operatives, and the trade unions of the fisherman and the cannery workers. Such activities show Norwegians' interest in the fisheries aside from their work as entrepreneurs and fishermen. It might be added that after the entry of the United States into World War II, the Alaska fishermen, particularly, were in a position to render important service to the Navy and the Coast Guard, by assisting in patrol and rescue work.

During the past forty years notable changes have occurred in the fisheries of the Pacific Northwest which have dramatically affected Norwegian participation in them, with the result that their activity is now confined to three or four branches of the trade, unlike the first sixty years when they were pursuing a dozen avenues. Norwegians no longer engage in the tuna fishery off the California coast nor do they fish for soupfin shark and dogfish on the Oregon and Washington coasts. Dogfish

109

is now commercially harvested, filleted, and shipped to England and West Germany for fish and chips. Whaling, of course, is no longer pursued. At one time, the craft fishing for herring were largely Norwegian, but this activity has virtually ceased. Salmon trolling on the Washington coast has been somewhat reduced, although Norwegians, aided by a marketing association, still constitute the major element in this fishery. Some schoolteachers on vacation and others who are seasonally unemployed fish during the summer if they can finance a modest operation. Norwegian trollers are still quite active in Alaska, but not nearly to the extent that they were in the 1920s and 1930s. Some Norwegians still fish for albacore tuna off the coast of Oregon and Washington, and Norwegians are still leaders in the yet flourishing cod fishery of Alaska.

Norwegians, as stated earlier, were the principal constructors and tenders of fishing traps in Alaska and on Puget Sound in the 1920s and early 1930s. Traps were the main source of fish for the canneries. Since traps were outlawed on Puget Sound in 1934 and in Alaska in the 1940s, these jobs have disappeared. When the traps were outlawed, the principal source of salmon for the canneries became the purse seine. Always active as purse seiners, the Yugoslavs (often referred to in the literature as Slovenians, though in Anacortes, Washington, they prefer to be called Croatians) became the principal commercial salmon fishermen. This situation changed drastically when the now famous Boldt decision of 1975 allotted half of the salmon catch in Puget Sound to the native Indians. Having fewer boats, the Indians are allowed to fish uninterruptedly, while other fishermen are drastically restricted.

Although few Norwegians are directly affected by this decision, it has been mentioned to show general trends in the fisheries. As a result of the Boldt decision, hundreds of fishing boats are now for sale, and many owners have gone bankrupt. Many more face a doubtful future because there are now far too many boats for the decreasing supply of salmon on the Oregon and Washington coasts and in Puget Sound; Alaska, however, is still productive, particularly Bristol Bay.

Fewer Norwegians than formerly are cannery superintendents, machinists, and carpenters in Alaska, and there are fewer Norwegian entrepreneurs in all these industries. They have, however, retained their relative share as ship chandlers and boat architects.

Two fisheries still attract numerous Norwegians: halibut, for decades a virtual Norwegian monopoly in Alaska based on boat ownership; and the king-crab fishery. A more recent development is the entry of Norwegians into the catcher-processor business. These three areas will now be examined.

Norwegian participation in the halibut fishery has changed in two essentials: those who now man the boats and own them are usually sons, grandsons, or sons-in-law of the original Norwegian immigrants; and the equipment now is more sophisticated and much more expensive. Looked at in the proper perspective, the earlier generation of halibut fishermen may prove to have been relatively as prosperous as the current ones. Several halibut fishermen built schooners valued at $40,000 in the early 1940s. But despite the drastic devaluation of the dollar in the past forty years, halibut boats built now for $800,000 are obviously more sophisticated and more expensive than those of four decades ago. While Norwegians are still very active in halibut fishing, they are no longer dominant as they were forty years ago. This is particularly true of Alaska-based boats.

The king-crab fishery is a different story. From rather modest beginnings several decades ago, the king-crab

111

industry has risen to a multi-million-dollar enterprise. In 1976, the United States established a 200-mile coastal limit and a three-mile management zone. This greatly enhanced the king-crab fishery for American fishermen, because it prevented the Japanese, Russian, and other fleets from exploiting or disrupting the breeding grounds of the king crab and taking unlimited quantities of fish on the high seas. It has had a similar effect on the halibut, cod, and salmon fisheries off the Alaska coast, principally in the Bering Sea and the Gulf of Alaska.

In 1980 there were 200 boats in the king-crab fishery with a total allotment of 185,000,000 pounds. The 1981 season had an augmented fleet of 225 boats but the king-crab population had declined and the allotted catch was reduced by more than one-half. In 1982, the allotment was reduced still further. Many of the king-crab fishermen who have been riding high on the accelerating crest are finding the immediate future crucial, as 1983 has shown. Poaching, always present to some extent, is also likely to increase.

In the king-crab fishery Norwegians have been the innovators in methods. In a letter of November 12, 1981, Harold Lokken states that while Norwegians do not own most of the boats, although they skipper more than they own, they have produced the most technical advances. These have then been exploited by others. So, while some Norwegians are doing exceptionally well as boat owners and fishermen, they are in the minority. A few of the more successful ones will be considered here, beginning with Oddbjørn Nordheim, Peter Njardvik, and Einar Pedersen.

Captain Nordheim came from Hallingdal in Norway in the late 1950s, and Njardvik arrived from Iceland as an adult. They engaged in crab fishing. With their shares of the catch, running into tens of thousands of dollars over the years, they formed a partnership and built their own boat. In 1980, Nordheim's daughter Birgit christened the third vessel in their growing fleet, a 122 × 32 × 16 foot super-boat, a crabber-trawler.

Nordheim and Njardvik have made their mark in the king-crab fishery; the Norwegian-born Einar Pedersen has also been important. His father, Reinhold, had come to Seattle in the middle 1920s and immediately found a job as a halibut fisherman. Soon he was able to bring his family over. In 1928, Einar arrived in Ballard with his mother, four brothers, and a sister. No sooner had he landed than Einar went to work as a doryman on the halibut schooner *Aleutian*. This was exhausting, grueling work, but in that first season, from March to late fall, he earned $800, good money in those days. Soon Pedersen bought a half-interest in the halibut boat *Oceanus* and skippered it to the halibut banks off Alaska. An enterprising man could rise rapidly in the trade; in 1940 Pedersen built the sixty-foot *Susan* and fished for many kinds of fish from the Bering Sea to Mexico. In 1958, Pedersen entered the king-crab fishery off Kodiak Island with the *Susan*, a kind of shoestring venture, it seems, but he succeeded.

In 1958, fishermen got 9¢ a pound for king crab, which gradually increased over the years so that now the price is $2.00 a pound or more. As a result of excellent management of resources and higher prices for king crab, Pedersen was able to build the $1,500,000 *Mark I*, with a 42.3 percent subsidy from the Federal Fishing Fleet Improvement Act. His son Mark, for whom the boat was named, still skippers it out of Dutch Harbor in the Aleutians. Pedersen sold the *Susan* in 1965, and she is still fishing halibut off Kodiak. By 1979 Pedersen, in addition to *Mark I*, owned or had an interest in five crab boats, from 94 feet to 110 feet in length. These are for the most part skippered and manned by Norwegians.

113

But Pedersen, although retired from active duty, was not through yet. In 1978 he, his son Mark, Stan Hovik, and Martin Stone discovered a mothballed AOG-I Navy gasoline tanker in Honolulu and paid about $400,000 for it. After being towed to Seattle, it was to have been converted into a processing ship at a cost of $7 or $8 million. Pedersen had intended to follow his fleet for crab, herring, salmon, and bottom fish from Alaska to Mexico. He predicted that his vessel would be processing quantities of abundant bottom fish all along the Pacific Coast, catching some species which are edible although they have not been marketed before. Unfortunately, lack of capital for remodeling has prevented his processor vessel from leaving Seattle.

The Norwegians who participated in the fisheries after 1940 were those who had risen from the ranks in the late 1920s and 1930s. They were replaced by a younger generation, who are now in their late fifties and early sixties. Several of these men were born in Norway, others, American born, are sons, sons-in-laws, grandsons, or more distant relatives of the older generation. Later, a select few from among this group will be considered individually.

Until fairly recently Norwegian fishermen on the Pacific Coast were either owners of their own boats or crew members for other individual owners. The halibut vessel owners would load their schooners at the fishing banks and transport them to receiving stations in Alaska, British Columbia, or Seattle, and then return for another catch. Over the past two decades, however, this pattern has changed. Before the establishment of the 200-mile limit, several foreign nations, notably Japan and Russia, brought their processor vessels into Alaskan waters and along the Washington and Oregon coasts. Russian vessels, particularly, have harvested tens of thousands of tons of hake (now called Pacific whiting) off the Washington and Oregon coasts. Fishing interests in Aberdeen, Hoquiam, and other Washington coastal communities, Norwegians among them, have considered establishing shore plants for Pacific whiting, but nothing has come of it because the fish are caught 150 or 200 miles offshore and they deteriorate very rapidly. They have to be processed almost immediately after being caught in order to retain their prime quality. This the Russians and others have been doing. Since the 200-mile limit was established, American boats are now catching this fish and selling it to the Russian processors and others.

It was noted earlier that Einar Pedersen had intended to enter the fish-processing business, which he described as "the wave of the future," but that he failed to accomplish his goal. Several Norwegians, however, are riding this wave, which may be characterized as the last phase of their hundred-year participation in the fisheries of Puget Sound, the California, Oregon, and Washington coasts, and Alaska. The most notable example of Norwegian activity in the fish-processing field is Trans Pacific Industries, whose subsidiary is Trans Pacific Seafoods, with head offices in Seattle. According to Michael Nordby, an officer of the firm, there are two Norwegian partners, John Sjong and Konrad Uri. Sjong is president, Uri vice president. Uri was born in America of Norwegian parents, but the family returned to Norway for a few years after World War II. Sjong, who was born in Sykkylven, where the Uri family came from originally, recalls that his introduction to Uri was by a swift kick in the pants. The boys were playing soccer. Both later migrated to Seattle, where they have made their homes since. They are now in their late fifties.

Konrad Uri's father was a dragger and halibut fisherman. The son worked on his father's boat when it operated off the Washington coast. Sjong and Uri became joint owners of a king-crab boat in 1971. They soon formed Trans Pacific Industries and it has had a phenomenal growth, with the result that it is, at present, an enterprise with assets of over $20 million. The company may be characterized as a catcher-processor operation, with five boats performing varied operations. The largest boat in the fleet is the *Arctic Trawler*, the only American factory trawler in Pacific waters and the largest fishing vessel in the United States, measuring 296 feet in length. It was built in 1961 by the United States government and remodeled by Trans Pacific at a cost of $3 million. This vessel harvests bottom fish in the Bering Sea carrying a crew of forty. The fish are cleaned and filleted immediately and packed and frozen in fifteen-pound cartons. By the end of September, 1981, the *Arctic Trawler* had brought to Seattle, in four trips, 4.65 million pounds of Pacific true-cod fillets. The trips lasted 98, 117, 86, and 98 days, with over a million pounds being processed on each trip. A fifth trip was completed before Christmas with equal results. These fish are sold by Trans Pacific to American markets.

The next two boats in size, which catch, cook, and freeze in sixty-five-pound boxes both king and Tanner crabs, are the *Pavlof* and the *Pengwin*. Michael Nordby explained that the latter boat was named with a Norwegian and an English component: *Peng*, money in Norwegian, and *win*. And in fact it and its companions live up to the *Pengwin*'s name. The fourth boat, the *Isafjord*, catches crab, which are processed aboard either the *Pavlof* or the *Pengwin*. The fifth boat is the small container ship *Trans Pack*, which carries eighteen refrigerated containers. With this fleet, Trans Pacific Seafoods grosses over $15 million annually. Although, as indicated elsewhere, numerous fishermen are experiencing difficult times, the people at Trans Pacific seem optimistic.

116

It is impossible to name all the Norwegians who are engaged in various branches of the industry at present, but a representative few will be mentioned. These men are all from Seattle. Bernie Hansen is part-owner with Kåre Ness and Rudy Pedersen of the *Pat San Marie*, a dragger which operates successfully out of Westport, Washington. They drag for rockfish, ling cod, Pacific cod, perch, and other fish. They deliver their catch to Westport, and the general view is that they operate one of the best draggers on the coast. Their boat is often commissioned to make resource assessments of fish all along the coast for the state of Washington, Alaska, and the United States government. Three other Norwegians now active are: Ken Pedersen, owner of two crab boats, one of which is *Americanus No. 1*, and Severin Hjelle and Reidar Tyness, who have operated two crab boats, but have now expanded significantly. In late December, 1983, these two men together with John Boggs, Alf Sorvik, Rich Hastings, and Eric Breivik, accepted delivery of a 201-foot trawler-processor, *Northern Glacier*. It was designed by the Norwegian-American firm of Jensen's Maritime Consultants in Seattle and cost $11,000,000. The Norwegian firms of A/S Atlantic and A/S Longvatrål are also partners in the venture. The firm has also acquired a warehouse in Seattle, the Glacier Fish Company, where the frozen cod will be stored. *Northern Glacier* carries a crew of forty and can take on board 40,000 cubic feet of cleaned and frozen cod in fifteen-pound cartons. The boat will fish for cod in the Bering Sea and is expected to return with its first load in January, 1984. According to Hjelle, cod is in good supply, and the owners express the same optimism that Michael Nordby did about the 296-foot *Arctic Trawler*, owned by Trans Pacific Industries in Seattle.

This section has emphasized the American catcher-processor to give credence to the idea that enterprising Norwegians do not have to remain dependent on

Sverre

Sverre Arestad

foreign processors. It should be emphasized that Norwegians do still participate extensively in halibut and cod fishing and salmon trolling and crab fishing in Alaska and elsewhere. So there are many successful men who have not been named in this short review. It may be of interest that various Norwegian bankers and doctors are now financial backers of some fishing ventures. The former banker, Asbjorn Nordheim, for example, is an owner of crab boats.

The preceding section ends on a somewhat sanguine note as far as many Norwegian fishermen are concerned. Since they are part of the larger picture, however, one must look briefly at the prospects for commercial fishing as a whole. The situation in all branches of the industry from California to Alaska may be said to be in a state of flux. The salmon population on the Oregon and Washington coasts and in Puget Sound falls far short of the demands of the overextended commercial fleet, not to mention the increasing number of sport fishermen. The Boldt decision in 1975, which allotted one-half of the salmon catch in Puget Sound to the native Indians, dealt a severe blow to the other gill netters and purse seiners there.

Despite a bonanza salmon run in the Bering Sea in 1982, the overpopulation of fishermen and the depressed prices, particularly for humpback salmon, called humpies, kept it from being a good year. The depressed prices were due in large part to the botulism scare: One man in Belgium died from eating a defective can of salmon from a cannery in Ketchikan and the Food and Drug Administration was forced to recall fifty million cans of salmon. This left a glut in the warehouses and caused the closing of several canneries in Alaska — at least for 1982. Also the salmon fishermen in the Bering Sea sat on the beach for two weeks in a dispute with

118

the cannery owners, with the result that millions of sockeye escaped, and the price of humpies fell from 37¢ a pound to 29¢. In Southeast Alaska humpies sold for 20¢ and many fishermen did not even bother to market them. The drastic reduction in the king-crab population has already been noted. During the past several years, cod and halibut are about holding their own, as is true also of such bottom fish as ocean perch, ling cod, snapper, and sole. And there seems to be an endless supply of Pacific whiting off the Oregon and Washington coasts and of pollock in Alaska.

Though not as dominant as they once were in the cod, halibut, king-crab, and salmon-trolling fisheries, the Norwegians are still active in all these branches. Now, however, the situation is quite different from what it was in 1940, when the only possible direction was up. As Michael Nordby so succinctly put it recently: "It is not as it once was. Licenses are going up, gear is going up, gas, wages, interest, and cost of equipment are all going up. The prospects for many of the thousands of fishermen — including Norwegians — are dismal, if not non-existent."

As indicated above, however, there is some feeling of optimism, especially among the successful. The enterprising will survive: by inventing and building better equipment; by entering the processing field; by encouraging bankers and doctors to invest in enterprises, as some have already done; and by cooperation with the several foreign countries which have an allotted quota of fish in American waters. Obviously, the 200-mile limit has aided American fishermen and entrepreneurs immensely.

The author's own experience with fishing in the Pacific Northwest goes back a long way. Seventy years ago our family caught fall salmon near our farm on Snus Hill,

119

twelve miles northwest of Bellingham, Washington, and we children pursued the fish half a mile through the woods along the big creek which emptied into Birch Bay. There we watched them spawn in a clear sand- and gravel-bottomed pool, thereby adding knowledge to our previous observation of the breeding habits of animals and fowl. As teenagers we learned about the relative costs of food, including salmon. The Indians fed humpies to their dogs and the early settlers found them a poor substitute for the superior species: sockeye, king, and silver. The story goes that it was not until an enterprising pre-Madison Avenue chap got the bright idea of putting this label on cans of humpie — "Guaranteed not to turn red in the can" — that the Scandinavians in the Middle West began buying them. Now they are one of the most widely distributed kinds of salmon, both here and in Europe.

During World War I our father hired a team of horses for $2.50 and a gravel box and we drove to Lummi Island and bought approximately a cubic yard of humpies for $1.25, probably about a cent per fish. We salted most of them and the rest we shared with our neighbors.

Many teenagers in our community had been in Alaska and soon our turn came. We hired out with the Fidalgo Island Packing Company, with headquarters in Anacortes, Washington, whose owner and president was "Old Sutter," a taciturn man who was constantly out where the action was, invariably sitting in his dark undertaker clothes and whittling away at a stick. He had disposed of his extensive holdings on Puget Sound in the early 1920s and had moved the company operations to Pillar Bay, Southeast Alaska.

My oldest brother Trygve, in his early twenties, myself, nineteen, my brother George who was seventeen, and a neighbor, Walter Oiness, who was my age, made up the capping crew. Our responsibility would be to lay the initial logs that are placed on top of the vertical pilings in constructing the fish traps. Trygve was to be "skipper" of our boat the *Wanderer*, a former purse seiner which bounced like a cork on any sea. He did not skipper the *Wanderer* independently but followed the *Mutual*, an eighty-foot diesel cannery tender, with William (Bill) Cackley as skipper. Cackley had run the tender aground once with slight damage, but he was retained because he was known as the best skipper on the Inside Passage. The *Mutual* was towing a scow of creosote pilings for a herring reduction plant at Pillar Bay. From Anacortes we had a marvelous cruise through the placid waters of northern Puget Sound, the American and Canadian San Juans, and finally the Inside Passage, which was like a trip through a Norwegian fjord. The only drawback was the cook, "High Pants," about five and half feet tall, whose hand-me-down trousers came just under his armpits. He was an abominable cook.

One evening toward dark we arrived at Swanson's Bay, just south of Queen Charlotte Sound. The tide was full and the lights from the dock cast a mellow pastel glow over the scene. During the night the wind came up and small-craft warnings were issued the next day for the Sound. But Bill and Barleycorn had been quite intimate in the skipper's cabin, so he ordered a departure at 4 p.m., with almost disastrous results. We set out bravely, following the lights of the *Mutual*, but soon the crew, including "High Pants," passed out, though Trygve remained at his post. Unfortunately, about midnight he got disoriented and forsook the swaying topmost light on the *Mutual* for the permanent glow of a lighthouse. We were rescued in the nick of time and when we entered calm waters again we realized what a near call it had been. We never encountered such adverse conditions again.

At Pillar Bay, we settled into roughhewn but comfortable quarters, with all the amenities and an abundance of excellent food. We made up the wire for the lead, the hearts, and the two pots for the fish trap. Then we moved onto the pile driver, where we had dismal facilities and High Pants as cook. He had been relegated to cook's helper at the cannery mess hall. Twelve men were quartered on the pile driver. The foreman and the engineer had quarters off the engine room and the cook slept somewhere in the galley, but the rest of us were quartered in between, where there were two three-tier bunks on one side and two two-tier bunks on the other, with the dining table in the middle. This was tolerable because both ends of the driver could be opened, so a few minutes of fresh air cleared the atmosphere. Our toilet facilities were the open sea, and a shallow, warm stream along shore was our bathtub. When adverse weather confined us to the driver, about all we would do was to play cards.

After trap no. 4 had been constructed, some of us moved to a spacious area just off the beach, which had ample accommodations. Here we had the most marvelous cook of all, a Swede. Our tasks were routine and undemanding, requiring at most ten or twelve hours a week to keep the trap clear of kelp and seaweed and assist with taking the salmon out of the trap. Time hung heavy on the hands of the non-readers, and I experienced vicariously something of the hopelessness of the young men who realized that they would be following this line of work all their lives. Boredom is difficult to live with when there is no apparent relief in sight. The only bright spot was that their work was limited to the summer months.

When one thinks now of the once seemingly inexhaustible supply of fish in the world's waters and realizes that in many areas this population has been sharply reduced, even to the point of marginal survival, one begins to wonder whether the fishermen of the world may not have been as shortsighted as the lumber barons once were. An experience in Alaska illustrates this.

All members of the company's boat and trap crews were allowed to take forty-eight cans of salmon and a ten-gallon keg of the salted fish home. About the fourth of July we had an exceptional run of salmon in trap No. 4. Our cannery could not handle them all, and boats came from Baranof Island to load the excess, but there were still a couple of thousand fish left in the spiller, which seemed lifeless because of the pressure on them. Old Sutter simply said: "Dump them overboard." Shortly after this it was my turn to salt my salmon. My Norwegian fellow crewmen insisted that the belly of the fish was the only suitable part to preserve, and they proceeded accordingly. The cannery did not process king salmon, although many were eaten there. One day a couple of dozen kings appeared in the trap, which I kept. Having filled my keg with the bellies, I consigned the carcasses, with most of the fish left on, to the waves. I can still see them floating out to sea, as I contemplate how many hours of fishing it now takes to catch even one of these thirty-pounders.

I was in Pillar Bay again in 1928, but that summer I was stationed on a new trap, No. 1. Three of us trap tenders — I a cook — lived in a 10 × 12 foot shack on top of the trap, with no room on shore. Monotonous, that is no name for it. The only break came one evening at dusk when a swarthy man in a small boat tied up to the trap. He produced a bottle of moonshine, and offered us $5.00 apiece for a certain number of fish. We innocents accepted. On the way home, one of my companions was horrified to read in the ship's newsletter that two of his friends had been arrested for selling fish.

In 1929, I was a trap tender on Salmon Banks, San Juan Island, which turned out to be the easiest job I have ever had, with ample time to read, flirt with the cook, and explore the island. Later in the summer I worked briefly in a cannery at Friday Harbor, San Juan Island. This was confining, mindless work in a smelly building, quite unlike the outside jobs I had always had. But there was one memorable man, a fish pitcher, short and sturdy, who wore the same shirt for a week — until the traditional Saturday night bath — with accumulated dried fish blood and scales on it. He informed us that his wife had tried to get him to remove the shirt, at least at night, but with no result, so she had to seek repose elsewhere.

In 1943 I was cook on the fish buyer *Sonja*, which ran out of Anacortes to Neah Bay and throughout the San Juan Islands to collect fish from the seiners — mostly Croatians — of the Fishermen's Packing Corporation. Our skipper was Scotty Lewis, a native of Guemes Island. He was typical of many in the industry. Telling of the summer he was in Ketchikan and his crew consisted of nothing but Indians and Norwegians, he commented: "I was the only white man on board." When I reminded him that I was Norwegian, he replied: "But you're different, Professor." So it was!

Norwegians operated as individual fishermen, using hook and line or the baited skein, working from oar-driven boats, almost from the moment they arrived from Norway. When the fisheries on the Pacific Coast were in their infancy, a century and a quarter ago, a fisherman's job was brutal. This was especially true in the coastal waters off Vancouver Island, the Gulf of Alaska, and the Bering Sea. The crew of a harpoon dory often encountered hazards when they left the security of the whaling vessel. Parent vessels fishing for cod launched a dozen or more one-man boats over a wide area before returning to their designated anchorage. The fishermen had to string out their baited skeins and wait several hours before hauling in the catch. Then the task of rowing back again began. In rough seas this was always difficult and at times hazardous. The waves were not the worst obstacle, however; the impenetrable fog, which could settle during the fisherman's wait for his haul, could sometimes be fatal when he could not find the parent vessel. These conditions had to be tolerated, in part because of the method of capture used and also because there were as yet no bargaining associations for the fisherman. Einar Pedersen stated that as late as 1938 he found the work of a halibut doryman as tedious as that of the cod fishermen decades earlier, although the risks were less. The doryman is now gone, but even on the larger and more sophisticated vessels the work still requires stamina.

Sometimes shoddy workmanship can cause disaster. A year or two ago, two modest-sized fishing boats, built in a New Orleans yard, sank off the Oregon coast. Recently a large Canadian factory-processor, on entering Queen Charlotte Sound, encountered mountainous waves and had its superstructure, along with the crew, washed overboard. The men survived a twenty-four-hour ordeal on a life raft. Oddly enough, the processor's motor kept running with the result that the boat was brought safely to port with its 600,000 pounds of frozen cod fillets. The young skipper, when questioned if he would go out on the boat again, replied: "What else is there to do?" In the fall of 1983, during the king-crab season in the Bering Sea, two boats built in Anacortes, Washington, as well as one built in Tacoma, sank on their first trip without a trace: boat, crew, and gear. Human error may have been a contributing cause. Deep-sea fishing is never risk-free.

It might be recalled, however, that the Norwegian immigrant fishermen in the North Pacific were veterans of equally forbidding fishing conditions, where the life toll was heavy even well into this century. Johan Bojer gives a vivid description of this in *Den siste viking* (The Last of the Vikings), published in 1918. Remember too that the successful entrepreneur Karl Hansen was driven from the Vesterålen Islands by the fury of the North Atlantic to the relative calm of Port Alexander, Southeast Alaska. Whatever the fishermen in the North Pacific had to endure was in no way comparable to the atrocities committed against crews on the early sailing vessels. Kenneth O. Bjork in *West of the Great Divide* gives a graphic example of several Scandinavian sailors, among them two Norwegians, who were either beaten to death on the spot or died from their injuries as late as 1872.

Rumblings of discontent were already evident in the mid-1920s. Some men in our crew found fault where none was called for, complaining about the food, and about having to sweep out their quarters. The latter would have required five minutes a day. One chap took the matter up with the superintendent and got the following valid response: "You've got brooms, but if you want to live like pigs, that's your business!" The same fellow became obsessed with the idea that the boat crew had canned strawberries, raspberries, and loganberries, which the trap tenders did not have. Not being too familiar with English, he dictated his complaint to me, laboriously copied it, and sent it off to the superintendent. It was the most abusive and vulgar message imaginable, but on the next boat he got his fruit. These were minor grievances, but they relieved frustration.

The only incident which could have been disastrous occurred when we were unloading material off a freighter for the herring plant and a loaded sling swerved toward the dock. We rushed out of the way and the sling crashed onto the dock. The foreman was furious: "Why didn't you prevent it?" We protested: "And be killed?" His response was: "Forget about the men, save the material." During the summer, however, he learned that matters were changing with respect to the workers' concern for their own safety, and he eventually agreed with our position. These incipient protests of the 1920s gradually resulted in better working conditions.

At times one wonders whether changes, supposedly for the better, always produce the desired results. In the early 1930s longshoremen won the right not to lift anything over fifty pounds — in general, a notable victory. But during World War II we unloaded forty-eight pound cases of canned salmon. With the weight of the case itself, they came to just under fifty pounds each. But if one stood in the hot hold of a freighter, lifting case after case for eight hours, he knew he had had a workout. Overbargaining by union members can in some instances be counter-productive, as illustrated in the Bering Sea salmon fishery in 1982, but workers will continue to bargain to try to secure what they hold to be their rights.

Few men could endure the rigors of the sea as do the men who fish the Pacific from Alaska to Chile or the Atlantic from Norway to Argentina. Lives are still lost occasionally on all oceans despite growing safety precautions. Television clips show fishing vessels out of Boston or those in the Bering Sea coming to port ice-laden. Arne Olson, a neighbor for some years, was a cook on crab boats in Alaska. He tells of times when there were sixty-mile winds and twenty-foot waves. The boat not only rolled but pitched, creating a heaving and twisting effect which made it necessary to secure cooking pots to the range with metal bars and the diners' dishes to the table in similar fashion. These conditions are not abnormal. Winds can attain 160 miles per hour and produce sixty-foot waves. Who would choose this kind of occupation? A lot of men do because, like those on oil rigs, fishing boat crews have made very good money.

In Pillar Bay, Alaska, from April 13 to August 27, 1928, I made $432.50, plus passage and my keep. My brother thinks I was overpaid because in the depression year 1932 he earned $231.00 for the same work. Today, fishermen who are regularly employed do exceptionally well, especially the crabbers. In a season some may earn between $40,000 and $80,000. One would think they could retire after a few years. Most men husband their earnings, but some novices squander their money on loose living. Others make reckless investments. Rob Betts, an estate planner with a Seattle law firm, conducts investment seminars. He tells of a young Norwegian crabber who returned with $60,000 for the season and invested all of it as a down payment on an expensive house in the Ballard section of Seattle. Out of cash and seasonally unemployed, he lost heavily because he could not meet his monthly payments.

So the substantial wages won by enduring the ardors of hell may slip through fingers unused to wealth. This situation fortunately is not universal; some men have prospered, but even for them circumstances grow more uncertain.

The testimony of a neighbor just returned from the Bering Sea after a short sockeye season will help to bring the story up to date. He said there were not nearly as many fish this year (1984) as last, but still enough for profitable fishing. Conditions from Southeast Alaska all the way to Oregon were again disappointing. The diminished salmon population is no doubt partly the result of overfishing, but may also be attributed to El Niño, the recurrent heating of the equatorial Pacific

Ocean which had unusually severe and widespread effects in 1982. King crab in Alaska has also been further reduced and more and more boats have been forced to withdraw, causing numerous bankruptcies.

Studies of Norwegian activity in all areas of the Pacific Northwest will no doubt be published in the coming decades. In the meantime, someone will write a definitive account of the fisheries, which will, I hope, corroborate some of the observations contained here and draw broader conclusions. There is a wealth of fascinating material awaiting the enterprising inquirer.

by KENNETH O. BJORK

5   *Reindeer, Gold, and Scandal*

IN 1893, H. C. Wahlberg, a businessman in Seattle, saw great economic possibilities in Alaska. It should, he thought, become to the Pacific Coast and to America what the Lofoten Islands and Finnmark were to Norway, and he urged the founding of a Norwegian or Scandinavian colony in the territory. He and others who expressed similar views in the early 1890s and spoke of another "Land of the Midnight Sun" or a "New Norway" were thinking of the rich harvest of the sea and a mixed economy of fishing, farming, and logging in southeastern Alaska. At a much later date, in 1944, C. L. Andrews, in a chapter titled "The Alaska of the Future," maintained that the territory "is the Greater Scandinavia," with vastly more resources than Sweden, Denmark, Norway, and Finland combined, but with only a tiny population.[1]

In dozens of letters written by Norwegians and Norwegian Americans in the late 1890s and the early 1900s the expressions "New Norway" and "New Scandinavia" appear as naturally, if not as frequently, as comments about weather, the sea, mountains, forests, and tundra. Unlike John Scudder McLain, who visited Alaska in 1903 with a party from the Senate committee

130

on territories, the Norwegian writers say very little about agricultural possibilities in the Far North, despite the fact that they were fully aware of similarities between their homeland and Alaska.[2]

It was the discovery of gold in the Klondike and Alaska that brought the north country into the full consciousness of the Norwegians and their Scandinavian cousins, not the views of farsighted men considering the total economy of Alaska. The lure of gold in the many rivers and creeks of the territory caused an increasing number of them to travel northward, and the rich findings in the Cape Nome area greatly stimulated the process and gave a strikingly Scandinavian coloring to the Alaska story.

If the gold fields near Nome were to become the magnet drawing argonauts of varied origin to Alaska, their discovery was the result of a quite different story, in which motivations were other than the search for the golden fleece. This story deals with the introduction of domestic reindeer into Alaska and is inseparably woven into the tale of greed and scandal that followed.

I

In 1884, Dr. Sheldon Jackson, who had served as a Presbyterian home missionary in Wisconsin and Minnesota and later in the Rocky Mountain area, sailed to Alaska as superintendent of missions in that territory. A year later he was also appointed federal superintendent of education for Alaska, and was charged with the responsibility of establishing a free school system. To this task he devoted the next two decades; in addition, he assisted in creating mail routes, aided in organizing the government of the territory, and was active in political life as leader of the so-called "missionary party."[3]

During his travels in the area of the Bering Sea, Jackson observed that the wholesale slaughter by whites of whales, walrus, even caribou and deer — together with irresponsible fishing — was rapidly destroying the very basis of life for the Eskimo. He visited native villages where the people were dying of hunger, and gradually came to the conclusion that there could be little hope for a school system until the Eskimo had the essentials for a normal existence. After careful study of the situation, he came to the further conclusion that the introduction of domestic reindeer would be the best solution to the problem of providing food, clothing, and necessary tools in the future.

Jackson secured the first few reindeer from the Chukchi (Chuckchees), the herders of eastern Siberia, with funds first raised by private subscription in the American East and later appropriated by Congress. The task of introducing and caring for the animals was given to the Office of Education in the Department of the Interior. This task was not easy, as events soon revealed that adequate buildings and corrals had to be provided and grazing land surveyed in an area extending from Bristol Bay to Point Barrow. Most important, experienced herders had to be found to train the Eskimo in the reindeer culture.[4]

Vast areas of land in western and northern Alaska were covered with moss, the chief reindeer food, and the climate there was found to be generally milder than in Siberia. The supply of animals across the Bering Strait was adequate. Obtaining the first reindeer, however, proved to be difficult in the extreme. Jackson and Captain J. Healy, who represented the government in the revenue cutter *Bear*, decided to place a few animals on one of the Aleutian Islands as an experiment. The Chukchi herdsmen, who were willing enough to exchange reindeer meat for inexpensive goods, were afraid to sell their animals on the hoof; their witch doctors (shamen) had taught them that, if they did, the spirits would cause the death of their herds and untold suffering for the herdsmen. Captain Healy was able to overcome the fears of the Siberians only after promising to feed them if such a calamity indeed occurred. Sixteen deer were bought in 1890. They thrived in Alaska, and in 1892 seventeen animals were brought to Teller on Port Clarence Bay in the Seward Peninsula, some sixty miles southeast of Cape Prince of Wales. A station was started there, and more deer were imported from about a hundred miles away. By 1902 a total of 1,280 had been brought in, all from Siberia. From these came all or almost all of the 350,000 reindeer estimated to be in Alaska in the 1920s.[5]

It was much more difficult to secure experienced herdsmen capable of training the Eskimo in the care of reindeer. The Chukchi, who had been employed for the first two years of the experiment, proved to be unsatisfactory, as the Eskimo regarded them as socially and culturally inferior to themselves and charged that they were cruel to the animals.

Readers of Norwegian-American newspapers saw, late in 1893, a story inspired by Sheldon Jackson. It stated that the government was seeking in the States and Canada men with practical experience with domestic reindeer. If readers knew of Finns or Lapps accustomed to their care and willing to go to Alaska, they should get in touch with Jackson at the Office of Education. None, it turned out, could be found in North America.[6]

What happened to solve the problem was explained in 1895 by William A. Kjellman (Kjellmann) of Stoughton, Wisconsin, who also took the opportunity to correct misunderstandings about the fate of the Siberian reindeer in Alaska. They had not been slaughtered, as some newspapers had reported, and indeed had increased in number. In 1893, he said, the government had imported 127 deer, together with four Siberian herders. Miner W. Bruce, who had been superintendent of the project, was replaced by W. T. Lapp. The failure of the Chukchi as instructors quickly caused the government to bring Lapps from Norway to take their place.

Kjellman, who was chosen to hire the Lapps and accompany them to Alaska, was born and raised in Finnmark, northern Norway, near the region occupied by the Lapps. He had learned their language as a boy and later, employed by a wholesale firm in Hammerfest, had bought reindeer meat and skins from the Lapps and sent these to England and Germany. Leaving for Finnmark in February, 1894, he proceeded to Kautokeino, where he hired seven Lapps, whose families accompanied them to Alaska. An additional 120 reindeer were imported from Siberia the same year, bringing the total to 418. Kjellman was soon forced by illness in his family to leave the Teller station, where he had been serving as superintendent, and to return to Wisconsin in August, 1894.

The government was fully satisfied with the new arrangement, especially after observing the manner in which the Lapps and the Norwegians who had accompanied them began the care of the reindeer, which soon increased in number to about 710 and were divided into three herds. Kjellman thought it would be of interest to many if *Skandinaven* of Chicago, the leading Norwegian-language newspaper in America, would follow the reindeer story in Alaska, especially now that it had become largely a Norwegian project, with Norwegian directors as well as Lapp herders. The acting superintendent in 1895 was J. C. Widsted, who had Norwegian assistants. In addition, there was also a Norwegian-American missionary and teacher at the Teller station, Pastor T. T. Brevig from Hudson, Wisconsin, a native of Norway.[7]

The Lapps, who unlike the Chukchi in Siberia had been Christianized as well as partially Europeanized, had requested as a condition of their leaving Norway a Lutheran minister as well as Norwegian supervisors in Alaska. The American government turned to the Norwegian Synod (Norwegian Evangelical Lutheran Church in America). In 1894, through the offices of Rasmus B. Anderson in Madison, Wisconsin, it inquired of the Reverend H. A. Preus, president of the Synod, whether he could provide a pastor to serve the Lapps and their Norwegian associates. Such a person would also be a teacher in a government school for native and other children, and would have the privilege of preaching the gospel to the Eskimo. Preus asked Brevig, who had taught in public schools in Minnesota, if he and his wife would serve in the dual role as teachers and missionaries at Teller.

Accepting, Brevig met and joined Kjellman and the Lapp party in Madison in May, 1894. A company of sixteen Lapps, Kjellman with his wife, a child, and his father, Brevig and his wife and one child, they proceeded to San Francisco by way of St. Paul, where they met Governor Knute Nelson — the "King of Minnesota." There and all along the train route to Seattle and San Francisco, the Lapps attracted interested crowds. On June 7, the party left by ship for Alaska and arrived at the Teller station on August 1. Four days later, Brevig held religious services in what was little better than a hut, one of several buildings the government had constructed as the Teller Reindeer Station. The buildings, 20 by 60 feet in size, with 8-foot studs, were, as Brevig remarked, better suited for California than for Alaska and were in great need of repair. The structure used for the school also provided an apartment in its east end for the Brevigs and another in its west end for the Kjellmans. To keep out the wind, they lined the interior with cotton cloth over which they painted.

On September 1, Brevig began teaching the Eskimo children, who numbered fifty the first day. The children learned the English words for objects and the instructor learned the corresponding Eskimo words. The task became almost impossibly difficult when the teacher turned to concepts, as abstractions such as numbers proved to be little more than puzzles to the pupils. The language problem was also complicated in religious services. Brevig preached every Sunday morning in Norwegian for the Lapps and the Norwegians, then in the afternoon in English for the Americans and the natives. At the afternoon service a young Eskimo, who was from a mission station and was learning to be a herder, served as interpreter for his people.[8]

Pastor Brevig's teaching-preaching mission at Teller is of absorbing interest in itself and should be studied with care. But his role in this study is primarily as a source of information for the reindeer and gold-strike saga in the Seward Peninsula. From 1897 to 1917, he served as official manager of the herds near Port Clarence. He received the animals imported from Siberia and dispatched herds to the north and south. He was also the first postmaster at the town later named Teller.[9]

On December 14–15, 1896, Brevig could report that the reindeer were doing well, and that Kjellman and two Lapps, Per Rist and Mikkel Nækkilæ (Nakkila, Nakkeli), were just setting out on a long journey to examine stretches of land, both nearby and at Cook's Inlet, considered suitable for raising deer. If their report was favorable, there was thought of creating a Lapp colony at the most convenient location and expanding reindeer production — thus far largely an experiment — into an industry.[10]

Two months later, Kjellman wrote to Rasmus B. Anderson, editor of *Amerika*, from the Bethel Mission

136

station on the Kuskokwim River, explaining that he was looking for a place to which the main reindeer station could be moved. He and his Lapp associates, traveling with deer, had already covered a distance of 950 miles and were as far south as they planned to go. They would now set out, by a different and far longer route, up the Yukon River to Nulato; they would go from there to Norton Bay and home, hoping to arrive in Teller by April 11, after completing a record trip of 2,000 miles without changing reindeer.

They had seen a vast area of wild land and experienced considerable hardship. They had slept in a sail-cloth tent in temperatures reaching $-75°$ Fahrenheit, and had encountered a storm so severe that neither they nor their animals could stand. The men had lain flat on the ground for sixteen hours, holding on to one another lest they be blown away. Such days were not uncommon in the mountainous areas. The men had been in places where no white man had ever set foot. Kjellman thought the reindeer industry had a great future, that much had been accomplished already with it, and that Congress should be more generous in appropriating funds. Reindeer were the only adequate means of transportation in Alaska, which was no longer an "icebox" but a "goldbox" that only the deer could open.[11]

The contract negotiated with the Lapps had stipulated that a physician should go to the reindeer station at Port Clarence, where his services would be available to them and to others at Teller. Dr. Albert N. Kittilsen (Kittleson), of Norwegian descent and familiar with the language of the Lapps, had been educated at the University of Wisconsin and the Rush Medical College in Chicago and lived in Mount Horeb, Wisconsin, at the time of his appointment to the station. He had traveled to Alaska in the spring of 1896. At Port Clarence he also served as assistant superintendent. When the main reindeer station was moved to Unalakleet in December of the next year, he went along and was there when gold was discovered nearby.

A letter written by Kittilsen a year before his transfer gives some idea of the experiences of a pioneer doctor in northwestern Alaska. His contract permitted him a limited private practice. "I am now," he wrote in December, "more than 200 miles from Port Clarence to call on a sick white child. A Lapp and I made the trip in five days with reindeer. We travel without tent or stove, hoping to arrive each evening at an Eskimo village and to sleep in a house; but one night we had to spend in the snow. This, however, did us no harm, as we are prepared for anything. We have sleeping bags made of reindeer skins; with them one can be warm anywhere.

"It is pleasant to travel with deer; on level surfaces they are much faster than horses, and they go through where it is so uneven that a horse wouldn't think of making it." His letter, he explained, would have to travel 2,000 miles by sled before it could reach a steamer. As for cold, the worst he had experienced was only −49°, and this was moderate for one dressed in deerskin from top to toe. He was traveling with two beautiful reindeer that had an unfortunate habit of running away. "Last year they did this three times. So far they have not got out of my control, although they have been able to smash two sleds for me." [12]

On June 22, 1897, Brevig had written in some detail about conditions at Port Clarence, and had informed readers of the Norwegian-American press about the decision to establish the Lapp colony and major reindeer station twelve miles from the mouth of the Unalakleet River, where there was an Eskimo village and a Swedish mission named for the river. There were, as he wrote, four reindeer herds in Alaska, with about 1,450 animals. Some 425 calves had been born during the year, 140 at Port Clarence and 115 at Cape Prince of Wales; sickness, misfortune, and the butcher's knife had taken about 100.[13]

Brevig reported in August of the same year that the "Wisconsin people" had already left his station, at least temporarily. Kjellman was with Sheldon Jackson up the Yukon River, and Dr. Kittilsen had just gone down to Unalakleet and St. Michael with supplies from the Port Clarence station. It was not certain that he would return, as the gold mines down there had a magnetic attraction for all who heard the rosy reports about them. Brevig was now alone with the Lapps and the Eskimo. He enclosed a copy of the July issue of what he called the most northwestern American newspaper, the *Eskimo Bulletin*. It had been written and printed solely by the Eskimo herders under W. T. Lapp, who was then in charge of the mission herd.[14]

Skandinaven carried a story dated October 20, 1897, from Seattle, reporting grim news from Sheldon Jackson. The missionary stated that half of the people at Dawson City had left the Klondike, and that the only way to avoid hunger there among Americans was for the government to set up reindeer stations throughout the Yukon Valley. The deer were necessary, not only for bringing food to the needy on claims as far as 150 miles from the Yukon, but also for bringing out the mineral wealth. Kjellman was now on his way to Finnmark to bring back more Lapp drivers to replace those who were returning to Norway with him after having fulfilled their three-year contracts. About fifteen Eskimo now knew how to herd reindeer, and by the following fall some 300 animals would have been trained for driving. According to Jackson, "If the government won't use them, they can be sold. We will receive $50 per head for them when hunger stalks the door, as it will next year and always in the Yukon Valley. Steamers cannot solve the problem of food supplies."[15]

The next month, *Washington Posten* noted that the revenue cutter *Bear* had arrived in Seattle. Aboard were some of the Lapps who were returning to their homeland. The climate in Alaska, they said, was much colder than in Norway, requiring two deerskin coats (*frakke*) instead of one as in Finnmark. The reindeer in Alaska were doing well but required more herders, who would earn $300 a year and their keep.[16]

Kjellman passed through Madison, Wisconsin, en route to Norway, accompanied by a dozen Lapps and a few Eskimo who were going to be educated at the government's Carlisle Indian School in Pennsylvania. He said, when interviewed, that the main reindeer station definitely would be moved to within forty-five miles of St. Michael, and thus much closer to the rest of the world. The new site, chosen by Kjellman as general superintendent of the reindeer project in Alaska, would also have better harbor facilities and other advantages over Port Clarence. He informed *Amerika og Norden* that he had visited the Klondike gold fields during the summer and thought it unlikely that miners there would be successful. He would return to Alaska to continue his work of instructing the Eskimo in the reindeer culture.[17]

Kjellman and his company spent a couple of weeks in Chicago, where he was interviewed at great length in their hotel. *Skandinaven*'s reporter described him as a tall, strongly-built man of about forty, with black hair and a full beard. The Lapps were dressed in the same skin and wool garments they wore in Norway. Kjellman recounted the whole sad story of why the reindeer had been introduced into Alaska, and added that in recent years not one whale had been seen in the Bering Sea. No less than 172 persons, he said, mostly Norwegians, had offered their services to Sheldon Jackson in bringing Lapps from Norway and supervising the reindeer project, some of them specifying that they would bring Lapp herding dogs as well. Kjellman, who received the appointment and brought the Lapps with their dogs in 1894, had found 151 reindeer at Teller. In the fall of 1897, there were 1,568 animals in the territory, divided among five stations: Teller, Cape Prince of Wales, the most western American point, Cape Nome, Golovnin Bay, and Eaton. These reindeer belonged to 500 Eskimo who had been taught to use the animals for transport, food, and clothing. In addition, there were another 500 Eskimo who, directly or indirectly, earned their living from the government's activity.

When Kjellman first went to Alaska, he remarked, the Eskimo were suspicious of the project, believing that whites would gain whatever benefits might ensue, as they had done in mining, whaling and sealing, and the canning of fish. They were won over only when it was made clear to them that all gains would be theirs. "Look here," Kjellman and others had said to the Eskimo, "you have a herd of 100 deer that we will give to a group of three families for a period of five years. You must not sell, slaughter, or lose them, but train them for transport as we do, and after the five years give us back 100 deer. The increase in the herd is your own property." Kjellman continued: "And we told them we believed they would become owners of 500 animals in these years, which would give them an adequate start in supporting themselves and their children for the rest of their lives. The project has been so successful in three years that the original units of 100 deer have increased to 368, which makes the owners . . . at least moderately well-off and independent. They are regarded by their own people as rich and are called umeliks or chieftains."

Kjellman added: "We gather from the various villages

141

young Eskimo who undergo a three-year learning period at one of the stations. During this time the government provides them with food, lodging, and clothes. If some of them at the end of the three years are found to be ready to care for a herd of reindeer, they are sent out with a number sufficiently large to begin sustaining them, their families, and others." The number of animals given them was determined by the size of their families as well as the number of learners in the group sent out. When the superintendent determined that three of them were ready to care for a herd and to work together, he gave them 100 reindeer. If he found only two who were willing to work together and were capable, he gave them 75, 80, or perhaps 100, depending on the size of their families. If a learner proved to be unprepared for the task of herding, he was given another year of training. If, after four years, he was still unqualified, he was given a share in a herd under the control of another native.

"As early as the summer of 1895," Kjellman said, "the Eskimo had become so interested in the project that we couldn't accept half of the applications we got from all corners of the country . . . as the government's appropriation for the operation of the school was too small for so many students. It became necessary, then, to cooperate with the various mission societies that are working in Alaska." A herd of 100 reindeer, accompanied by a Lapp, would be lent to a mission for a five-year period, with the understanding that the Eskimo in the mission would train under the Lapp, that the society would clothe and feed the natives, and that part of the herd's increase in five years would become the property of the mission and part would go to the Eskimo. "Now five times as many Eskimo are being trained as herders than would have been possible if the government were alone in the program." The mission societies were required to

142

report on their activities, and the superintendent had the power to recall the original number of reindeer lent out if he thought there was danger of losses caused by neglect. There had been no need to enforce this regulation, however, as the relationship with the missions had been one of full cooperation and success. The societies the superintendent had worked with were the American Mission Association, the Swedish Evangelical Mission Association, and the Episcopalian Mission.

The government was also supporting fifty-four Eskimo directly with food, lodging, and clothes. These were the students' wives, families, and other relatives who were not able to support themselves. "As the young men we are training will be the future leaders of the reindeer industry," Kjellman explained, "we are careful to choose the best, most trustworthy, and strongest among the Eskimo. To do this, we must often support their elderly parents and other relatives who previously had depended on them for their daily bread." Such persons normally contributed to the station the products of their hunting and fishing.

Twelve of the Lapps who had gone to Alaska in 1894 and whose contracts had expired were returning to Norway with him, but had not yet decided whether to renew their contracts. It was possible, Kjellman said, that he might bring back to Alaska as many as 100 families. In general, the Lapps had liked the territory, although they had found the winter climate more trying than in the birch forests of northern Norway. In order to secure moss for the deer, they had been compelled to stay in the western part of Alaska that stretches out into the Bering Strait. On its treeless heights they were exposed to winter-long and ice-cold northwestern winds. At times, even in their deerskin clothing, they were unable to leave their houses. The reindeer, however, did well even in the cold. The stretches of land in the interior, with their pristine forests and extended valleys, had a much milder winter climate, but in summer were extremely warm, and people there complained about the mosquitoes.[18]

The reindeer story took a new and exciting turn late in 1897, with further reports of threatened hunger among the miners in the Yukon. *Nordvesten,* for example, carried a story from New York to the effect that 1,000 animals might be imported from Norway. Kjellman went to Washington to receive instructions in the event that Congress approved the plan to acquire these reindeer. From Røros, via *Aftenposten* in Kristiania, came the news that Kjellman had arrived in Finnmark on a much larger undertaking than the one of 1894. Horses had failed in their effort to bring supplies into the Yukon. Kjellman hoped to take back with him not only 1,000 deer, but 100 Lapps for a new colony in Alaska. He had said it would be relatively easy to buy the deer at $10 a head in Nordland and Finnmark, but moss in quantity sufficient to feed the animals during the journey presented a real problem in winter.

Kjellman, in Norway, explained that two transport ships, each of 250 tons, had brought food to the mining districts in the Yukon. Despite the great care that was being taken in distributing the food, with 200 Canadian mounted police rationing it, the supply could not last beyond the beginning of April. If the rivers were not open before July, enabling steamers to go in with new provisions, the mining population of from 6,000 to 8,000 would suffer real want unless food could be transported overland in one way or another. Of this fact the government was fully aware, and the three states of Oregon, California, and Washington had volunteered to contribute the necessary provisions free of charge if a means of transportation could be found. Hence the need for the reindeer, Kjellman said. He would be able to take back

144

100 pounds of food for each animal. Asked how many Norwegians were in the Klondike, he answered that there were between 400 and 500.[19]

Kjellman presumably had some difficulty in recruiting Lapps. According to one Norwegian newspaper, the herders who returned to Kautokeino had lodged complaints. They had been well paid, they said, each adult male receiving by contract 100 *kroner* (about $20) per month in Alaska, and they had been given free board and clothing. All had gone well on the Thingvalla ship *Island*, and, on arriving at Port Clarence in 1894, some of the Lapps had set about building houses and caring for the reindeer. Others had fished for salmon. Until the houses were completed, they had been forced to live with the Eskimo in crude dirt dwellings. In summer they lived in tents. The work had not been hard, but they had found it difficult to adjust to the food they were given, especially the salted meat, which they left in water for eight days before they could eat it. Only when they became sick did they receive small portions of fresh deer meat, despite the fact that they had been promised fresh meat in their contracts. They had been assured, too, that they would be permitted to take their dogs back to Norway, free of charge, but had been forced to return without them. Their children had suffered from convulsions, and all of them had found it difficult to adjust to the climate during their early months in the territory. One herder had lost his young wife. But the Lapps admitted that the Eskimo had been willing to learn the care of the deer. They would agree to return to Alaska, as they had been able to save about 3,000 *kroner* per family, if they were assured that contracts would be strictly honored.[20]

Kjellman was forced to travel over 3,000 miles in Finnmark and was reported from Alta to have secured only about 500 animals. After much effort, he had been

145

able to persuade fifty Lapps to accompany him. Sheldon Jackson had shared his search and had found the region more challenging for winter travel than Chilkoot Pass in Alaska. But they were partially successful, and Dr. Jackson wired the Department of War early in February, 1898, that the Allan Line's *Manitoba* had left Norway with 530 deer and 87 Lapp men and women.[21]

For some weeks the Norwegian-American press had been exaggerating the number of Lapps and reindeer, but *Skandinaven* was close to the truth in reporting that on February 27 the *Manitoba* had arrived in New York, after a trip lasting 24 days, with 537 deer, 43 Lapps, 10 Finns, and 15 Norwegians who had brought their families with them — in all 68 men, 19 women, and 26 children. The group included six newly-married couples, Samuel Balto, a Lapp who had been with Fridtjof Nansen in his famous trip over Greenland, and Johan Peter Skalogare (Johannesen), a Finn who had carried mail on his back for eight years in Finnmark. The cargo included 418 pulkas (Lapp sledges), 511 sacks of sailcloth, and 4,000 sacks of moss.[22]

The train bearing the reindeer expedition, thirty-nine cars divided into two sections, stopped off in Chicago on March 6, 1898, and, after the animals had been given some rest in the stockyards, went on to Seattle. *Skandinaven* took the occasion to announce that it was possible the deer and the sleighs would be sold on the West Coast, as the government had learned that help was no longer needed for the miners in the Yukon and Alaska. The number of Finns in the party was now reported as two.[23]

When the train arrived in Seattle, the reindeer were taken to Woodland Park, where crowds of people gathered to see them and the Lapps. The government definitely had given up the original plan for a relief expedition to the Yukon, according to *Washington Posten*, but

The reindeer grazing in Woodland Park in Seattle in 1898 before going on to Alaska. The photograph is by the well-known Norwegian photographer Anders Wilse. COURTESY OF THE HISTORICAL PHOTOGRAPHY COLLECTION, UNIVERSITY OF WASHINGTON LIBRARIES

the deer nevertheless would be sent to Alaska. The new plan was to divide the herd into two parts; one with 337 animals would go to Pyramid Harbor, and from there by the Dalton route to a place under American jurisdiction, possibly Circle City, where a relief station would be set up under Kjellman's direction. The remaining 200 deer would be sent to Prince William Sound with about fifty attendants under the leadership of Captain W. R. Abercrombie. The second expedition would investigate the Copper River (Port Valdez) area, where it was hoped they could find a way, over only American soil, by which to reach the gold fields in the Yukon. The general attitude seemed to be that, although the government had given up its original plan for which the reindeer had

147

been purchased, much good would still come from their use in Alaska.[24]

The first and larger expedition left Seattle aboard the bark *Seminole* in March, sailing first to Port Townsend, where women and children were to be put ashore temporarily, then going on to Pyramid Harbor, where the reindeer were to be stationed for a couple of months. It was reported that 200 of the animals already had been sold to private individuals for $100 each. In April, the second expedition, under Abercrombie and with Martin Bjørnstad, an experienced miner, as interpreter, left for Copper River.[25]

Kjellman returned to Wisconsin in the summer of 1898 to spend some time with his family in Mount Horeb. Interviewed by *Amerika og Norden* in Madison, he reported that he had had amazingly good fortune with his reindeer in Alaska and likely would continue to serve as superintendent. He also stated that there had been three expeditions similar to his but under other leaders during the past winter. In one instance, the last deer had died when the ship from Norway anchored in New York. A second expedition brought a couple of live animals as far as Seattle, but these had died en route to Skagway. The third had five live reindeer when it arrived in Skagway, but the last of them had died at Lake Bennett. Kjellman had brought 536 of his 537 deer to Alaska in good condition. He informed the newspaper that Pastor Brevig would return to the States in the summer, as the government would soon end its work at Port Clarence, where only a few families remained after the reindeer station had been moved to its more favorable location. Kjellman said he would go back to Alaska soon, and would proceed to Siberia to secure more animals.[26]

Martin Bjørnstad, with Captain Abercrombie's exploring party in the Copper River country, wrote a series of

The Norwegian Lapps who were hired as herders attracted much attention. ANDERS WILSE. COURTESY OF THE HISTORICAL PHOTOGRAPHY COL-LECTION, UNIVERSITY OF WASHINGTON LIBRARIES

long letters to *Washington Posten* late in 1898, but these reports deal largely with mining prospects — or lack of them — in the region. Abercrombie had been generous in providing stranded gold-seekers with lodging and food — presumably including reindeer meat — in Port Valdez. Traveling over the Valdez Glacier was extremely difficult. Abercrombie's expedition had left in the summer to cross the glacier and explore the region beyond as far as Mount Wrangell. It apparently found a better route to Copper River than the one by way of Valdez Glacier, but it could be used only in late fall or winter. Bjørnstad was one of the party that had found it.[27]

Pastor Brevig, home in Wisconsin after his four-year period of service at Port Clarence, also visited the offices of *Amerika og Norden* and presented a lecture in Madison and elsewhere on his Alaska experience. He

149

naturally hoped to arouse interest in his mission and to promote support for his work with the Eskimo. He reviewed the entire reindeer story and said he thought the government's program was successful. Those involved in it had discovered in time that at least half of Alaska was clearly suited for grazing ground, and that the wilderness could sustain millions of deer and serve the native population well.[28]

On January 1, 1899, Lapps delivered at St. Michael what remained of the main herd of reindeer transported from Norway. With them were also a number of missionaries on the way to stations along the coast. Significantly, the men brought news of a remarkable discovery of gold in 1898 in small streams flowing into the Snake River, which had its mouth at Cape Nome. Prospectors had begun a stampede to Nome, some pulling their sleds themselves because of the high price and shortage of dogs. Dr. Kittilsen, who had been with the first Norwegians and Lapps to locate claims, had been living at St. Michael for more than a month, but returned to Nome on January 9 with an ample supply of provisions.[29]

After the discovery of gold at Cape Nome, the reindeer program was to play a secondary but not unimportant role in the overall story of Alaska. But the people who had been and in part still were involved in it — Lapps, Finns, and Norwegians — were to be major characters in the new saga of gold.

II

As late as the summer of 1899, *Washington Posten*, which reported faithfully on incoming ships from Alaska, wrote mainly of mines owned by Seattle Norwegians and of the successes, failures, and tragedies among these people in the Yukon and Alaska. But it also gave tentative reports of the gold find at Cape Nome.

Hundreds of gold-seekers, the newspaper said, were going there and to the Klondike daily, but Nome was being favored, in part because it was on American soil. On June 30 it reported that rich gold fields "really have been discovered" in the Seward Peninsula. In July, "gold ships" began to arrive from St. Michael, and the *Alliance* brought the first substantial news about Nome. Later ships brought the report that there were more people than mines at Cape Nome and advised people not to go there.[30]

The press had a reliable source of information from Nome during the early fall of 1899 in Magnus Kjeldsberg, who had been in charge of the reindeer sent to Norton Sound. When he arrived at the station there, he learned of a gold discovery on Anvil Creek. He had gone immediately to the Nome area and had been fortunate in securing some of the best claims in the new mining district. He, Dr. Kittilsen, and a few other Norwegians could be said to be the richest men at Cape Nome. Kjeldsberg had left Norway a little more than two years before with hardly a cent in his pocket; now he counted his money in the thousands of dollars. With another Norwegian, he later operated a saloon on Anvil Creek. In September, *Washington Posten* announced a second discovery of gold along the beaches at Cape Nome; there, too, Norwegians had been among the fortunate.[31]

Once fully aware of the importance of the discovery on Anvil Creek, the Norwegian-language newspapers carried many stories about it and Nome, often with exaggerated estimates of the riches taken. Although most of the miners had earned good money, many were nevertheless sick because they lacked fuel for heating, and among them was Jafet Lindeberg, the chief discoverer on Anvil Creek. A little over two years before, he had come with the Lapps in the second reindeer expedition, and had gone to Norton Sound with Magnus

151

Kjeldsberg and his brother. Lindeberg recovered and arrived in Seattle aboard the gold ship *Roanoke*, which carried $1,500,000 in the precious metal. Lindeberg and John Brynteson were reported to have $400,000 each, J. R. Anderson, $100,000, H. C. Wilhelmson, $30,000, and William A. Kjellman, $75,000. Kjellman, who planned to spend the winter in Wisconsin, was accompanied by Dr. Kittilsen, who also had rich claims.[32]

Late in 1899, *Skandinaven* ran a long but misleading story about Cape Nome, among other things stating that the chief discoverer of gold there had been a Swedish Covenant missionary from Chicago, the Reverend Nels O. Hultberg.[33] This and other inaccurate articles in the Norwegian-American press also had implied less than honest actions by Hultberg and another Covenant missionary, P. H. Anderson. Kjellman felt impelled to write an article correcting these errors, and he sent copies of it to various newspapers from his home at Mount Horeb. He described the "gold belt" to which Nome belonged. Paying sand had been found at various places in the belt; each had its own "discoverer," Kjellman wrote, "and I think that, if one knew the whole truth, Scandinavians without doubt hold the record. This, in any case, is true along the Bering Sea coast" — a fitting consequence, he added, of the fact that Vitus Bering, the first European to sail those waters, was a Scandinavian.

Kjellman explained that the discovery at Cape Nome was made in 1898 by the Swedes Erik O. Lindblom and John Brynteson and the Norwegian Jafet Lindeberg. The three men had sailed from Golovnin Bay on September 11 in a flat-bottomed boat "in which few would have risked their lives." On September 18, coming to one of the Snake River's tributaries — later named Anvil Creek — they had found coarse gold in paying quantities. The men had remained long enough on Anvil Creek to seek out and stake what they thought were —

and what proved to be — the best claims. They had returned to Golovnin Bay on October 5 to get several more men to join them and to agree on the necessary bylaws for the new district.

Dr. Kittilsen, who was then at Golovnin Bay, Gabe Price of San Francisco, Johan I. Tornanses (Tornensis), a Lapp, and the three discoverers had set out for Nome on October 12 in a small schooner belonging to the Swedish mission and had arrived at Snake River on the 15th. There they had organized a mining district, staked their claims, opened a recorder's office, and chosen Kittilsen recorder. They had worked at their tasks until the freeze set in, then had returned overland to Golovnin Bay and given out the news of their actions. These, Kjellman maintained, were the naked facts about Anvil Creek. Stories in *Skandinaven* and other newspapers some time earlier had tended to blacken the reputations of two honorable Swedish missionaries. He thought the much publicized "beach diggings" at Nome would yield little gold but that the rivers and creeks, as well as the tundra in the Cape Nome district, would give up a great deal of treasure; they were already largely "located." [34]

There was a measure of truth in *Skandinaven*'s story about Hultberg as the discoverer of gold at Cape Nome. Captain Daniel B. Libby, who had been a member of the Western Union Telegraph construction corps in Alaska, was among those who had found evidence of gold on Mesling and Ophir creeks in 1897. After spending the winter at Golovnin, he and his associates had resumed prospecting and founded Council City. Hultberg, who had established and was in charge of the Swedish Covenant mission at Cheenik on Golovnin Bay, came to Libby's camp on April 23, 1898, and took part in the organization of the Discovery mining district, the first placer district on the Seward Peninsula. Soon

153

after, he participated in the creation of the Eldorado (El Dorado) mining district, adjoining Discovery, and the Bonanza district on Golovnin Bay.

Hultberg had actually prospected before Libby's arrival. One result of this activity had been a rush of prospectors to the Kotzebue area in the summer of 1898. No promising discovery resulted there, however, and the Ophir Creek findings were soon "eclipsed by strikes on Anvil Creek." Natives had reported gold on the beach of the Sinuk River, information that led Hultberg, Brynteson, H. L. Blake, and others to set out in a schooner for the site. A storm forced them to take refuge at the mouth of the Snake River. Prospecting there, they crossed Anvil Creek but found little gold and failed to stake out claims. Similarly, they did not find gold in sufficient amounts in the beach sands of the Sinuk River.[35]

By far the most important account of the gold discovery on Anvil Creek was written in later years by Jafet Lindeberg. A trader in Golovnin Bay named John Dexter, he wrote, had provided a few natives with gold pans and instructed them in their use. While on a fishing and hunting trip, an Eskimo named Tom Gaurik found gold on Ophir Creek in the Council City area. When he returned in August, 1897, he reported his find. Shortly thereafter, a few prospectors representing San Francisco capitalists under a grubstake contract learned of the native's experience from Dexter. Prospecting there with others during the winter and spring of 1897–1898, they staked claims on Ophir and Melsing creeks and organized the Eldorado mining district, elected a recorder, and drafted rules. When news of their success slipped out, a rush followed from nearby places. He continued:

"I, Jafet Lindeberg, a native of Norway, came to this country in the spring of 1898 with Sheldon Jackson . . . for the express purpose of going to Plover Bay, in Eastern Siberia, to relieve Captain Kelly, who was trading at that place for reindeer. . . . I left Seattle on the steamer *Del Norte* . . . taking with me a stock of provisions. . . . On arrival at St. Michael, news was brought to Doctor Jackson that Captain Kelly had been driven away from Plover Bay by hostile natives. It was then decided that it would be unwise to send me over there and, being left without a suitable position, Doctor Jackson gave me permission to leave Government employ. This I did, and, taking my outfit, made for the new diggings at Council City, which had been located on the banks of the Niukluk River, near Ophir Creek."

Lindeberg introduced his major associates in this manner: "John Brynteson, a native of Sweden and an experienced coal and iron miner who for seven years had worked in the mines of Michigan, determined to go to Alaska and look for coal. Arriving in St. Michael and hearing of the discoveries on Ophir Creek he promptly left St. Michael for Council City, arriving there early in the summer of 1898.

"Erik O. Lindblom, a native of Sweden, by profession a tailor, and for years following his trade in San Francisco, while there, hearing of the fabulous reports from Kotzebue Sound, joined the stampede, going north on the bark *Alaska.* Arriving at Port Clarence on his way . . . and hearing of the gold discovery on Ophir Creek, he left the ship and proceeded to Golofin [*sic*] Bay, then to Council City.

"We three men," Lindeberg continued, "met by chance at Council City in August, 1898; after prospecting around in that district for some time and staking some claims, we formed a prospecting companionship and decided to prospect over a wider range of territory. Even at this early date the Council City district was overrun by stampeders and staked to the mountain tops; so we proceeded to Golofin Bay and taking a large open

155

boat and an outfit of provisions, on September 11, 1898, started up the coast toward Port Clarence, stopping at various rivers to prospect on the way, in which we found signs of gold, but not in paying quantities, and finally arriving at what is now known as the town of Nome, which we named, and camped at the mouth of Glacier Creek, prospecting as we went along. The first encouraging sign of gold we found on the banks of the Snake River. . . . After locating our camp as before mentioned, we proceeded to prospect along the tributaries of Snake River, which tributaries we named as follows: Anvil Creek (taking the name from an anvil-shaped rock which stands on the mountain on the east side of the creek), Snow Gulch, Glacier Creek, Rock Creek and Dry Creek, in all of which we found gold in paying quantities and proceeded to locate claims, first on Anvil Creek because we found better prospects in that creek than in the others, and where we located the 'discovery claim' in the name of us three jointly. In addition to this, each man staked a separate claim in his own name on the creek. This was the universal custom in Alaska, as it was conceded that the discoverer was entitled to a discovery claim and one other. After locating on Anvil Creek, claims were staked on Snow Gulch, Dry Creek and Rock Creek, after which we returned to Golofin Bay and reported the discovery.

"It was then decided to form a mining district, so we three original discoverers organized a party, taking with us Dr. A. N. Kittleson, G. W. Price, P. H. Anderson and a few others, again proceeded to Nome in a small schooner which we charted in Golofin Bay, purchasing as many provisions as we could carry on the boat, and on our arrival the Cape Nome mining district was organized and Dr. A. N. Kittleson elected the first recorder. Rules were formulated, after which the party prospected and staked claims, finally returning to Golofin

Bay for winter quarters. The news spread like wildfire and soon a wild stampede was made to the new diggings from Council City, St. Michael and the far-off Yukon.

"At this point very few mining men were in the country, the newcomers in many instances being from every trade known. The consequences of this were soon well known; a few men with a smattering of education gave their own interpretation of the mining laws, hence jumping mining claims soon became an active industry. . . . They were angry to think that they had not been taken in at the beginning, so a few of them jumped nearly every claim on Anvil Creek, although there was an abundance of vacant and unlocated ground left which has since proved to be more valuable than the original claims located by us and our second party who helped us to form the district. This jumping, or relocating of claims by the parties above mentioned, poisoned the minds of all the newcomers against every original locator of mining claims and as a consequence every original claim was relocated by from one to a dozen different parties. . . .

"In the early months of 1899 we hauled supplies to the creeks and as soon as the thaw came began active mining on Snow Gulch and on Anvil Creek. Soon a large crowd flocked to Nome, which was then known as Anvil Creek. Among this crowd was a large element of lawless men who soon joined forces with the Council City jumpers and every effort was made by them to create trouble. . . . and had it not been for the military, who proved themselves to be true men to the American Government, much riot and bloodshed would have resulted from the conduct of the aforementioned parties. . . .

"The situation was suddenly relieved in an unexpected manner. It was accidently discovered that the beach sands were rich in gold. . . . Within a few weeks

157

the mutterings of discontent were almost silenced because it was found that good wages could be made with rockers on the beach. All the idle men went to work as fast as they could obtain implements."[36]

Something of what it meant to come to Nome from northern Norway and to work in one of Jafet Lindeberg's mines is told in the story of Leonhard Seppala, who later won fame as a dog racer in the 408-mile All-Alaska Sweepstakes and the Ruby Derby. Lindeberg financed the trip of this young fisherman, who in turn was to repay its cost from wages, a sum of $300. On arrival, Seppala and his fellow immigrants wandered about the sprawling town of Nome for several days, finally taking shelter in a cabin owned by Lapps, where they slept on the floor. There they waited for word from Lindeberg. It finally came in the form of a request that Seppala and his partner Magnus, also a fisherman, drive a heavily loaded wagon to Discovery on Anvil Creek. Neither had ever driven a horse and they found it necessary to bribe a stableboy to harness a lively team and hitch it to the wagon. Beyond the firm beach, out on the tundra, their troubles began. "The horses went down in the soft mud and the wagon sank to the axles. Time and again we unloaded the wagon, carrying the burden by hand until we found more solid footing." Almost ready to give up, they were saved by a prospector familiar with their problem. In all, it took eleven hours to make the five-mile trip to the mine.

Leonhard and Magnus were separated the next day. Seppala's account of the job he was assigned suggests the demands made on the workers in the mines. He was ordered to hold a horse-pulled slip-scraper, "which was used to clear away the tailing at the lower end of the sluice boxes. It looked simple enough, but the teamster kept the horses at a trot all the forenoon while I followed filling the scraper and then running behind and dumping it. Later I found out that the dumping was supposed to be the teamster's job." Seppala was saved from total exhaustion by transferring to another job, which was only a bit less strenuous. After the scraper was damaged and taken to the shop for repair, he was put to work shoveling gravel into the sluice boxes, an activity that at first "seemed child's play to me"; but he soon realized that he was falling behind another miner opposite him who "worked like a machine." When the day ended, Seppala's arms "ached and throbbed" and his "blistered hands burned" so he could not sleep.

What any worker in the mines along Anvil Creek confronted in addition to meager wages was a group of "slave-driving bosses. . . . It was a case of the survival of the fittest." The result was discouragement and disillusion on every side. "Men who had never done a day's hard work in their lives toiled and struggled trying to earn enough money to leave the country." After a ten-hour day of shoveling and a sleepless night, Seppala said, "I was in a sort of daze from fatigue. They told me it was time for me to do some real work — I was to go on night shift." For mineowners, the almost impossible efforts of the workers were profitable indeed. Discovery Mine on Anvil Creek yielded "from six to fifteen thousand dollars in a two-day run of each string of boxes. I saw gold dust and nuggets by the pan and bucketful."

Seppala went on at least one prospecting trip at Lindeberg's request, with negative results. When the prospectors returned, he went back to his night shift. "All that September the rain never stopped." His new foreman was a well-read American who taught the newcomer English and the ways of the country. But the work continued to be unbearable. Seppala stated that his arms burned so with fever that he would go out of his tent and "thrust them into the cold water in one of the pits to cool them and so relieve the pain. . . . After insufficient rest, the men would drag themselves to the pits, stiff and sore in every limb, dressed in oil-skins, sou'westers, and rubber boots, with coal-oil headlights making a weak light." Water "ran in streams down our necks as we bent over, and trickled up our arms as we lifted them with each shovelful of gravel — a process repeated probably two thousand times in a night. . . . Men came, worked a shift or more, and left. Some did not last a single shift."

Seppala, when each evening approached, thought of his home in Norway. In his words, "I . . . regretted that I had listened to the golden-tongued orators who had persuaded me to come to Alaska. . . . I wanted adventure and I was getting it. . . . Often when I awoke . . . I would try to console myself with the thought that after all this life had one advantage over that of the Norse fisherman — we at least had ground under our feet, and not hundreds of fathoms of roaring Arctic Ocean. . . . If only the gold had not beckoned and I had been able to stay in Southeastern Alaska and fish as I had planned so long ago!" Daylight brought new hope. At breakfast, "which was supper for us . . . we would build a crackling fire in the little tent stove. It was so cozy in there that we would fire up and talk for hours while our clothes dried and the boys from neighboring tents dropped in and exchanged stories with us. . . . Our troubles were forgotten until we went to bed and the pain and fever returned."

Lindeberg, a major victim of mine-jumping, was not averse to using violence himself in defense of his claims. One night he ordered Seppala and four other men to report at his office. There he told them and additional men to go quietly in pairs to his No. 2 mine on Glacier Creek and to meet him at the southeast corner stake. All received guns, left at ten-minute intervals to walk the six miles in darkness to Glacier, and, arriving, were stationed at various points on the property. Jumpers made two attempts to relocate the claim, and failed. Shots were fired and three intruders were captured. Seppala, who was involved in the fighting, injured one of the jumpers by hitting him with his rifle.

One morning late in October, Ole, boss of a nearby group of night workers, stuck his head into Seppala's tent and announced, "Well, it's all off. She froze up on us last night. You clean up the boxes for the last time to-day." Seppala then found a temporary job in a small camp where the men did their own "sourdough cooking." He worked with two young Norwegian Americans just out of school and unused to hard work, but the demands were not great and they got along well.

In December, Lindeberg brought news of the gold discovery in the Kougarok and of a plan to send out four men and two dog teams to prospect in the area. He invited three Swedes and Seppala to join the party, causing the latter to dream of making a strike, staking a claim, and becoming rich. The trip with his congenial partners was rich in experience and tragic in its revelation of what white civilization had done to the Eskimo, but it failed in its search for gold. Seppala never "struck it rich," but, as he told the writer in 1948, he was glad of it. He had seen enough of what the metal could do to people like himself.

When asked his opinion of Jafet Lindeberg, Seppala described him as a strong, natural leader of men, but lacking in education. Tall and athletic, he had been a fine seaman and fisherman in Norway. His parents, both of Finnish origin, had come to Finnmark by way of Sweden. (Seppala's mother was Norwegian; his father was half Finnish.) Lindeberg, something of a "plunger," who was forced to spend a fortune in the litigation resulting from an effort to steal his mines, had later lost much of his money in Nevada. Speaking of the

161

Nome of the early 1900s, Seppala said it was full of Norwegians, some from Finnmark and other parts of Norway, others from the States. Swedes, also deeply involved in the gold discoveries, were perhaps equally numerous. But the workers in the mines had come from everywhere. Seppala, while directing operations in an underground mine, had had employees from Russia, Portugal, Egypt, Montenegro, and other countries under his supervision.[37]

III

The discovery of gold on Cape Nome was followed by what must be described as one of the most notorious and infamous judicial scandals in American history. It involved the theft, by legal action, of the rich placer mines largely owned by Scandinavians, and it was perpetrated by the judge of a district court in Alaska in collaboration with a prominent national politician.

The Norwegian press in America covered the Nome scandal thoroughly and, on the whole, accurately, but it is best to hear this story of intrigue and conspiracy first from a person trained in the law and familiar with the Alaskan scene. Perhaps no one was better qualified to interpret its legal aspects than James Wickersham, who served as a district judge in Alaska after 1900 and was later the territorial delegate to Congress for fourteen years. He was editor of seven volumes of *Alaska Law Reports* and author of *A Bibliography of Alaskan Literature*.

Wickersham writes that among those who went to Nome in 1899 were lawyers to whom it seemed "wickedly unfair that the rich claims, so few in number, should fall to a few 'lucky Swedes' and Lapland reindeer-herders, and loud protests began to rise above the warm stoves in the straggling new town. Then some 'sea lawyer' raised the question whether these aliens could legally locate and hold mining claims in Alaska." When

162

the Nome lawyers answered this question in the negative, the protests grew into threats, and the threats led to action.

Certain discontented miners shared his view and at a meeting on July 10, 1899, a resolution was drafted declaring the claims of the Scandinavians illegal and therefore open to relocation. The leaders among the protesters had men stationed on Anvil Mountain, near the mines; the understanding was that when they saw a signal fire in Nome they would know that the resolution had passed and that they should get on with jumping the claims. Word of this scheme, however, had got to Fort St. Michael. A Lieutenant Spaulding and two of his soldiers proceeded to Nome, attended the miners' meeting, and forced adjournment by motion.

Frustrated in their claim-jumping plan, the Nome lawyers sought to have the mining laws altered in their favor, and sent one of their men to Washington, D.C., where a bill was pending in the Senate in the fall of 1899 for civil government in Alaska. An act of 1884 had stated that the laws of Oregon "are hereby declared to be the law in said district so far as the same may be applicable." According to the civil code of Oregon, an "alien may acquire and hold lands, or interest therein, by purchase, devise, or descent, and he may convey, mortgage, and devise the same, and if he shall die intestate, the same shall descend to his heirs; and in all cases such lands shall be held, conveyed, mortgaged, or devised or shall descend in like manner and with like effect as if such alien were a native citizen of this state or the United States." Section 73 of the Oregon civil code specifically stated that the "title to any lands heretofore conveyed shall not be questioned, nor in any manner affected, by reason of the alienage of any person from or through whom such title may have been derived."

These parts of the Oregon code had been put into

163

Senate bill 3919, which was introduced on March 1, 1900, by Senator T. H. Carter of Montana. When the bill came up for discussion, Senator H. C. Hansbrough of North Dakota moved their elimination and offered what came to be known as the "Hansbrough amendment," which declared invalid the claims on Anvil Creek and permitted relocation by jumpers ready to act. The amendment was immediately opposed by senators W. M. Stewart of Nevada, J. C. Spooner of Wisconsin, Knute Nelson of Minnesota, H. M. Teller of Colorado, and others.

Finding the Hansbrough motion inadequate, the senators who had favored it gave their support to another amendment introduced by Hansbrough on April 4: "That persons who are not citizens of the United States or who prior to making location had not legally declared that intention to become such, shall not be permitted to locate, hold, or convey mining claims in said district of Alaska, nor shall any title to a mining claim acquired by location or purchase through any such person or persons be legal." This altered motion also led to vigorous objection and heated debate in what Wickersham likens to a lawsuit in the Senate. When it appeared that the debate might prevent passage of the bill, which also provided for needed civil government in Alaska, the senators arrived at a compromise that eliminated the controversial sections from the Oregon civil code on alien property rights, and the bill was passed. Nothing in American law, however, denied aliens the right to own or to sell mines.

As Wickersham asserts and the Norwegian-American press had charged all along, the leader and moving spirit in the struggle to get approval of the Hansbrough amendment and its revision had been Alexander McKenzie, a Republican national committeeman from North Dakota who had strong political influence in the capital and in the states of Minnesota, North Dakota, and Montana. He had been a receiver for the Northern Pacific Railway during its financially difficult years and subsequently chief lobbyist in Washington for this and other railroads. It was to him that the lawyers representing the jumpers in Alaska turned in their effort to secure the Anvil Creek mines. He failed to steer the Hansbrough amendment through the Senate, but succeeded in eliminating the controversial Oregon sections from the Alaska bill. He also had become interested in the Nome gold field and had set his mind on securing what he could of it.

McKenzie, together with his friends in the Senate, next had to make sure that his nominees were chosen for the new United States First District Court in Alaska. President William McKinley obliged by appointing Arthur H. Noyes of Minnesota as judge, C. L. Vawter of Montana as marshal, and Joseph K. Wood, also of Montana, as district attorney. McKenzie even influenced the selection of minor officers. He then organized, under the laws of Arizona, a corporation with authorized capital stock of $15,000,000. He became president and general manager of this firm, the Alaska Gold Mining Company, and later arranged with Hubbard, Beeman, and Hume, attorneys for the jumpers in Nome, to buy from their clients titles to the mines they had taken. Payment for the claims was made in stock in his company. McKenzie also doled out shares to friends who would help him in his scheme, put some in reserve for other purchases, and was believed to have kept the majority of the shares for himself. It was clear that, in Wickersham's words, he was "intent on capturing a fortune by piratic force from a few simple-minded Lapp reindeer-herders and hard-digging Scandinavian miners. It looked to the boss like an easy job!"[38]

If what had happened in the Senate was part of a

165

carefully worked out plan to justify the seizure of mines from their rightful owners, what followed was nothing less than a colossal swindle. Judge Noyes, an old friend of McKenzie's in Minnesota who had been in Washington during the hearings on the Alaska bill, sailed to Nome from Seattle on the *Senator* in the company of McKenzie and Robert Chipps, jumper claimant of Discovery mine on Anvil Creek. Noyes remained aboard ship after McKenzie and Chipps went ashore in Nome. On the day of landing, July 19, 1900, McKenzie met with the attorney W. T. Hume of the firm Hubbard, Beeman, and Hume; the result was the transfer to McKenzie's company of a half-interest in the disputed mines. Noyes then entered Nome on July 21. When Wood, the district attorney, became a member of Hubbard, Beeman, and Hume, McKenzie also received a quarter-interest in the legal firm.

It was at once clear that McKenzie faced strong opposition in Charles D. Lane, a successful miner from California, Jafet Lindeberg, whom Wickersham describes as a shrewd businessman who had the witnesses essential to fighting the schemers, and two young San Francisco lawyers, Samuel Knight and W. H. Metson. Lane had organized the Wild Goose Mining Company, which did battle beside Lindeberg's Pioneer Mining Company. McKenzie and his attorneys relied on Judge Noyes to put into effect the plan prepared by them to make McKenzie receiver of the claims and to protect him as he worked out the mines. Knowing of the relationship between the two men, Lindeberg and Lane understood that they could have no justice in Nome: their lawyers therefore prepared to appeal to the United States Circuit Court of Appeals in San Francisco.

According to Wickersham, McKenzie's lawyers "had four actions pending in the court over which Judge Noyes would preside, attacking the right of the original

166

locators to four of the most valuable claims on Anvil Creek. Another case was brought . . . by Chipps, who had previously jumped Discovery claim, and on . . . the 24th, at six o'clock p.m., in Judge Noyes' private room in his hotel, applications were presented by Hume to the Judge to appoint receivers for these five claims. Without notice to the defendants, and without even reading the papers or the orders he signed, as his first judicial act at Nome, Judge Noyes appointed McKenzie receiver for these five claims, with instructions to take immediate possession and extract the gold therefrom." He ordered those who held the mines to deliver them to McKenzie and to refrain from any kind of interference in working them. "The receiver's bond was fixed at $5,000 in each case, though the output from one of the claims alone was stated to be $15,000 a day. The receiver had two wagons ready and he and his men raced to Anvil Creek that night and took immediate possession of the claims and all personal property thereon, to the surprise of the owners who had not expected such quick work."

When Noyes refused to listen to the mineowners' attorneys or even to grant them the right of appeal in Nome, they sent lawyers to San Francisco who delivered Noyes's papers to Judge William W. Morrow of the federal court of appeals. This court was not sitting, but Morrow prepared orders permitting appeals in the five cases and "directed that writs of supersedeas issue thereon . . . directed to McKenzie and Judge Noyes commanding Noyes to desist from any further proceedings on account of said orders, and commanding McKenzie to restore to the defendants in said cases all property which he had taken as receiver. Certified copies of the orders allowing appeals and writs of supersedeas in all such cases were returned to and filed in the district court at Nome, and served upon Judge

167

Noyes and McKenzie. The receiver refused to enter orders requiring him to do so, and denied the right of the Circuit Court of Appeals to allow the appeals and to issue the writs of supersedeas."

The owners' attorneys thus failed in their effort to get the judge and receiver to comply with the orders of the San Francisco court. Noyes and McKenzie were taking the advice of Wood, the district attorney, McKenzie's private lawyer, and C. A. S. Frost, an examiner in the Department of Justice who was then serving in Alaska and who stated his views "in violent and defiant language." The defendants, having no other course, then "made up the record and filed it in the Circuit Court of Appeals . . . with an application for its mandatory action." That court on October 1 found that the receiver "had continued to refuse to restore the gold and gold dust and other personal property." It also ordered two deputy marshals "to proceed to Nome, to enforce its writs of supersedeas, arrest the offending receiver . . . and produce him at the bar of that court at San Francisco."

McKenzie and his men again refusing to comply with the writs, the marshals proceeded "to secure the large amount of gold dust deposited in the Nome bank (the Alaska Banking and Safe-Deposit Company) in McKenzie's private deposit boxes." Their task was no easy one, as McKenzie resisted physically and provoked "a violent altercation" at the bank counter. The marshals called upon the army at Fort Davis, and a guard of soldiers came to their assistance. They then broke open the boxes, extracted the gold dust, delivered it to the mineowners, arrested McKenzie, and "boarded the last boat for San Francisco."

McKenzie was tried on February 11, 1901, was found guilty in two cases, and was sentenced to imprisonment for one year in the Alameda county jail. The court of appeals used blunt, harsh language in sentencing him and praised the people of Alaska for depending "solely upon the courts for the correction of the wrongs." McKenzie's attorneys applied to the United States Supreme Court for a writ of habeas corpus testing the legality of his sentence; it reviewed his case but refused to prepare the writ. His many political friends rallied to support him and in May, 1901, President McKinley, on tour in San Francisco, received an appeal for a pardon from McKenzie, who claimed ill health. The appeal was granted reluctantly after McKenzie returned the gold dust he had shipped to Seattle.

According to Wickersham, McKenzie's "notorious criminal activities as the head of the most flagrant prostitution of American courts known in our history, and his other offenses were all forgiven by the President's pardon. He returned to North Dakota, where his health quickly recovered its normal condition, and continued in his activities as a leading citizen." In July, citations were issued by the San Francisco court, taken to Nome, and served on Noyes, Wood, Dudley Du Bose and Thomas J. Geary, McKenzie's legal advisers, and Frost. They were ordered to appear before the court of appeals, where they were charged with contempt. All but Geary were found guilty. Noyes was sentenced to pay a fine of $1,000; Wood was given four months in jail, Du Bose, six, and Frost, twelve; all served their terms. Noyes and Wood were subsequently removed from office.[39]

Unfortunately, others had followed the example of McKenzie and his associates in the Nome area. When Wickersham arrived there on September 16, 1901, he found that with the excuse that the locators had not been citizens, many claims had been jumped, and the original owners had had little chance to defend their rights. Lawsuits had been started but not tried. After the San

Francisco decisions, the miners naturally expected that they would recover their property. When Noyes sailed for San Francisco, the owners had joined forces and driven off the jumpers, in effect setting themselves above the law. Soldiers had seized the claims but had not worked them. With Wickersham's appearance, they withdrew and civil authority was restored. The judge had some 200 cases before him, but speed in dealing with them was possible because of the San Francisco interpretation of the law. Case after case involving jumping and disputed ownership was tried during the winter of 1901–1902. The "business of the town and district began to respond to the settlement of title." The "cleansing of the Augean stables at Nome," begun by Wickersham, was continued by Judge Alfred A. Moore of Pennsylvania, who arrived on July 13, 1902, to fill the bench vacated by Noyes.[40]

IV

Meanwhile, the Norwegian-American newspapers carried numerous stories, often written as letters from Alaska, about the discoveries at Nome and the subsequent attempts to steal the mines.

One of the first and most competent correspondents to write from Nome was Captain E. M. Cederbergh of Portland, Oregon, who went to Alaska early in 1900 as director of the Arctic Trading and Mining Company.[41] His reports to the Norwegian-American press were detailed, reflecting sound judgment. The same can be said of the letters from C. M. Thuland, who after graduation from Luther College and a short course at the University of Minnesota law school published and edited newspapers in both English and Norwegian. Going to Seattle in 1889, he started *Washington Tidende*, which later merged with *Washington Posten*. He continued his studies in law, was admitted to the bar, and opened an office in Seattle. He went to Nome in the spring of 1900 to defend the interests of clients and remained there, gaining some notoriety in suits involving mining property. As a journalist, he also wrote interesting stories about Scandinavian social life in Nome.[42]

Skandinaven was quick to publicize the efforts to deprive the Scandinavians of their rightful claims to mines. Beginning with its April 27, 1900, issue, it covered the debates in the Senate, April 18–19, under the caption *Guldtyve* (Gold Thieves).[43] The editors expressed their indignation at the shameful treatment of the Norwegians, Swedes, and Lapps in Nome and also the misrepresentations of the situation in the English-language press. The newspaper promised its readers to expose the whole story of the "Laplanders," as all the Scandinavians and Finns were labeled by those who sought to rob them, and spared no words in condemning a so-called Law and Order League for trying to secure the help of Congress in carrying out its plans. It praised Senator Knute Nelson for his defense of the Scandinavians in Nome and such senators as Teller, Stewart, Spooner, and others who supported him. As for Senator Hansbrough, *Skandinaven* said the Norwegians in North Dakota knew him well as an enemy of Scandinavians but never dreamed that he would sink to the level of becoming the congressional spokesman and tool for a gang of lawless thieves.[44]

The next month, with a clearer view of what had gone on in the Senate, *Skandinaven* loaded both editorial barrels for an article called "Covering up His Tracks." It charged that Hansbrough, after having been "compelled to abandon his dishonorable plot of robbing the discoverers . . . by means of retroactive legislation," was making "vigorous efforts to enlist some of the Washington correspondents in his cause. In this he appears to have been rather successful. W. E. Curtis had

171

come to his rescue in the Chicago *Record.*" The editorial quoted Curtis as saying that the Alaska bill "would have been defeated in the Senate and Alaska would have been left another year without any laws if Senator Hansbrough and Senator Carter had not yielded the amendment prohibiting the location of mining claims by aliens which they had advocated so earnestly. Senator Stewart . . . and others whose friends are interested in a syndicate that has purchased a lot of claims at Cape Nome from the Laplanders . . . showed a determination to defeat the bill by talking it to death rather than accept the Hansbrough amendment, which canceled the Laplander claims and left them open to relocation by American miners. Most of the claims . . . have been 'jumped' by genuine miners, and the titles will now be settled either by shotguns or the courts. Alaska people report a general and determined hostility against the syndicate, and the miners profess to be able to take care of themselves."

Skandinaven's reply to the *Record* was a simple statement of the facts in the conflict. It pointed to the "fine Italian hand of Hansbrough" in the Curtis account, which it described as "nothing but a maze of misrepresentations. It conceals the fact that the amendment . . . was smuggled in as a substitute for a unanimous committee report; it describes the original claimholders as alien Laplanders, whereas the truth is that nearly all of them are Scandinavians and citizens or intended citizens; it represents the contest as a fight between individual American miners and a powerful California syndicate, while, as a matter of fact, it is a fight between the . . . discoverers and lawful claimholders . . . and a lawless mob, many of whom were aliens. . . . Mr. Curtis conceals the fact that Senator Hansbrough himself is one of the claim-jumpers, by proxy or otherwise, while he insinuates that those who opposed the Hansbrough outrage were working on behalf of interested friends! . . . He has been misled into fathering a veiled charge of which there is no trace even in Hansbrough's curious argument."

Skandinaven also called attention to an article written by the Washington correspondent of the *Minneapolis Journal*, who "tells the same story . . . and it is very evident that both gentlemen have drawn upon the same source." The *Journal* scribe "dons the mask of impartiality and appears to be very much concerned about the truth. But the burden, not to say purpose, of the article is to mislead the reader — to befog what must have been perfectly clear to the writer himself if he had made any attempt at all to ascertain the facts." *Skandinaven* was indignant over the fact that the *Journal*'s writer "gravely informs his readers that a California syndicate sent the 'Laplanders' to a district where gold was not known to exist, for the purpose of gobbling up all the gold there; and that such simple-minded fellows as senators Nelson and Spooner were caught in a Democratic trap and — 'unbeknownst to themselves,' of course — were aiding a Democratic scheme of securing a million dollars of Cape Nome gold for the Bryan campaign fund!"

"Here," according to *Skandinaven* "are some of the pertinent, incontestable facts that the *Journal* man has neglected to state:

"1. The so-called 'Laplanders' were mostly Scandinavians or Finns. Some of them were United States citizens; others had declared their intention to become citizens in the manner prescribed by law, while the rest (including Lindeberg) had declared such intention in good faith before a United States commissioner in Alaska.

"2. Even if they had been aliens, their right to hold claims is indisputable according to the act of 1897, as interpreted by the Supreme Court of the United States. . . .

"3. Some of the members of the so-called Law and

173

Order League were, or are, aliens in the service of English syndicates.

"4. The Hansbrough amendment was presented, surreptitiously, as a substitute for a unanimous committee report. Senator Carter, the chief champion of the amendment on the floor of the Senate, had given his cordial support in committee to the section he had subsequently, at the solicitation of Hansbrough, sought to defeat.

"5. The Hansbrough amendment was an attempt at retroactive legislation, one of the most odious forms of injustice and oppression.

"6. Senator Hansbrough is himself one of the claim-jumpers at Cape Nome.

"7. Senator Stewart stated upon the floor of the Senate that, if the claims of certain people (Senator Hansbrough) had been good, the amendment would not have been presented. To this Senator Hansbrough made no reply."[45]

William A. Kjellman was delighted with *Skandinaven*'s exposé. Writing to the newspaper from his home in Mount Horeb, he maintained that the affair was "far more important for the Scandinavian population in this country than it would first appear to be. The assault against some of them at Cape Nome by 'American tramps' for whom Senator Hansbrough . . . has made himself spokesman is one of the worst and most infamous attacks that has ever been made against our people." The same was true, he wrote, of Hansbrough's shameful performance in the Senate, and he hoped the Norwegians in North Dakota would not forget it. He had been in Nome after December, 1898, and knew very well how the jumpers went about their work. "If it hadn't been for the timely help that the Scandinavians received from the military authorities, one would have heard long ago of bloody conflict up there, as well as complaints that in this country there is no law or justice." Kjellman did not know Senator Nelson, but he expressed gratitude for Nelson's skillful defense of the mineowners. He was less enthusiastic about the Scandinavian press in America; during the two weeks he had followed events in the Senate, he had looked for articles in support of their people and those who defended them in Washington, but, until *Skandinaven* spoke out, he had waited in vain. He hoped now that other newspapers would follow its example.[46]

If the other Norwegian-American newspapers gave less attention than *Skandinaven* to the Senate debates, they were nevertheless keenly interested in the Nome story. *Washington Posten* reported in July, 1900, that since General Randall had taken command in the city, lawlessness had decreased significantly. But mine-jumping remained common. Many persons from the States had bought "claims" whose location was a mystery to all but God. Many in the great mass of people that made Nome a city "stand with empty pockets." *Nordvesten* quoted O. Ellingson of St. Paul, who had just returned from Nome, as reporting that most of the gold up there had been taken, and that hundreds of gold-seekers would die of hunger if the government did not bring them home. *Washington Posten* published a long and interesting description of the Nome area written by C. M. Thuland. It pointed to the shortage of water for the mines on Anvil, Dexter, Snow Gulch, and Glacier creeks, where people were waiting for the rains that might give them employment and a chance to earn money enough to pay their passage home. Along the beach, one could still wash out about $5.00 a day in gold. Despite all its problems, in 1901 Nome would be a lively mining town of about 3,000 people; there really was not room for more, he said. By the next spring, pending litigation would be disposed of, new claims

175

would be made, and there would be water for the mines, as a pumping station would be constructed in the mountains to supply the creeks.[47]

Kjellman, still in Wisconsin, provided *Amerika* with thoughtful accounts of the situation in Alaska in late summer, 1900, correcting mistaken and exaggerated statements in the American newspapers. The winter postal service had been irregular in the interior of Alaska, he reported, but a great improvement had resulted from the work of Norwegians in the service. Johan P. Johannesen (Skalogare), who had gone to Alaska in Kjellman's last expedition and who had previously carried mail across Finnmark, had delivered it on skis during the past winter from Eaton on Norton Sound to Kotzebue Sound. Another man, a Lapp, had brought mail by reindeer from St. Michael via Eaton, Golovnin Bay, and Council City to Nome, bringing dependability into the service and winning high praise.

In a later report Kjellman quoted the *Cape Nome Gold Digger* as saying that, in all, gold to the value of $15,000,000 would be sent out of Nome; Kjellman thought that, for 1900, $10,000,000 would be closer to the truth. The feeling was growing in Nome that the problem of how to continue mining operations in winter would soon be overcome, to the benefit of owners and workers alike. Eskimo, sick with diseases brought by whites, had been taken to Nome for medical care, and some people thought that the natives should be set apart from gold-seekers on a reservation, a plan Kjellman approved.[48]

When the government transport *Lawton* returned from Nome in August, 1900, it carried 150 gold-seekers "without a red cent" and twenty-six Lapps on their way to Norway. The Lapps, who were tired of life in Alaska, would be accompanied home by Sheldon Jackson; about eighty, who were well satisfied with their rein-

176

deer culture and some of whom had made rich gold finds, remained in the North. *Skandinaven* in September of the same year printed a long interview with a Norwegian from Stoughton, Wisconsin, who had toured Cape Nome and Cape York during the summer. He gave a balanced evaluation of conditions there but advised against rash migration to Alaska. Another man spoke of "disappointment on top of disappointment."[49]

The newspapers naturally followed closely and gave full publicity to news from the Circuit Court of Appeals in San Francisco. In October, 1900, *Washington Posten* reported the arrest of McKenzie. He had so often, according to *Posten* "'greased his stockings' at the expense of Norwegian farmers in North Dakota, that he was happy to reap a rich harvest in Nome." The newspaper then recounted the whole sordid story and correctly stated that the only justification for the robbery was the fact that a few of the Scandinavian mineowners were not yet citizens of the United States. The jumpers knew that only a law passed by Congress could legalize their actions, and they had found the man to do this in McKenzie, "who had done the political bidding of James Hill in North Dakota, had thwarted M. N. Johnson when he tried to run for the Senate and got Hansbrough elected in his place, had begun his public life as a United States marshal and in time became one of the receivers for the Northern Pacific Railway as a reward for his services."

The account continued: "Unfortunately for McKenzie and his gang, some of the Lapps had sold their claims to Charles D. Lane, treasurer of the national Free Silver Committee, and among his close friends in the Senate were some who immediately saw what Hansbrough had in mind." Knute Nelson, too, had struck a blow for his countrymen in all of Alaska, and his clear presentation of the case in the Senate influenced others in their favor.

Lindeberg, Brynteson, and Lindblom had their mines again and would also get back their gold, "but for them it has been a costly affair." Nome had had little sickness during the past summer, thanks to Lindeberg, R. T. Lyng, a Swede, Thoralf and Magnus Kjeldsberg, and other Norwegians, who had brought spring water to town from Anvil Mountain. Also, a hospital had been built in Nome, paid for by Lindeberg, Brynteson, and Lindblom.

Both Norwegians and Lapps, *Washington Posten* stated, were dissatisfied with the treatment they had received on the most recent reindeer expedition. "They were treated like dogs and received wretched food. A complaint was sent to the Swedish-Norwegian minister in Washington, who gave it to the Department of the Interior, where it went into the wastebasket." The contract with the United States government had given the parties a period of six months within which they might terminate their agreement. Many in the expedition had taken advantage of this right, but when they came to Sheldon Jackson for settlement, they had to "bite into the sour apple." The contract also stated that the Lapps should have free clothing. They were enjoined to buy clothes in Norway at the cheapest possible prices, and assured that the government would repay them. When the time came to settle for the clothing, the Lapps were credited for the amount they had paid out in Norway, but Jackson had debited them for the clothes they had been wearing for half a year — at Klondike prices!

The petition to the Swedish-Norwegian minister, reprinted in *Washington Posten,* quoted the assurance in the contract that the reindeer people would have "good and safe food" as well as clothes. They claimed they did not receive it and, "because of this," the protest stated, "many have been sick." In Port Townsend, Washington, the government had told them that they would obtain at the station all things not included in rations at the same prices they cost at Port Townsend, but this promise was not kept. Nothing had come of their complaints. "Many have sought their release, and all of us are more or less unhappily silenced as inexperienced strangers in a strange land." Returning to the food problem, the petition said: "We think that the total lack of berries or dried fruit during the entire winter has been in part the cause of all our sickness." It also expressed the hope that the American people, who, they were told, fought for those who were hungry and oppressed, "would also grant justice to us who are having trouble in the service of that people." The petition was signed by twenty-six of the Norwegians and witnessed by J. Werner Sverdrup and Thomas Rudd.[50]

When the returning Lapps stopped off in Minneapolis, attracting considerable attention, a reporter from *Nordvesten* interviewed them. The spokesman for the group, Jacob Larson Hatta, was of the opinion that Alaska would not turn out to be a good place for raising reindeer, in part because of its unfavorable climate but also because its moss was of too poor a quality to sustain the animals. *Nordvesten* also commented editorially on the matter. At Port Hope, where Hatta had delivered some deer, a bitter wind blew constantly, whereas in Finnmark it did not, and the moss was covered by snow. The reindeer almost froze where he was; within a few years they might adjust to the climate, but they would never thrive as in Norway.[51]

E. M. Cederbergh, writing to *Skandinaven* in June, 1901, saw a great future for Alaska and gold production, which he thought was only in its infancy. Anvil Creek was a mere beginning. Thus far placer mining and sluice boxes had dominated the story, but now it was clear that gold quartz would have its day. Machinery would be brought in the next summer for hydraulic use.

He was less optimistic about Alaska for growing crops, but he pointed to places, on Golovnin Bay and Norton Sound, where vegetables could be raised, and of course there was forest in abundance. Reindeer, he insisted, did well in the country. The governor was reported as favoring populating Alaska with Scandinavians. Tundra was similar to Norwegian peat and could be used as fuel — an attractive prospect where coal cost $75 per ton and wood was $40 per cord. G. J. Lomen had written to a newspaper in Kristiania asking for information about processing the tundra. He reported that the Eskimo population was dying out because of white man's food. Prices generally were lower, Nome enjoyed excellent water supplied by the Nome Water Company, which was largely owned by Scandinavians, and there was ample social life in the city. Cederbergh concluded by urging persons coming to Alaska to have money enough with them to live on for a time — and for a return ticket.[52]

On August 16, 1901, C. M. Thuland wrote to *Washington Posten* to report an extraordinary meeting of the legal profession in Nome. They had decided unanimously on the previous day to send a resolution to President McKinley by telegraph from Seattle requesting the dismissal of Arthur H. Noyes and the appointment of a fair, honest, and capable judge. They accused Noyes of being incapable, vacillating, weak, partisan, and careless. The telegram was signed by all the lawyers in Nome, except for a few who had been appointed commissioners or clerks and who therefore could not have been practicing law. The resolution was a mild expression of what 99 percent of the people thought of the judge. Noyes had left Nome without giving even a couple of hours' notice. Claim-jumping continued. Things had been bad before; they were worse now. It was likely that the mineowners and townsfolk would organ-

180

ize a vigilance committee that would also serve as a court of conciliation, as they expected no help from the government. "Up on Ivan Creek the miners have joined together, and if a jumper tries to take a claim, word is sent to all and they meet at the disputed claim to throw the jumper off. This is easier and cheaper and possibly more just than to appeal to the federal law and Noyes."[53]

Of great interest to the reader must have been Thuland's statement in October, 1901, that a lawsuit had begun as a result of disturbances on Glacier Creek. About sixty masked and armed men had attacked the workers there the month before and seriously wounded one person. The aggressors in this attack were Lindeberg and Lane people, and among the leaders were Lindeberg and G. W. Price, Lane's brother-in-law. When the grand jury met and began to investigate the action, Lindeberg, Price, and several other leaders had left Nome, and charges had been filed against them and warrants were in the hands of the federal marshal. A week later Thuland reported more specifically about the affair. Preliminary hearings had been held against J. W. Griffin and J. T. Price, two of these arrested who, on August 14, had driven claim-jumpers from the California Fraction on Glacier. The jury was divided and new preliminary hearings were to be held later.[54]

A news item from Washington, D.C., on January 23, 1902, reported that Attorney General P. C. Knox, after a talk with the President, had stated that, regardless of any action to the contrary by the Department of Justice, Noyes would not be invited to refill the bench he had left in Nome. *Skandinaven* reported in detail that President Theodore Roosevelt had sent a letter to Noyes removing him from office. The newspaper also stated that Knox had studied the whole Nome scandal thoroughly, had publicly branded Noyes's actions as shameful, and

181

had listed and denounced them one by one. In March the newspaper printed an announcement that the Pioneer Mining Company, following the dissolution of the Lindeberg, Brynteson, and Lindblom organization, would now give the public an opportunity to buy stock in the reorganized company and share in the profits of the rich placer gold fields at Nome. The company would sell shares with par value of $1.00 for 50¢ apiece. The advertisement maintained that $2,463,705.10 in gold had been taken on less than ten percent of the area owned by the company in the preceding three years. This statement, it said, had been verified by banks.[55]

Skandinaven then recounted the whole story of the attempted gold steal in Nome, as told by the San Francisco court, and accompanied its long article with an editorial on the "black conspiracy," which it said had broad ramifications. Alexander McKenzie had been the "controlling force" in North Dakota politics for years; "he had made, or unmade, United States senators, governors, and other public officials whom he cared to control. . . . Fortunately, the cause of justice has equally determined champions in the Senate, chief among them senators Nelson, Spooner, and Stewart."

Skandinaven followed this editorial the next month with another on the Nome judiciary. Numerous letters the newspaper received from northwestern and western states, the editorial stated, disclosed a lively interest in the pending appointment of judge and clerk of court for the Nome district. "Our enterprising and hardy young men are beginning to realize the magnificent possibilities of the vast territory. They are eager to contribute to its development and are ready to face the hardships of arctic winters if they can be assured of an honest enforcement of the laws by the federal courts. Such assurance is entirely lacking at present." But *Skandinaven* thought President Roosevelt, who was familiar with affairs in Alaska, could be trusted to make the right appointment to the court. The newspaper thought George N. Borchsenius of Madison, Wisconsin, a fine person for clerk of court, as he had stood firmly opposed to the corruption in Nome as clerk under Noyes. But for him, the crimes would have been even more numerous and shameful. He would have the vigorous support of senators Spooner and Nelson.[56]

C. M. Thuland usually included references to mining activities in his frequent letters to *Washington Posten*. His own Bench Claim No. 4 on Specimen Gulch was prospected during the winter and yielded paying gravel. The Pioneer Mining Company was washing on No. 1 Anvil, with good results. The Reverend P. H. Anderson, a Swedish missionary, was being sued for $400,000. The case concerned No. 9 Anvil Creek, which Anderson had held and worked since the fall of 1898. The charge against him was that he had cheated two Eskimo, Constantine Uparazuck and Gabriel Adams, of their title to the mine. Adams died in 1900 and Uparazuck and K. Hendricksen were administrators of his estate. Erik O. Lindblom had staked No. 9 for Adams and No. 8 for Uparazuck; both natives were members of the Swedish Covenant mission congregation at Chivik. A month later, Thuland reported, Anderson had taken it on himself to function for the Eskimo, as he had heard that natives could not hold mine claims in Alaska. He had joined with G. W. Price to reclaim No. 8 and with R. L. Price to reclaim No. 9. R. L. Price had later surrendered his right to claim 9 to Anderson, "to hold and keep in trust for Gabriel Adams." Anderson had told the Eskimo that they could not have mining claims and that he would hold this claim for them. They believed him. All that the natives had received to date from Anderson was $400, but gold in the amount of $400,000 had been taken from the mine, the richest on Anvil. Thuland and

183

T. M. Reed, serving as lawyers for the Eskimo, were requesting that the claim be returned to the Eskimo and their heirs and that Pastor Anderson return to them the value of the gold that had been removed.[57]

In July, 1902, the steamer *Kimball* arrived in Nome from Seattle. Among its passengers were Alfred A. Moore, the newly appointed district judge, G. N. Borchsenius, reappointed clerk of court, and B. E. Rogers, also of Madison, Wisconsin, who would hold a position in the court. The ship also carried E. M. Cederbergh. In Madison Borchsenius had organized the Arctic Gold Mining Company; he was said to be part or sole owner of about 100 gold claims in Alaska. Borchsenius' return was warmly received and better days were anticipated by the *Nome Gold-Digger*.[58]

William A. Kjellman stopped off in Madison on his way to Chicago after a long rest at his home in Mount Horeb. Now full of energy, he wrote to *Amerika*, he had new plans for Alaska that had little to do with gold. He spoke of Norway and Alaska as if they were neighbors, for he saw a striking resemblance between the two countries in geography, economy, and future development.[59]

Disputes over gold continued late in 1902 to put Nome in the news. *Washington Posten* stated that in San Francisco Thomas J. Duffy, a mine operator in Nome, had begun a suit against Jafet Lindeberg for $900,000. Duffy charged that Lindeberg had jumped valuable claims belonging to him and had taken gold out of the mines in the amount he was being sued for. The newspaper continued to report on arrivals from Nome and their success in the gold fields.[60] In March and April of 1903, it printed a series of wide-ranging articles about Alaska — the land of the future.

By 1904, Nome occupied a less prominent place in the columns of the Norwegian-American press. But *Skan-*

dinaven printed an article from the *Minneapolis Journal* about Knute Nelson's six bills for Alaska. These provided for a second judge and another judicial district, construction and maintenance of wagon roads, establishment of schools, care of the insane and destitute, codification of laws pertaining to municipalities, election of a delegate to the House of Representatives, changes in the criminal code, and construction of a bridge across the Snake River at Nome. His bills were tangible results of a visit of senators to Alaska in the summer of 1903.[61]

Skandinaven had followed with interest the activities of E. M. Cederbergh and in fact had first learned the real facts about the Nome gold fields from him when he visited Chicago. In May, 1904, the newspaper announced that he was leaving for Alaska after having spent a period of about five months in Chicago. He had been about three years in Alaska as director of a New York firm, then had come to Chicago on the invitation of friends who requested that he buy claims for them on the Seward Peninsula. The result had been Cederbergh's leadership in organizing the Good Hope Bay Mining Company, of which he was president. He was optimistic about Alaska and thought the Seward Peninsula the richest mineral district in the world. According to the article, many Chicago Scandinavians had invested in his company.[62]

V

Life went on at Teller and the other reindeer stations despite the more dramatic events at Nome and the departure of superintendents and Lapps for the gold fields. The Reverend T. L. Brevig, who had left Alaska in 1898 and had been in the States on leave since then, returned to his mission in the summer of 1900. Seeking support from the Norwegian Synod and from friends while in the States, he had received a little more than $900 from the church and was hoping for $1,000 per year from it in the future. As *Nordvesten* put it, he had real need for this money, since he intended to start a day school for Eskimo children as well as continue work with Lapp families and gold-seekers. With him when he left the Midwest in late May was A. Hovig, a young man who would assist him in his many activities.

How isolated Brevig was at Port Clarence is indicated by the fact that he received mail twice a month during the summer and at best once in winter, by an overland route. He was grateful for the help given him by friends, but cautioned them to send money, as supplies sometimes arrived at ports in the States too late to catch cargo ships and, as a result, lay over until the next year. Money was being used in Alaska, and so cash gifts could be sent to the Norwegian Synod's treasurer, who would see to their delivery; it was also possible now to send registered letters to the new post office, where he was serving as postmaster.[63]

When Brevig arrived at his mission on June 30, he found its buildings basically as he had left them, but in terrible disorder after their use by mine workers. Teller, the town, had been laid out two miles from the station, and people were streaming into it. The creeks nearby were promising. The schooner *Cosca* arrived about ten days later and included among its passengers a Lapp family who would serve as reindeer caretakers. The station had received an additional 100 deer, all lively and in good health, but Teller was no longer the chief center for the reindeer industry.[64]

In the late spring of 1900 Theodor Lindseth of Benicia, California, left Seattle on the *Cosca* to take over direction of the reindeer station at Yacucatta, where Kjellman formerly had been in charge. He had been employed by the Department of Agriculture. Lindseth was born in northern Norway and had known and worked with Lapps.[65]

When Brevig wrote in the winter, he reported that things were going well at the station; everyone was cheerful and healthy. The Eskimo children ate heartily and played; the young men worked every day with enthusiasm, and at the moment were occupied with the woodpile. There had been no hunger among the Eskimo, as the tomcod, a small fish that often came close to the shore, had been available in abundance during the fall. Later in winter the fish had gone away for a while, causing the first food shortage. Some of the natives now lived around Teller and had become acquainted with liquor. "I have been able to get some of them to settle on a point of land west of the station where they are on their own, and they get help where it is needed. I heard yesterday that up on the Govirok River 65 miles to the east there were 24 parentless children who were supported by a young Eskimo and his mother. The need was great. Travel has been such that we have been unable to get up there to investigate. We are now so many at the station that we can't take in more, but we will send up food and clothing as soon as we have the opportunity. In the town of Teller the supply of provisions is small, and so at present it is almost impossible to buy anything there. Coal is $160 a ton but unavailable. Many are seeking to leave for Nome, as food is cheaper there. Many here have nothing to eat except the fish they can catch. Reports of gold one hears everywhere, but these are surely only rumors."[66]

Husbibliothek, a literary supplement to *Skandinaven*, published an article in November, 1901, on the Lapp women in Alaska. It revealed that there were about a dozen reindeer stations in the territory and that more would be started. It also ran a picture of a Lapp woman in traditional attire at Eaton, then the main sta-

187

tion. She carried a baby on her back in a cradle hand-carved from a log and held in place by a strap. The Lapp women played a vital role in training the Eskimo in the reindeer culture. They taught the natives how to make clothes from skins and butter and cheese from milk, and how to cook and dry reindeer meat. Eskimo women gathered at the various stations, often coming from a distance of 100 miles or more, to receive instruction.[67]

Brevig, whose story is closely involved with Lapps, Eskimo, and reindeer, seemed proudest of his work in starting a home for children at the Teller station, the most northerly institution of its kind in North America. In a long letter to *Amerika* written in October, 1901, he explained that the children in it were Eskimo or of mixed Eskimo and white origin, the latter usually deserted or otherwise parentless. He gave the names of fourteen children, with explanations of the meaning of these names, and added to his list five adult natives who were reindeer herders. These had all been taken in at the station after his return to Alaska and were attached to his home.

Brevig also wrote about fourteen Eskimo who had obtained their reindeer before he left Teller in 1898 and who owned from 75 to 160 animals each. They supported themselves but were under the leadership of the mission, and they received from it and the government whatever they required as payment for their services. This arrangement, Brevig explained, was necessary to protect the Eskimo from exploitation. All their business was handled for them by the mission. He also named three Lapps, two young men and a woman, who were given food and clothing by the mission and were paid by the government. Alfred Nilima, one of the Lapps, would soon take a herd of about 200 reindeer to the Quaker mission on Kotzebue Sound. Brevig's own family numbered five. In addition, there were Hovig and Lucalia

Krukoff, a single lady, both of whom had been with his family from Wisconsin — a total of forty-three persons who gathered together on Sundays, with the exception of one or two who tended the deer. They were joined by people living near the mission and by some from islands in the Bering Strait and from East Cape, Siberia.

When a child or an adult came to the mission to be supported there, the first step in the admission process was a warm bath, then clean clothes from tip to toe. Next, the hair was cut and the head treated with paraffin to keep uninvited guests away. Clothes soaked with blubber were burned, but otherwise serviceable garments were put in sacks until they could be used away from the station or when the newcomer left. The children were cooperative and easy to work with. The half-breeds, he wrote, were more stubborn and willful than the Eskimo. The government was giving no help that year, but Captain F. Tuttle of the *Bear* had put ashore some flour and General Randall had sent in the same boat flour, bacon, and "ship's bread" from his own supply. The mission now had 160 reindeer, of which number it owned 60; 100 would have to be returned in four years, but the mission would keep the natural increase and would have temporary use of the animals it would later return.

More children wished to come to the home, but there was no room for them, and cost prohibited enlargement of the place. Everything would depend on the support that friends would give the home. He did not know how much money had come in for the mission, as he had received no report from the Synod since his return to Alaska. Brevig wrote an eloquent appeal for help, but made it in terms of the Eskimo, who should be aided in defending themselves, largely against the rapidly increasing white population. The mission was a secure place for the natives. Widows with their children and

189

grown daughters came to it to escape the unwelcome attentions of all kinds of men. Many of the problems faced by the Eskimo had been created by whites in the past several years, and those who cared would have to act soon or it would be too late.[68]

At a later date, Mrs. Julia M. Brevig was interviewed in Stanwood, Washington, about the mission at Teller. She used stronger words than her husband in discussing the gold-seekers in Alaska. She answered her own question, whether or not the successful ones visited the children's home and contributed to its work, with these words: "Far from it. The lucky ones have never been of any joy or advantage to us or our work. . . . But trouble we have had, and I can say pleasure in a certain sense, as it is a pleasure to give food to the hungry."[69]

Earlier, Mrs. Brevig had written from Teller welcoming the arrival of an early spring and announcing that the children at the home had come through the winter without illness, the great trial of other years. All the same she and her husband were eager to have a separate room for the sick, and hoped that funds for it could be raised. No new parentless children had come to the home since the previous fall until a month ago, when Brevig went up to Cape Prince of Wales and returned with four little boys and a girl. When the girl had been with them for two weeks, she ran away to the town of Teller and there found refuge in a house of ill repute. Brevig and one of the young men at the station had gone after her and talked with her, but she had refused to return. Brevig then spoke with the local judge, who brought her back to the mission. Next day she was taken overland to Cape Prince of Wales by a herder; there she was turned over to a missionary.

Since the arrival of miners in the area, according to Mrs. Brevig, the shameful influence of whites had increased greatly; young Eskimo girls suffered especially

190

from it. If those who supported the mission only knew of its work during the past three years, she believed they would rejoice indeed. The last mail had brought the good news that something would be done for the mission by friends. They had often been discouraged; Brevig had written a number of times to the Reverend U. V. Koren, president of the Synod, for help, but had not yet received a reply. Mrs. Brevig had suffered during the winter from a heart ailment and her husband had said she must not spend another winter in Alaska. The young men had traveled with sleds and deer during the past week bringing in fuel; the animals were tired and had to rest, as good wood was found only far away. She had taken all the children for a sleigh ride and picnic in Teller; this treat was repeated each year in the spring. A person with a camera had been out on the ice and taken pictures of the "Santa Claus children." [70]

Brevig returned to the States in 1903 and went back to Teller on the *Charles Nelson* in June, 1904. With him were an Eskimo boy and Ludvig Larsen, who would take over his position at the station. Also on the ship were Olaus Alseth and Oscar Finley, who would erect schoolhouses for the government at Cape Prince of Wales and St. Michael. On August 8 Brevig joyfully reported that on the preceding day he had baptized 19 Eskimo — 5 adults and 14 children aged 6 to 15.[71]

Although reindeer were not the main interest of the churches, the story of the reindeer in Alaska was closely interwoven with that of the Christian missions in the territory, as Sheldon Jackson, the moving force in introducing them to the Eskimo, liked to point out. *Skandinaven* as early as 1902 editorially supported his claim that in a short time reindeer would become the chief means of travel between Alaska and the outer world. They were already in service in moving mail in winter, and many mineowners used them to carry supplies to

191

Kenneth O. Bjork

the claims. The Congregational mission on Bering Strait had a herd of 1,000 animals. Jackson said there were about 4,100 deer in the territory and that the annual increase was between 30 and 40 percent. About 4,500 animals had been born in Alaska since the reindeer were first brought in in 1892. The government was lending them out both to the missions and to private persons for five-year periods. Deer were better for travel than dogs, because of the necessity of carrying heavy and expensive food for the dogs and buying more along the way on trips longer than a week. Reindeer, on the other hand, could go anywhere with a pack of 200 pounds on their backs or pull a sleigh with a 300-pound load — and find their own food along the way.[72]

For some time reindeer were to play a vital part in the lives of the Eskimo. The herds around the stations at Port Clarence, Golovin, Eaton, and Wales grew in number to at least a half million by 1930. The Eskimo owned about 70 percent of them, to a value of about $1,000,000. According to C. L. Andrews, the deer sustained from 5,000 to 10,000 natives and supplied them with virtually all necessities. Management of the herds was transferred from the Office of Education to the governor of Alaska in 1929, and in 1937 the service was placed under the Bureau of Indian Affairs. The reindeer industry was later taken from the Eskimo and given over to white owners. The number of animals declined after 1940.[73]

NOTES

[1] *Skandinaven*, February 15, 1893, reprinted from *Tacoma Tidende*; C. L. Andrews, *The Story of Alaska* (Caldwell, Idaho, 1944), 247–248.

[2] For John Scudder McLain's views, see his *Alaska and the Klondike* (New York, 1905).

[3] For a brief account of Sheldon Jackson's career, see *Dictionary of American Biography*, 9:555–556.

[4] For brief accounts of the introduction of reindeer, see Andrews, *Story of Alaska*, 178–179, and his "Reindeer in the Arctic," in *Washington Historical Quarterly*, 17 (1926), 14–17. Arthur S. Peterson, in "The Introduction of Do-

mesticated Reindeer into Alaska," in *Norwegian-American Studies and Records*, 11 (Northfield, Minnesota, 1940), 98–113, summarizes briefly Sheldon Jackson's official reports on the subject together with several other accounts in English.

[5] *Washington Posten*, December 23, 1893; Andrews, "Reindeer in the Arctic," 14–17. The *D.A.B.* gives the total number of reindeer for 1928 as 675,000.

[6] *Washington Posten*, December 23, 1893.

[7] *Skandinaven*, October 16, 1895.

[8] J. Walter Johnshoy, *Apaurak in Alaska: Social Pioneering among the Eskimos* (Philadelphia, 1944), 24–37.

[9] For his earliest reports, see *Amerika*, June 22, September 12, 19, November 7, 1894, July 31, October 28, 1896.

[10] *Tacoma Tidende*, May 15, 1897; *Amerika*, May 19, 1897.

[11] *Amerika*, May 19, 1897.

[12] *Amerika*, May 26, 1897.

[13] *Amerika*, July 21, 1897.

[14] *Amerika og Norden*, November 3, 1897.

[15] *Skandinaven*, October 27, 1897. Judge William W. Morrow later told the story of an ice-bound whaling fleet near Point Barrow. Its partially Scandinavian crews were relieved in March, 1898, when an expedition, traveling overland with dog teams from Cape Vancouver and adding reindeer with Lapp drivers up the coast, arrived at Point Barrow. See his "The Spoilers," in *California Law Review*, 2 (Berkeley, 1916), 89–113.

[16] *Washington Posten*, November 12, 1897.

[17] *Amerika og Norden*, November 17, 24, 1897.

[18] *Skandinaven*, December 15, 1897.

[19] *Nordvesten*, December 16, 1897; *Minneapolis Tidende*, January 14, 1898.

[20] *Nordvesten*, January 20, 1898.

[21] *Washington Posten*, January 14, February 18, 1898; *Skandinaven*, February 16, 1898; *Nordvesten*, February 10, 1898.

[22] *Skandinaven*, March 2, 1898.

[23] *Skandinaven*, March 9, 1898.

[24] *Washington Posten*, March 11, 1898.

[25] *Washington Posten*, March 18, April 8, 1898.

[26] *Amerika og Norden*, June 8, 1898.

[27] *Washington Posten*, August 5, November 25, December 2, 1898, January 20, 1899.

[28] *Amerika og Norden*, December 28, 1898.

[29] *Washington Posten*, May 12, 1899.

[30] *Washington Posten*, June 2, 9, 30, July 7, 21, August 18, September 1, 1899.

[31] *Washington Posten*, September 22, 29, 1899.

[32] *Washington Posten*, October 27, November 3, December 14, 22, 1899, January 12, 1900; *Nordvesten*, December 14, 1899.

[33] *Skandinaven*, December 27, 1899.

[34] *Amerika*, May 2, 1900; *Minneapolis Tidende*, May 11, 1900; *Washington Posten*, May 11, 1900.

[35] E. S. Harrison, *Nome and Seward Peninsula: History, Description, Biographies and Stories* (Seattle, 1905), 47–51.

Kenneth O. Bjork

[36] Quoted in J. D. Harlan, "The Nome Gold Placer Fields," in *Ax-i-Dent Axe*, 16 (Salt Lake City, 1931), 31–35.

[37] Elizabeth M. Ricker, *Seppala: Alaskan Dog Driver* (Boston, 1931), 97–145; interview with Seppala in Seattle, July 7, 1948.

[38] James Wickersham, *Old Yukon: Tales-Trails-and-Trials* (Washington, D.C., 1938), 337–347. For the debate in the Senate, see the *Congressional Record* for March and April of 1900.

[39] Wickersham, *Old Yukon*, 348–361. For the trials in San Francisco, see *Federal Reporter: Cases Argued and Determined in the Circuit Courts*, 106 (St. Paul, 1901), 775–790; 109 (1901), 971–976; 121 (1903), 209–233. For the verdict of the Supreme Court on McKenzie, see *United States Reports: Cases Adjudged in the Supreme Court at October Term, 1900*, 180 (New York, 1901), 536–551. Judge Morrow's "The Spoilers" throws interesting light on several phases of the court cases, all of which were favorable to the mineowners.

[40] Wickersham, *Old Yukon*, 362–378.

[41] See Cederbergh's comprehensive account of the gold discovery at Nome in *Skandinaven*, April 25, 1900.

[42] For short sketches of Cederbergh and Thuland, see Harrison, *Nome and Seward Peninsula*, 288–289, 336–337. Thuland published a brief work in Norwegian on American mining laws, *Amerikanske minelove: En haandbog for menigmand i amerikansk mineret* (Seattle, 1908).

[43] *Skandinaven*, April 27–May 9, 1900.

[44] *Skandinaven*, April 27, 1900.

[45] *Skandinaven*, May 16, 1900.

[46] *Skandinaven*, May 9, 1900.

[47] *Washington Posten*, July 20, August 3, 1900; *Nordvesten*, July 26, 1900; *Amerika*, August 1, 1900.

[48] *Amerika*, August 8, 22, 1900.

[49] *Washington Posten*, August 31, 1900; *Skandinaven*, September 5, 7, 1900; *Amerika*, September 26, 1900.

[50] *Washington Posten*, October 5, 12, 1900.

[51] *Nordvesten*, December 6, 27, 1900.

[52] *Skandinaven*, June 26, 1901.

[53] *Washington Posten*, August 30, 1901.

[54] *Washington Posten*, November 1, 15, 1901.

[55] *Nordvesten*, January 30, 1902; *Skandinaven*, February 28, March 5, 1902.

[56] *Skandinaven*, March 12, April 23, 1902.

[57] *Washington Posten*, May 2, June 27, 1902. For a full account of No. 9 Anvil Creek, see Leland H. Carlson, *The Story of No. 9 Above* (Chicago, n.d.).

[58] *Skandinaven*, August 22, 1902.

[59] *Amerika*, September 12, 1902.

[60] *Washington Posten*, September 19, October 17, 24, November 14, 1902.

[61] *Skandinaven*, January 29, 1904.

[62] *Skandinaven*, May 27, 1904.

[63] *Nordvesten*, June 7, 21, 1900.

[64] *Amerika*, August 8, 1900.

[65] *Washington Posten*, May 4, 1900.

[66] *Amerika*, April 17, 1901.

[67] *Husbibliothek*, November 15, 1901.

194

[68] *Amerika*, November 20, 1901.
[69] *Amerika*, February 26, 1904.
[70] *Amerika*, August 14, 1903.
[71] *Amerika*, June 24, 1904; *Nordvesten*, September 8, 1904.
[72] *Skandinaven*, July 11, 1902.
[73] Andrews, *Story of Alaska*, 178–179, 188–189, 224, 240–242.

by Rangvald Kvelstad

6 *The Pioneers of Dog Fish Bay*

O<small>NLY FOUR YEARS</small> after the boundary between Canada and the United States was set at the 49th Parallel, the first Norwegian arrived in the Pacific Northwest. It was 1849, the year of the great gold rush to California, and his name was Zachariah Martin Toftezen. Exact details of his trek are wanting, but it is known that at age twenty-eight he had shipped out as a sailor and landed in New Orleans. Thomas Ostenson Stine in his book *Scandinavians on the Pacific* (1900) says of him: "He was a pioneer of heart and courage — chivalrous Martin Toftezen. He had drifted around the Horn on a ship, and was tossed into the mouth of Puget Sound, where the breath of the deep calmed to a gentle zephyr, and the wings of speed flapped in disconsolation."

In a less flowery vein, Alice Essex in her *Stanwood Story* (1975) says of his landing on Whidbey Island: "Enroute, he met Col. Ulrich Freud of Switzerland, who was also seeking a land of promise . . . . they were joined by C. W. Sumner, a Yankee from New England with the same yearning. The three teamed up, hired a sloop, and via Indian canoe and guide found themselves

196

in Crescent Harbor, where they landed at a spot called 'Big Springs' in December, 1849. After climbing to the top of a high hill, Toftezen pronounced the view 'the most glorious on earth' and shouted to his companions, 'Our search is over — we have at last found our earthly paradise.'" The "paradise" Toftezen saw was from a hill now overlooking the town of Oak Harbor. Alice Essex continues her story: "Stirred with a tinge of wanderlust, Toftezen left his Paradise three times, but always returned to the island he loved, where he died in 1901 at the age of 80. He was buried in an old cemetery in Oak Harbor, the place that was his first love in the West."

The remains of the first Norwegian settler in what is now the state of Washington were consigned to a forgotten grave in an abandoned cemetery. Thirty years later compassionate fellow Norwegians on Whidbey Island and in the Stanwood community were instrumental in having the body moved to the Lutheran cemetery in Stanwood. A marker was erected over his grave by the Pioneer Historical Society of the Stillaquamish Valley and the Sons of Norway. Suitably, the monument was dedicated by the future King Olav V of Norway, on May 27, 1939.

The founders of what was to become the city of Seattle followed Toftezen by two years, in 1851. The Arthur Denny party came over the Oregon Trail from Illinois to Portland, and then by ship to the Puget Sound. They landed on what is now known as Alki Point. In the party was Mary Denny's newborn baby boy. Eighty years later he was still alive and well. Rolland Denny had spanned the years from the Indian cayuse to the automobile, from the canoe to the airplane. He saw Seattle grow from one roofless cabin in the wilderness to a city of towering buildings.

When the Norwegians moved into the Pacific Northwest they found a land very similar in climate and scenery to their homeland. The surprising difference was the huge stands of big trees. The forests provided them with a livelihood until they could clear a piece of land and begin to grow their food. Dozens of sawmills sprang up, some the largest in the world, and the timber products found a worldwide market. Amidst this abundance of timber, game, waterfowl, fish, shellfish, wild berries, and fruit lived the children of Nature, the Indians. At first the white man posed no threat to their livelihood and the relationship was amicable. There were here none of the fierce military confrontations that shook the Midwest, though the Indians' lack of a sense of ownership of land was later to create problems. The Indian tribes limited their activities within fairly well defined areas. A tribe would usually number only a few hundred souls. Since here there was very little need for extended travel as with the nomadic tribes of the plains, each tribe developed its own customs, culture, and language, somewhat like the fjord and mountain communities of Norway. The Indians around Seattle, Bainbridge, and parts of Kitsap county were called the Suquamish. Chief Seattle, for whom the city is named, was a member of that tribe. The Point Elliott Treaty in 1855 set aside a tract of land for the Suquamish tribe and they still own a part of it.

To the west of Seattle, across Puget Sound, lies the Kitsap peninsula. Bainbridge Island lies as a sort of buffer between the peninsula and the mainland. A quiet, tranquil bay lies between the peninsula and the island. When the white man first came, the bay was teeming with dogfish, hence the name Dog Fish Bay. The name has since been changed to Liberty Bay. At the head of the bay lies Poulsbo. At the neck where it enters the Sound lies Keyport, now the United States Naval

Ole Anderson Stubbhaug (1821–1916), known as Ole Stubb in America, was the first white man to move to the Dog Fish Bay area. He came in 1875.

Torpedo Station. In 1875 the bay was uninhabited except for an occasional Indian who came in to hunt or fish. That was the year the first white man entered the bay with the object of establishing a home. He was Ole Anderson Stubbhaug, known in America as Ole Stubb, who was born in Naustdal, Førdefjord, Norway, in 1821. Very little has been written about Ole Stubb. He is barely mentioned in passing in a number of historical accounts about the first settlers. The writer discovered a great-grandson of Ole Stubb, Donald Stubb of Aberdeen, Washington. Through his genealogical research

199

this void in the story of the first Norwegians to settle in western Washington can now be filled.

Ole's father died in 1860 and Ole, the eldest son, inherited the family farm, which was said to be the finest in the Naustdal valley. A census report from 1860 showed a 25-acre (99 *dekar*) field and a 27-acre (105 *dekar*) pasture — a sizable spread in that time and place. The livestock included three horses, eighteen cows, ten calves, and seventy-six sheep and goats. An illustration in the family history from Sunnfjord, *Henrikslekta*, by Andreas Karstad, published in Bergen, Norway, in 1968, shows some very imposing farm buildings. Ole Stubb was no pauper who had to go out into the world to seek his fortune.

Ole Stubb married Danele Solem. A son, Anders, was born on March 26, 1850, and the mother died nine days later. The boy was reared by his maternal grandparents and took their name. In 1855 Ole then married Gunhild Hafstad from Førde. Four sons were born to the couple while they were living in Naustdal: Ludvig Daniel, 1856–1933; Matias Olai, 1858–1894; Andreas, 1860–1961; and Olai Andreas, who was born in 1862 and died as a child in America. In 1866 this family, including Anders Solem, left Førdefjord for Stony Lake, Michigan. There is some evidence that Ole came to America alone in 1864, then returned and sold his farm in 1865. The families of his brother, Kristian Anderson Stubbhaug, and his cousin, Kristian Larsen Karstad, accompanied him to settle in Michigan.

In 1868, Ole and his family left Michigan for Spink township in Union county, South Dakota, and then, in 1875, they headed west again. It is known that Ole visited the Norwegian settlement at Stanwood but he finally chose Dog Fish Bay in Kitsap county as his permanent residence. There is some uncertainty about his arrival there but he very likely went back to South Da-

200

kota and brought the family out in 1876. His wife did not come to Washington. After a lingering illness she died on December 28, 1876. She was cared for by her stepson Anders Solem. Ole was apparently not at home when she died. Ole and Gunhild had two children that were born in America: Helle Johanne was born in 1868 and died at the age of four; Henrik was born in 1872 and died October 28, 1944.

Ole's matrimonial ventures were not yet at an end. Sometime after coming to the West Coast he met and married a widow by the name of Ingeborg Erikson Peterson. Nothing is known concerning her except that she was born in Norway on February 18, 1821, and died October 28, 1907. She is buried in the cemetery by the First Lutheran Church in Poulsbo.

What sort of person was Ole Stubb? A passage from the genealogical study by Donald Stubb attempts to answer this question: "Very little is known of his characteristics, as no one now alive knew him intimately. His son, Andreas, once said he was a 'very restless man.' Captain J. Chris Moe, who first met him in 1883 when Mr. Moe was a small boy, pictured him as a very independent and self-sufficient man who believed in direct action and was not inclined toward compromise or bargaining. . . . Mr. Moe told these two stories: His father, two brothers and himself had rowed the three miles from Poulsbo to visit Ole Stubb. During their visit a rather violent storm came up and they were afraid to row home. They remained with Ole for three days. Finally Ole, tired of hearing them worry about the rest of the family at Poulsbo, said, 'If you cowards are afraid to go home alone, I'll take you.' So he herded them into his boat, took their boat in tow and rowed the three miles across the stormy bay and then returned home. He was then about 65 years old. Mr. Moe also told about bargaining for apples with Ole who had the only orchard in the area at the time. Being boys they always tried to get him to lower his prices. The old man's firm reply was, 'Well, boys, the apples are mine and the money is yours; if each one of us keeps what belongs to him we'll both be satisfied.'"

A Norwegian Christmas magazine, *Jul i Sunnfjord* (1932), printed a rather farfetched account written by Andreas Johan Sørebøe, who had some years earlier paid a visit to Ole Stubb and was now regaling his readers with vignettes of life in America. A translation of one section of the article follows:

WHEN 1,000 INDIANS CONDEMNED TO DEATH ONE SUNNFJORDING
THE FIRST EMIGRANT FROM NAUSTDAL
by Andreas Johan Sørebøe

"It wasn't completely a romantic life to be a pioneer in those days. The Indians paddled their canoes in and out among the many bays and fjords and kept their eyes on the scattered whites. Then something happened. An Indian disappeared without a trace. A Norwegian named Benson and a Finn were suspected of having done away with him. While this was going on Ole Stubb came rowing back from Seattle with food supplies and headed for a visit with his friend Benson. He was told of what had happened. While they were sitting discussing this something else happened to make the situation more ominous. An Indian's dog had come in and molested a milk cow in the pasture. Tired of this one of the men had gone out and shot the dog, thrown the dog in the boat, rowed out and dumped the dog in the bay.

"The next morning there was a band of Indians at the house. The three men went out to meet them. The chief pointed to the blood in the boat and demanded an explanation. It was given but the Indians did not believe

202

the story. They insisted the blood in the boat was evidence of what had happened to the missing Indian.

"The three men were taken prisoner and conveyed to Bainbridge Island. There at least a thousand Indians had gathered, all the way from British Columbia. A trial was held and a disposition was to be made of the matter. The cross-examination and final arguments of the Indians was an amazing performance and their whole demeanor was cool, calm, and collected. The result was that the three men were found guilty of murdering the vanished Indian.

"An Indian with a feather headdress hanging down his back quietly told the men they had been found guilty and proceeded to pronounce the sentence. He pointed to the Olympic Mountains to the west and said in a few simple words, Indian style, 'See the sinking sun. When that has dropped below the mountain's rim, your life will end.'

"But then suddenly, like a miracle, a troop of soldiers appeared in the arena. They had been alerted in Seattle that something unusual was going on on the island. Against them the Indians dared not put up resistance, so the three men who had stood at Death's door were saved."

For seven years, from 1876 to 1883, the Stubbs were the lone settlers on Dog Fish Bay. A couple of hours by rowboat would take Ole to Port Madison with its mill and probably a company store. A day's rowing, making use of the tide, would take him to Seattle, a bustling city of 16,000 people, and the next day's tide would carry him home. Though he came from the finest farm in Naustdal, Førdefjord, here Ole Stubb, imbued with the pioneering spirit, was willing to grub and hoe to create a farm from the wilderness. He had found his Shangri-La. Ole Stubb died at his home in Kitsap county in 1916, at the age of 95. He is buried in the Island Lake cemetery in Poulsbo in an unmarked grave.

Five sons of Ole Stubb reached maturity. Information on each, garnered from Donald Stubb's genealogical study, follows:

1. Anders Olai Olsen (Stubbhaug) Solem, born in 1850, came to America with his father in 1866. He worked in the sawmills and logging camps in Michigan until 1874, when he made a trip back to Norway. He returned in 1875 and went to South Dakota, where he took care of his stepmother in her final illness. He held a number of elective offices, including that of county assessor in Union county, South Dakota. He died January 24, 1935.

2. Ludvig Daniel Olsen Stubb, born in 1856, farmed in South Dakota until he went west in 1880. He came to his father in Kitsap county and worked in the sawmill at Port Madison for a year and a half. In 1882 he moved to the Stillaquamish valley, settling at Norman, Washington, which is five miles upriver from Stanwood. He bought 140 acres of land which was densely covered with timber. Before buying the land he started a logging business with his brother Andreas. He continued logging while clearing his land in preparation for farming. He put up a log house and other buildings which were used until 1903, when a large house and other new buildings were constructed. He operated a shingle mill for a period of time. Later he confined his activities to dairy farming, maintaining a herd of forty milk cows. Their feed was raised on the farm. Cash crops such as spinach, beets, and other vegetables were raised, as well as field peas for canning and freezing. He was also involved in mining ventures in the Cascade Mountains. He served on the school board for many years, was on the election board as a representative of the Republican party for forty-nine years, and was county road supervisor in his district for a time. He was one of the five original directors of the Josephine Old People's Home at Stanwood and one of its trustees for eleven years.

Ludvig married Nele Marie Samsonsdatter Leknes. They had eleven children. They were a musical family; a picture in *The Stanwood Story* shows three of the boys in the Silvana Concert Band. The picture must have been taken around 1900 because one of the boys, Anton, died of a ruptured appendix in 1906. Ludvig died on the Stubb farm at Norman, Washington, on November 4, 1933. His obituary in the *Stanwood Twin City News* says of him, "He was a kind and helpful neighbor and possessed the courage and perseverance so necessary to him who would follow the frontier and develop new states. The pallbearers were his six sons."

3. Matias Olai Olsen Stubb, born in 1858, came to America with the family in 1866. While he was living in South Dakota he suffered a severe sunstroke which affected his mind. It is quite probable that he went west with his father in 1875. He lived with his father in Kitsap county but spent his last years with his brother Ludvig. He contracted tuberculosis in 1894 and soon died, at the age of thirty-six.

4. Andreas Olsen Stubb, born in 1860, came to America with the family in 1866. He went to Washington to join his father in Kitsap county in 1878. He followed his brother Ludvig to the Stillaquamish valley, where he and Ludvig were engaged in logging. After they quit logging, Andreas operated a packtrain carrying mining machinery into the Cascade Mountains. In 1898 he took his horses to Alaska where he carried miners and their equipment from Skagway to Lake Bennett over the Chilkoot Pass. After the gold rush he came back to Washington. From then until his retirement he operated hotels and apartment houses and for a time farmed near Kent, Washington. Andreas married Karoline (maiden name unknown). They had two children, Hazel Oline, born July 1, 1892, and Albert Charles, whose birth date is unknown. According to the genealogical records, Andreas died at the home of his daugh-

ter in Palo Alto, California, in February, 1961. He would
have been 101 years old.

5. Henrik (Henry) Olsen Stubb was born in 1872 on
the Stubb farm in South Dakota. He went west to his
father in company with his brother Andreas in 1878. He
worked in the logging camps and farmed his father's
homestead in Kitsap county. He is the only Stubb the
residents of the Poulsbo area have any recollection of.
Henrik married Sofia Pearson, a widow, sometime
around 1907. They had no children. Sofia died August 20,
1944, and Henrik died October 28, 1944. They are both
buried in unmarked graves in the Island Lake cemetery
not far from Poulsbo.

The summer of 1883 was unusually hot and dry in
western Washington. Forest fires raged unchecked
through the magnificent stands of timber. There was no
way of fighting the fires, so they just burned themselves
out. The smoke hung so heavy in the air that it shut out
light. For weeks neither sun nor moon had been visible.

Through this smoke one day came two men in a rowboat from Seattle to visit Ole Stubb. Without benefit of
compass and without visible landmarks to steer by, they
had let out and dragged a long anchor rope behind their
boat to keep from rowing in a circle and thus they had
kept the course. The men were Jorgen Martinus Eliason
and his friend Peter Olsen. Eliason, like Stubb., was
from Førde, which undoubtedly prompted the visit.
The men were seeking land and there are several accounts of the welcome they received from Stubb. According to one account, Stubb told them, "No one else is
going to come to this part of the country. I have been
here six years and I am still the only settler." Another
account has Stubb taking them about three miles up the
bay to where Poulsbo is now located. There each man
finally filed a claim, up the hill and away from the water.

The waterfront had already been acquired for logging, the earliest logging being done where the logs could be felled right into the water.

Jorgen Martinus Eliason was born in Førde, Sunnfjord, Norway, on November 20, 1847. The family had financial problems and the father lost the farm. At age nine, Jorgen had to go out and earn his living by herding sheep. As a thirteen year old he sought work in a neighboring community, where he stayed for five years. His next job was assistant to the *lensmann* (sheriff) in Førde. He saved enough money to buy a steamer ticket and after a three-week trip he landed in New York in 1868, when he was barely twenty-one years old.

From New York, Jorgen Eliason headed for Whitehall, Michigan. He spent fifteen years there working in sawmills and a tannery. In 1875 he married Martha Solem, who was also from his home region of Norway. She was probably a relative of the Solem family Ole Stubb first married into. In 1881 Martha died, leaving a six-year-old son, Elias, who in later years was always referred to as E. J. Eliason. Jorgen Eliason found it too difficult to continue to live in Michigan now that his wife was gone, so he sold his home, took his son Elias and his sister Rakel, and headed for Seattle. They traveled by Union Pacific to San Francisco, since there was no railroad to Seattle, and on to Seattle by ship.

The sister, Rakel, took a job at the Occidental Hotel in Seattle and at the same time took care of little Elias. Jorgen was determined to acquire a homestead. With several others, he rowed across Lake Washington and headed north up the valley past the present location of Bothell. They cut trails about four miles through the timber and each of them staked out a tract of land and a site for a house. They soon ran out of provisions and wandered about without food for three days. They estimated that they were about twenty miles from the

207

nearest source of supply, Seattle. Packing supplies that distance through the wilds of western Washington, they realized, was out of the question, so they went back to Seattle. Jorgen Eliason decided a water route was preferable and headed across Puget Sound for Ole Stubb and Dog Fish Bay. After that visit, after the smoke and the fog, after the backbreaking work of rowing his boat across the Sound, and then the endless prospect of clearing the forest to make a farm out of the land he had filed on, Jorgen Eliason was not eager to remain in Washington. If he had had the money, he would have returned to Michigan with another party that had come out with them. Jorgen conferred with his sister and she recommended that they stay; in later years he often said he never regretted the decision. Jorgen Eliason lived until 1937.

The early Kitsap county historian, E. E. Riddell, who knew the Eliasons quite well, writes thus of him in *Kitsap County, a History*: "Mr. Jorgen Eliason represents the early pioneer and his many hardships, among which were to row many miles to Port Madison for provisions and mail. Or sometimes setting out for Seattle or Olympia in their rowboats, having to camp on the way while waiting for suitable weather or tides, so it sometimes took them a whole week for the trip. When traveling by rowboat they took their blankets, cooking utensils, two or three loaves of bread, some potatoes, an axe and matches. Their meat supply was plentiful when the tide was out. It is hard for us to realize the difficulties which they underwent. For days after rowing to Seattle and back, their fingers were cramped in the position of holding the oars, and would not straighten out until the tired muscles relaxed again. But knowing nothing but hardships, they proceeded to hew out their homes, and being few neighbors they gladly took turns in rowing to Port Madison for supplies or mail for each other."

Riddell relates several other interesting incidents about the Eliasons: "The first cow was brought in by Mr. Eliason on a narrow three log float which was so tippy that whenever the cow moved, Mr. Eliason had to jump to the other side to balance it. However, he managed to get the cow home safely. But the cow did not seem to care much for her new home as she ran away the next day toward Suquamish where young E. J. and a neighbor cornered her and started homeward along the beach, but in the meantime the tide had come in and it was necessary to cross a deep creek. The neighbor finally succeeded to lead the cow into the water, but E. J. was too small to wade or swim and seeing himself left alone, he made a desperate grab for the last thing in sight which was the cow's tail and hanging on for dear life, she pulled him through the water while he was whirling somewhat like a trolling spoon."

The first wedding in Poulsbo was that of Nels Olsen and Rachel (Rakel) Eliason, Jorgen's sister and housekeeper. They wanted a Norwegian minister to perform the ceremony. The nearest one was in Stanwood. He came to Seattle by boat and on to Port Madison. When he found he had to row the rest of the way to Poulsbo he refused and sent word for the bridal couple to come to Port Madison by six o'clock the following morning. They got the message at eleven o'clock in the evening and with a lot of hurrying and a midnight row to Port Madison they made it in time for the wedding.

The third permanent settlers on Dog Fish Bay were the family of Iver B. Moe, who arrived about a month after the Eliasons. They came from Paulsbo, Norway, a small community between Halden and Kornsjø. The story of the Moe family is well recorded. Captain Torger (Tom) Birkland interviewed one of the sons, Chris Moe, for a series of articles for the monthly newsletter of the

Puget Sound Maritime Historical Society, from which excerpts will be taken.

Iver Moe (1843–1927) had a small sawmill in Norway but the work was slow and hard and he could see no future in it. The America fever was raging in Norway, and in 1880 Iver left by himself for New York to see what the New World had to offer. He went to Minneapolis and got work in a sawmill. In the fall he sent for his family, which included his wife Anne, a daughter Mina, and two sons, Albert and Chris. They traveled from Hamburg, Germany, to Baltimore, Maryland, and thence to Minneapolis. An older son, Andrew, was at sea in the Baltic at the time so did not come to America until the spring of 1881.

In the fall of 1881, Moe went to the Red River valley in Minnesota and took up a homestead. In the spring of 1882 he went for a second look and found it all under water. It was then that he decided to head for the Puget Sound country. He hired out to work for the Northern Pacific Railroad which was then building through Montana. The family lived in a boxcar which was moved westward as the construction advanced. Railroading was not to Moe's liking, so he managed to land a contract with a gold-mining operation near Helena in Montana Territory to provide cordwood for their steam boilers. The mining company advanced him money to buy four horses and the equipment to get the wood to the mines, deducting one dollar per cord until it was paid back. The family now experienced life in a cabin dug out of the hillside. Their worst hardship was the necessity of melting snow for water for themselves and their horses. By spring there was plenty of water; the roof leaked so badly that puddles stood on the floor.

Their mecca was Seattle on Puget Sound. They had two wagons with canvas covers and one pony for Moe to ride scouting the trail ahead. There were no roads. Part of the time their trail led them through Indian reservations where they were rudely treated. Over the Bitterroot Mountains in Idaho they followed a trail used by the cattlemen to get their stock to market. Driving steadily they made their first major stop at Ellensburg.

Let Chris Moe continue the story here: "When we finally saw the lovely valley where Ellensburg is located it was indeed a beautiful sight of deep green fields and alfalfa, lovely homes and the abundance of precious water. At this time most of the farmers in and around Ellensburg were of Scandinavian descent. They went all out to help us. They wanted us to remain there and take up land. There was a lot of good land to be had for free, but father said he was no farmer and would rest a few days and be on his way. There was a lake up in the mountains and there was a road to the lake, but he was told that was as far as he could possibly go. Father, of course, was determined to get there. He left us to see for himself; when he returned he had it all figured out. He said he would build a raft of logs to cross the lake. There was lots of timber near the lake and with large oars he would row the raft across. This was Lake Kechelus. At that time it was about two miles long. We remained with the good people in Ellensburg for about two weeks. By that time the horses, as well as ourselves, were all rested so we were on our way again.

"It required about two weeks to build the raft. We made two trips across the lake but our troubles began again. No road at all, just a pack trail. Whenever possible to do so we cut trail but in some places we could not cut large trees which had blown down. They simply were too large to cut. We had to pile brush on each side of the logs so it was possible to lift the wagons over. It took two weeks from Lake Kechelus in the Cascade Mountains to Issaquah.

"Well, at last we were near our destination [Seattle].

211

Rangvald Kvelstad

In this town [Issaquah] we again met some very nice
people. Father rode his pony in to Seattle. Now we had
a very good road compared to the trails we had traveled
here-to-fore. My father had arranged for a place in Seattle where we could pitch our tent for a time at 5th and
Madison, which is now the site of the Seattle Public Library. This was late September and the woods were
very dry. While in this location someone set fire to the
woods which spread rapidly and it became necessary to
move our tent several times. Fires were a common thing
in those days. Many thousands of acres of the finest
timber went up in smoke and there was nothing that
could be done about it. There was so much smoke a
person could not see the sun for days at a time.

"Father put the horses to work grading part of what is
now First Avenue. He then found a better job on a
railroad that was being built into the Black Diamond
coal mines east of Seattle. Andrew, my oldest brother,
was old enough to drive one team of horses and father
hired another man to drive the other team. This left father free to locate land and look for timber. He rented a
row boat and procured some maps. He first landed on
Bainbridge Island."

One of the first people Moe met on the island was the
owner of a logging operation who offered to sell him
forty acres of land on Mosquito Bay very cheaply. A deal
was made, an agreement signed, and a down payment
made. There was a lot of discarded lumber from the
sawmills along the beach so the family soon had a two-
room cabin to move into. In an interview in 1962, Chris
Moe relates what happened: "It was a lovely little bay
and a nice creek ran right by our house. Beautiful green
timber grew all the way to the water's edge. Fish were
so plentiful they would jump right out of the water onto
dry land. It was a wonderful place to live. We needed
some more lumber and other supplies. Port Madison, a
mill town, was about four miles away. Father went there

212

and was told it was the county seat for Kitsap county.

"Father wanted to get some information as to taxes regarding the land he had purchased and much to his surprise was told the land he had bought did not belong to the man who sold it to him. We did not have it after all. While he was in Port Madison he was told there was good timber land that he could take up as a homestead at that time, called Dog Fish Bay. Here he located on 150 acres of large timber and underbrush right down to salt water. Father then went to the courthouse in Port Madison to have his homestead recorded.

"In the fall of 1883 a man by the name of Jorgen Eliason had homesteaded on land a little east of the town of Poulsbo. He was the first settler and my father was next, following one month after Eliason. Where the town of Poulsbo is now located was an abandoned logging camp. There were two bunk houses with no windows and no doors. Mr. Eliason had moved into one of them. My father decided to move his family into the other one until such a time as he could build on his own claim. Mr. Eliason, a widower, had a sister and a small boy. So now it was back to Mosquito Bay to get someone to move us to Dog Fish Bay. Now for the first time since leaving Minneapolis, my mother had a woman companion, who was Mr. Eliason's sister."

Iver Moe now homesteaded a 160-acre tract at what was known as the head of the bay. He rowed to the Port Madison mill, about eight miles away, where he bought lumber for a house. He made a raft, secured it with a rope, and towed it behind his rowboat, a trip requiring several days. It was difficult to know exactly where the property lines were, which had been surveyed some years before. A timber cruiser came along and informed them they were on mill-company land, so they had to move again. Chris says it was the first time he ever saw his mother cry.

This time they built a better house on their own land.

213

Iver had to leave his family to go to work in Seattle. On one trip he brought home two little pigs. The family cleared a plot of ground for a garden. The big problem was to protect both the pigs and the garden from the bears that would come right up to the door. In the spring of 1884, Moe decided to log for himself. The mill at Port Madison, owned by Mr. Meigs, would buy his logs. Meigs would bring his horses over to Port Madison on the steamboat and Moe would raft them across to the Kitsap peninsula shoreline. From there they followed the beach to Moe's home near Poulsbo. Chris says they bought a Jersey cow about this time which they swam across the Agate Pass channel and then led it along the beach as they had done with the horses. By then they had added a stable, a chicken house, and a bunkhouse, and had a large garden with excellent soil. In the pigpen were many young porkers. But timber was the cash crop, so logging would be their business.

More settlers arrived. Chris says, "In 1885, my father petitioned the government for a post office with himself as postmaster." The date on the application, however, is September 9, 1886. In six places on the application the name of the new post office is to be filled in. Iver Moe decided to use the name of his home community in Norway, but his handwriting was not too precise. Three times it looks like an *a*, three times it looks like an *o*. The Post Office Department chose the *o* and thus Paulsbo became Poulsbo. In 1886, Adolph Hostmark had come to Poulsbo and opened a store. It was logical that the post office should be in the store, which was the central meeting place for the community, so in September, 1887, Adolph Hostmark became the postmaster. His building still stands and is the oldest building in Poulsbo.

The first schoolhouse was built on the Moe land. The first teacher was Miss Nellie Kiddy, who had a three-month contract. There were six pupils, all boys: Sam Olson, Paul and Theodore Thompson, Albert and Chris Moe, and E. J. Eliason. Nellie Kiddy was only sixteen years old and this was her first school. The boys were determined to make things as miserable for her as they could, and she resigned after six weeks. A new teacher came to complete the term and the boys vowed to get rid of her, too, but they were not successful this time. Chris says, "The jig was up. She just beat the tar out of us. This was all the schooling I ever had. To me it was just a waste of time."

With the Norwegian pioneers, it was first a school and then a church, and so it was in Poulsbo. By 1886 some additional families had moved in along Dog Fish Bay. A Lutheran home missionary pastor who visited the area encouraged them to form a congregation. A meeting was called in Jorgen Eliason's home. Iver B. Moe was elected secretary and apparently the pastor served as chairman. The following men also signed as charter members: Ole Thoresen, Stener Thoresen, Johannes Olson, Nels Olson, Edvart Bjermeland, Ole Asplund, Paul Wahl, Iver Thomsen, and T. B. Moe. Jorgen Eliason donated the land for the church and cemetery. It was named Førdefjord Lutheran Church for Eliason's home parish in Norway; it has since become First Lutheran. Pastor Ingebricht Tollefson was called to serve the new congregation as well as parishes in Bothell and Tacoma. His salary was $200 a year. The new church was dedicated in 1887. Many of the charter members are buried in the churchyard.

Logging was Moe's business. He found Meigs at the Port Madison mill difficult to deal with. There was another sawmill at Port Gamble about twelve miles north of Moe's home, but there was no trail, just dense forest. He started for the Port Gamble mill one day equipped with a compass, a hand axe, and some sandwiches. He

215

guessed on direction and blazed the trees as he went. The trip took three days. To prove he had been to Port Gamble he brought back a bottle of liquor. The present highway from Poulsbo to Port Gamble follows the trail Moe blazed.

The most lucrative logging involved taking out spar trees to be used for masts on sailing vessels. They had to be straight trees of good grain from sixty to one hundred feet tall. The Moes found a good source of such trees in the Miller Bay area on the Kitsap peninsula several miles from Port Madison. Large spar trees would bring one hundred dollars each. They would be made up into rafts and towed to the Port Blakely mill on Bainbridge Island. There the poles had to be scored on four sides to make them square. The spars would then take up less room and any defects would show up. Port Blakely was at one time the largest mill in the world. Five full shiploads of spars were shipped from there to Boston. From the profits of this business the Moes were able to expand their operations elsewhere. Logging had hitherto been done with oxen and horses, but now the steam engine was replacing them. Locomotives and logging trains were now being used to haul the logs down to the salt water to be made up into rafts. Let Chris Moe tell about it: "We started our first railroad in 1907. Logging, of course, was still our business, but logging, too, was due for a change. Timber was getting farther away and the old method of logging was not practical or profitable and the only answer was the railroad. Most logging companies were changing over to railroad operation. Rails were in such demand they were not procurable on the Sound. Father made the trip east to the rail manufacturers at some point in Ohio to secure the necessary rails. He also went to Cory, Pennsylvania, to order a locomotive. We had about thirty miles of railroad not including the side tracks. This was a tremendous improvement over the old method of logging. In 1907 we built our own standard gauge railroad." Andrew, the oldest Moe brother, was supervisor of the logging and railroading operations. The Moe railroad carried the logs to be dumped into Hood Canal on the west side of the Kitsap peninsula. From there they were rafted to the Port Gamble mill. There are pictures to prove that quite often there were half a dozen sailing vessels anchored in Port Gamble waiting for cargo. Port Gamble lumber was carried all around the world. The mill is still in use and at 130 years it is the oldest operating mill in the United States.

The Moes expanded into another venture. Transportation by steamboat between Poulsbo and Seattle was not satisfactory. The Moes bought a steamboat, the *Dauntless*, and put it on the run. There were no dock facilities in Poulsbo, so passengers had to row out to a raft anchored in the bay and wait to board the boat. As the business grew, the Moes expanded by purchasing faster and more comfortable ships. The pride of their fleet was the *Reliance*. They put the *Advance* on the Seattle-Port Gamble-Port Townsend run. In 1905 they got the government contract to carry the mail, but in the same year they sold their ships and gave up the transportation business.

When city government was first set up in Poulsbo in 1908, Andrew Moe was the first mayor and Chris Moe was elected councilman. At the first meeting of the town council, when one of the members resigned, Iver B. was appointed to fill the vacancy. Thus there were three Moes on the first town council.

Fishing was now on the upswing in Poulsbo. Halibut, salmon, and codfish were the main catch. The Moe family were determined to try for halibut, which is deep-sea fishing. Again let Chris tell of their experience: "In 1912 we built the halibut schooner *Tyee* at a cost of $30,000. The halibut business was good, especially if the owner himself was on the boat. But hiring all the crew, and especially the captain, did not work out so well, as we soon found out. The boat operated at a loss every trip. We received an offer from the New England Fish Company of Bellingham, Washington, for the halibut schooner. We accepted the offer and sold to them at a loss charging it to experience. Fishing is an unprofitable business and especially so for loggers."

A codfish venture came next. The Pacific Coast Cod Fish Company of Poulsbo was organized about 1911. It was a stock company and the Moes invested with the stipulation that the plant be located in Poulsbo. The company purchased three- and four-masted schooners that had been engaged in the lumber trade, which had now changed over to steam-driven vessels. The Poulsbo company eventually owned four of these sailing ships. Without engines they would be able to bring back larger loads of fish. They would leave the Poulsbo plant about the first of April for the Bering Sea, where the codfish were caught by hook and line in one-man dories, and would return about the middle of September. They would carry supplies to last for six months and employ about forty-five men on each vessel. Each ship would return with about 500 tons of codfish salted down. Much of the codfish was dried to be made into *lutefisk*. The cod would be brought back to the plant in Poulsbo, hung on racks to dry, and then piled like cordwood. By that time it had lost ninety percent of its weight of liquid, was very light, and required no refrigeration. To return the cod to its original state it was soaked in a lye-water solution. Modern refrigeration has done away with the *lutefisk* business in Poulsbo.

The Moe family did not find the codfish business to their liking and sold out after the first season. The family had now moved into Poulsbo. All the timber had been cut and they had done very well financially and thought it was time to quit. Chris, however, had to take one more fling in the business world. In his own words: "In those days the only lighting was coal lamps. The nearest electric power lines were at Keyport four miles away. In 1917, I made a twenty-five-year contract with Olympic Power Company of Port Angeles, Washington. I built four miles of power lines into the town of Poulsbo and the surrounding district. I was not interested in operating the system but just to get the lights into town."

Because Chris Moe was more verbal than the rest of the family, he is the source of much historical information that might otherwise have been forgotten. He seemed always eager and ready to try something new. In 1911, he brought the first automobile into Poulsbo, a 1911 Studebaker for which he paid $1,200. The contract is in the Kitsap County Historical Society archives. It was purchased from E. M. F. Studebaker Company in Seattle. The company was jokingly referred to as Every-Morning-Fix-it Studebaker Company. Chris does best at relating his adventures: "In 1911 I bought my first automobile, a Studebaker. It was also the first car north of Bremerton in Kitsap county. I had it shipped from Seattle to Port Gamble on a steamer. I had only one hour's instruction in driving. The roads were only for wagons. Stumps in the middle of the road some places were so high the car had to be lifted over them. If I met someone with horses the driver would have to unhitch them and take them into the woods, but the horses did not seem to mind after a time. Speed of from fifteen to twenty miles an hour seemed rather fast.

"It was not long until almost everyone had a car. On my first trip to Shelton, Washington, a distance of about eighty miles from Poulsbo, it took all day. From Shelton to Seattle by way of Olympia, there were good dust

219

roads. A Dr. Slippern went with me, and our neighbors said it was smart to take a doctor along on the trip."

The Moes sold their interests in Poulsbo in 1918 and moved to Seattle, where they built a house in the Magnolia Bluff section of that city. Chris had married Oline Marie Olson in 1905. Here again Chris speaks: "Just why she came out west I cannot say. Anyway she was and is the most beautiful and the sweetest girl in the whole world. We have been married for 52 years. To my dear wife I owe a lot. She has been an inspiration and in pouring oil on sometimes troubled waters made it possible for the family ship to survive and come through undamaged. We celebrated our Golden Anniversary in 1955." Chris Moe died in 1966. His wife, Oline, was later taken to the Martha-Mary Rest Home in Poulsbo where she died November 11, 1978, at age ninety-three. And so a chapter of pioneer history came to an end.

by JAMES S. HAMRE

7 *Three Spokesmen for Norwegian Lutheran Academies: Schools for Church, Heritage, Society*

D URING THE nineteenth century significant changes in the American educational system took place. On the elementary level the free public school system — the "common" school — was firmly established. At the secondary level an important change occurred in the type of school: whereas academies supported by private or religious sponsors were the most widespread secondary schools at the beginning of the century, by the end of the century the public high schools had outstripped them in numbers of students enrolled. At the college or university level the development of the elective system heralded important alterations in the patterns and goals of these institutions. Many of these changes involved debates and discussions, which in turn reflected profound differences in philosophy.[1]

The Norwegian immigrants and their descendants have shared this concern for education. One expression of it is the academy movement that flourished among them for about three-quarters of a century. Starting in the 1860s and 1870s, the movement gained momentum and was especially popular around the turn of the century. E. Clifford Nelson has written that the great initial interest "led many to assume this kind of education would be a permanent characteristic of the Norwegian Lutherans in America." But that did not prove to be the case. Many Norwegian Lutherans saw matters differently. The improvement of the public schools meant that increasing numbers of young people were drawn to them, leading to a decline in the enrollment in the academies after World War I. The Great Depression "administered the *coup de grace* to the academy movement."[2] It might be noted, however, that a number of the still functioning colleges started by Norwegian Lutherans either began as academies or had academy departments connected to them.

In 1944 B. H. Narveson published an article on the Norwegian Lutheran academies. His discussion provides a good overview of the character, purpose, and daily life of these institutions. One very helpful feature of his article is a list of these schools. It includes a total of seventy-five academies founded by Norwegians. It also gives such information as years of operation, enrollment figures, number of teachers, value of buildings, religious affiliation, and location of each school. A second list provides the names of the presidents who served these institutions. Narveson contended that "the academy has made a larger contribution to church and nation than is generally appreciated."[3] His discussion is a good starting point for anyone who wishes to understand the academy movement among Norwegians in America.

In a sense the present article can be viewed as an extended footnote to Narveson's discussion. It seeks to present the underlying philosophy of those who advocated these schools by discussing the views of three men who spoke out in their behalf. One of them, H. A. Preus, provided some of the ideas that initiated the academy movement. The second, D. G. Ristad, presented his views shortly after the turn of the century, when the movement had reached its highest point. The third figure, Olaf M. Norlie, wrote when the decline of the academies was underway. Together their writings help us to understand more fully the fundamental convictions of those who believed that the Norwegian Lutheran academies provided the best pattern of secondary education for Norwegian Lutheran young people in America.

Herman Amberg Preus (1825–1894) was born and educated in Norway. He studied at the Christianssand Cathedral School and received a degree in theology from Christiania University. He served briefly as a teacher in Norway before emigrating to America in 1851. Preus was a pastor in Spring Prairie, Wisconsin, from 1851 to 1894 and was one of seven pastors who organized the Norwegian Synod in 1853. He served as president of that body for many years and helped to shape its outlook.[4]

Preus was concerned that the children of Norwegian immigrants be provided with what he considered to be the proper type of education. During the "common" school controversy which developed in the 1860s and 1870s he was one of the persons who promoted the establishment of Lutheran parochial schools, in opposition to those who encouraged the immigrants to send their children to the public elementary schools. The parochial schools would teach all of the required elementary school subjects plus Norwegian and religion.[5]

The academy impulse grew out of a similar concern.

223

To set the beginnings of the academy movement in their proper context it is necessary to refer to several persons with a different point of view. Rasmus B. Anderson was an energetic and articulate figure motivated by a vision of securing a role for Norwegian Americans in the broader American culture. One of the ways to do that, he felt, was to secure "the appointment of Norwegian teachers and professors in American schools" of higher learning. Such persons would be in a position to assist and guide young people from the Norwegian immigrant communities who might come to these institutions for an education. The young people would then be able to return to their communities as teachers and leaders. Anderson sought the support of such persons as Knud Langeland, John A. Johnson, and the pastor C. L. Clausen.

These men responded positively to Anderson's initiatives. Clausen issued a call for a meeting in Madison, Wisconsin, on March 4, 1869, of those persons interested in promoting "true popular enlightenment" (*sand folkeoplysning*). Out of that meeting came the short-lived Scandinavian Lutheran Educational Society, one of whose main goals was the establishment of Scandinavian professorships in American universities.[6]

H. A. Preus was among those present at the Madison meeting. He had earlier prepared a statement on the topic of "true popular enlightenment." It was published the same day as the Madison meeting, in the March 4 issue of *Fædrelandet og Emigranten*. At the Madison meeting Preus objected to the manner of proceeding that Clausen insisted on: only those were permitted to speak and vote who would sign a statement supporting the idea of the Scandinavian professorships. Preus and a number of others refused to sign because they felt the procedure was unparliamentary and would commit them in advance not just to a worthy goal but also to the means of achieving that goal. Those who refused to sign felt themselves excluded from the meeting and a number of them decided to hold their own meeting the next day to take up the topic. Preus was chosen as their chairman. A detailed statement was issued by Preus's group indicating wherein it differed from the approach favored by the Scandinavian Lutheran Educational Society. It is clear that two different philosophies were operative. The March 5 meeting of these "dissenters" was "the start of an academy program that was to flourish among the Norwegian Americans for three-quarters of a century."[7]

The statement prepared by Preus for *Fædrelandet og Emigranten* and the one issued by the dissenting group that he led contain many of the same ideas. Both statements will be utilized in the discussion that follows. It is clear that Preus agreed that "true popular enlightenment" is a very important goal; he did not agree that the best way to achieve it was by establishing Scandinavian professorships in American institutions of higher learning.

Before turning to the question of means, however, Preus raised a preliminary question: What is it that constitutes "true popular enlightenment"? His answer was religious in nature: "In the fullest sense it is that enlightenment worked by the Holy Spirit by means of God's Word concerning God and His gracious will" which is applicable to the individual and the entire people. A people without that light, according to Preus, are still walking in darkness "in spite of the brilliant appearance of enlightenment with which worldly education and civilization, arts and sciences, can surround them."

It is important to note that Preus sought to guard against the appearance of a sectarian rejection of or withdrawal from the affairs of this world. He stressed

225

that those who do walk in the true light will seek to acquire useful knowledge for the benefit of themselves and others, for "Christians are also for a time citizens of this world, and it is God's will that all the talents He has given them should receive the greatest possible cultivation." From this perspective Christianity's task is "to penetrate, cleanse, and hallow all other knowledge and learning." In fact, a true understanding of worldly learning is regarded as possible only when it is viewed from the perspective of the light that shines from God's Word.

Preus noted also that from the early centuries Christians have established schools and encouraged learning in ways that contributed significantly to true popular enlightenment. He felt that in America there is a double challenge to work toward that goal: a free church encourages more active participation on the part of its members than does a state church, and the American system of government offers citizens a chance for a larger role in the affairs of state. It would therefore be a blessing if more Lutherans were involved in the affairs of state, for "if we believe that our Lutheran Church is the orthodox, visible church on earth and that our teaching and confession are the pure, unadulterated gospel, we should strive to place the light of God's Word on a candlestick before all the people and permit our church more and more to become 'a city on a hill that cannot be hid.'"

With that understanding of "true popular enlightenment" Preus then proceeded to indicate why the means promoted by the Scandinavian Lutheran Educational Society — appointment of Scandinavian Lutheran professors — was unsatisfactory. For one thing, he held, we must keep in mind the nature of American schools: in the statement issued by the Preus group they are described as "either religionless or sectarian or even dominated by a purely unbelieving and anti-Christian spirit."

Preus felt too that it was important to be aware of the influence that professors and fellow-students would have on Lutheran young people: instead of being permeated by and strengthened in their love for the Lutheran Church they might be tempted to deny Christ, drawn into sectarian errors, or led into an indifference that makes no distinction between the Lutheran Church and the teachings of other groups. Further, at these American schools they would be exposed to "the results of modern research in the fields of philosophy and natural science which tend to tear down the Bible and Christian faith, without at the same time receiving the necessary Christian guidance and warning." They would also be exposed to "modern false philanthropic and humanistic ideas and teachings" and the danger that "an essentially pagan morality would be impressed on them." All of these factors would tend to have destructive effects.

Preus then asked whether such schools are suitable places for the education of Lutheran youth. Can parents with a good conscience send their children to these schools with the hope that their stay will be a true blessing to the children? Preus answered with a decisive no. He felt that young people fifteen or sixteen years of age would not be equipped to meet the challenges of such a situation. They needed instead "careful tending" (*omhyggelig pleie*) which would build on the basis that had been laid in confirmation, constant instruction in the word of truth, and the reminder and strengthening that come with regular association with serious, experienced Christians. Such "tending" would not be provided for Norwegian Lutheran young people in the American schools.

But wouldn't the results be different if there were

Lutheran professors in these schools? Preus acknowledged that such might be the case if there could be a guarantee that such professors would be "faithful Lutherans," although even then the young people might be influenced by the other professors and students. But it was the matter of a guarantee that was the stumbling block for Preus. What guarantee, he asked, would the congregations have that these professors would be "confessional Lutherans" and not false friends or open enemies of our Lutheran Church? He felt that such professors must be competent in Norwegian as well as English and possess a solid grounding in the Lutheran faith. He asked where persons with such qualifications could be found. And even if they could be found, what assurance was there that they would be sought out and appointed? Given the many divisions among the Norwegian Lutherans in America, he felt that it was unlikely they would agree in their choices. And as far as the Scandinavian Lutheran Educational Society was concerned, Preus noted that some of its members had deserted the Lutheran Church. To work with such persons to promote "Lutheran popular enlightenment" seemed both "un-Lutheran and unreasonable."

What, then, in Preus's view, would be the best means for promoting "true popular enlightenment"? The program that he proposed dealt with schools at several levels. At the elementary level he stressed the importance of having "qualified Lutheran teachers" take over the English district schools. If this could not be done, the Norwegian Lutheran congregations should initiate separate parochial schools where the children could be instructed in Christianity as well as all other necessary subjects, "all in a Christian spirit and under Christian discipline."

Luther College, the college established by the Norwegian Synod in 1861, also played a part in Preus's thinking. He noted that its original purpose was to educate pastors and teachers. The more the college came to fulfill this purpose the more the need for an additional type of institution — "middle schools" or academies — would be felt. Such schools would provide education beyond the elementary level whereby the confirmed young people could be fitted to "fulfill their duties as Christians and citizens and work for the blessing of church and state."

These "middle schools," Preus held, should be established in the areas having the largest concentrations of Scandinavians so that the young people could obtain additional education without neglecting the farm work during the busiest time of the year. "I call them middle schools," said Preus, "because they must be intended to form a link, a transitional stage, between the elementary school and the various institutions at which the young person will seek the final preparation for the particular earthly calling or life's work which he intends to enter." As such the academies could prepare the young people to enter either Luther College or some technical institute. The academies would provide instruction in various subjects. They would also offer religious instruction so that young people would get a better knowledge of Scripture, be established in Lutheran doctrine, and become acquainted with the confessional writings of the Lutheran Church, church history, and the main teachings of the most common sects. These schools must also provide "thorough instruction" in the Norwegian and English languages.

Preus acknowledged that his proposals would cost money. But he felt they offered a far better means of promoting "true popular enlightenment" than would the installation of Norwegian professors in American colleges and universities. And it seems clear that many persons within the Norwegian-American community

James S. Hamre

came to share his views. In the years that followed, quite a number of academies came into being in areas of heavy Norwegian settlement.

D. G. Ristad (1863–1938) was born in Norway, received part of his education in that country, and taught school there for several years before emigrating. In 1887 he came to the United States, where he received his theological education. His career as a clergyman in America included several pastorates and the presidencies of Albion (Preus) Academy, Albion, Wisconsin (1901–1906), Park Region College, Fergus Falls, Minnesota (1906–1916), and Lutheran Ladies Seminary, Red Wing, Minnesota (1916–1919). He belonged to the Norwegian Synod and, after the church merger of 1917, the Norwegian Lutheran Church of America, which he served as vice president and president of its Eastern district.[8]

Ristad was also interested in fostering and preserving the Norwegian cultural heritage in America. He was involved in the *bygdelag* movement. He also served as the first president of the Norwegian-American Historical Association, from 1925 to 1930, and later as its vice president.[9]

In 1906 *Symra*, the periodical of the Decorah-based literary organization of the same name, published a fifteen-page article by Ristad dealing with the Norwegian Lutheran institutions of higher education in America (*Om de norsk-lutherske høiskoler i Amerika*). His discussion does not deal with individual schools but seeks rather to present a general statement of the character and purpose of these institutions.[10]

Written at a time when interest in and support of the academies seemed to be at a high point, Ristad's article breathes a spirit of confidence concerning their future. "Their activity," he said, "is still in its beginnings, in

230

the first period of development." Later in the article, after noting what the people who belong to the Norwegian Lutheran churches in America have accomplished in the field of education, he offers this observation: "On the basis of what has taken place we venture to conclude that the Norwegian Lutheran schools are still in their infancy; what they have accomplished, and what they are, are but a herald of what they ought to become and can become."

In the opening part of his article — which contains observations that apply to the colleges as well as the academies — Ristad noted that "it is common to call the schools that Lutherans of Norwegian descent have established and operate in America *Norwegian-Lutheran*." He felt the name was appropriate, for in their origin, activity, and purpose these schools were both Norwegian and Lutheran. He regarded the adjective "Lutheran" as the most descriptive one, for "it is with the intention of educating the young as Lutheran Christians and thereby preserving and strengthening the Lutheran Church in America that these schools are operated."

But, asserted Ristad, these schools are also Norwegian, in that they are owned and utilized primarily by Norwegians and their descendants. Beyond that their purpose is also Norwegian: "Not only is there instruction in Norwegian language, history, and literature, but the schools' entire relationship toward everything Norwegian — especially Norwegian cultural life — is of an intimate nature. The schools are — together with the Norwegian-American press — the living connecting link between Norway and its people and Norwegian America." Ristad pointed also to another factor that made it possible to call these schools Norwegian: they "present Norwegian-American youth with an understanding of their distinctive features as children with a

Norwegian quality (*norskhed*) marked deeply in their dispositions." And the schools can help the young people to bring out the beneficial features and subdue those that are harmful.

Having characterized these schools as both Lutheran and Norwegian, Ristad then added a third adjective: "It is obvious that these schools are also American." The fact that they were both Lutheran and Norwegian did not, in Ristad's view, make them any less American. He spoke of the schools as being American in such things as organization, plan of instruction, and language, and essentially also in method and the most immediate practical purposes. The schools are American, said Ristad, because the Norwegian-American people *want* their schools to be American — "in this word's best and most correct meaning." These schools are as like the American schools as possible without adopting the public schools' "religious and pedagogical principles." Later in the article Ristad noted points at which these principles clashed with those of the Norwegian Lutheran schools.

Ristad saw the academies and other Lutheran institutions of higher education as a result of the unique demands that life in America presented to the Norwegian Lutheran immigrants and their descendants. He said that the Norwegian immigrants had come to America to better their economic condition. After they had established themselves, other interests came to the fore. Religion was one factor that bound them to one another, yet religious conditions in the New World were different from what they had known in Norway. There the state had provided for religious instruction. Here they had to take action themselves. To give their children the type of education they wanted became for them "a matter of conscience."

The church realized the necessity of educating pastors. Out of that realization came colleges and seminaries. But, said Ristad, the church people realized that a well-educated clergy was not enough. It was also necessary to educate the young people who did not feel called to the ministry. The academies have their origin in this demand. If, asserted Ristad, the public high schools, which deal with young people from ages fifteen to nineteen, can with a certain right be called "folk universities," then the academies can certainly with even more right be called "the Norwegian congregations' folk universities." The tasks of the academies include providing further education for Norwegian Lutheran young people who have completed elementary education, as well as preparing these young people for college, teaching, or other practical roles in life. As that is being done the main emphasis is placed on the growth and unfolding of the Christian personality. And since the academies point rather in the direction of general enlightenment and education for the masses than toward serving those few individuals who are preparing for the learned professions, they can be called "the people's high schools — the organized institutions of the Norwegian Lutheran free church for the furtherance of Christian general education in America." Ristad, it is clear, regarded the academies as having an important role among the Norwegian immigrants and their descendants.

But he was also aware that these schools faced difficulties. He spoke of two major obstacles. One of them came from the state. He granted that there were no laws against establishing private schools, but he felt that the laws did favor the public institutions. And "because of the strong tendency to accelerate the assimilation of nationalities" there were laws that had made the existence of private church schools difficult.

Another facet of this first major obstacle was the chal-

233

lenge coming from the public high schools with their tendency to present a different ideal or philosophy of life. Ristad spoke of the appeal of success. In America, he said, the heroes are the self-made men in business and politics. The emphasis in the public schools is that the way is open to all "to dare and to do." But the church operates with a different philosophy of life and so must present the students with a different ideal. The principle of obedience and the ideal of service should have a more prominent role in education than self-assertion and the right to dominate. Quite clearly, this is a different understanding of "success." Ristad was convinced that the Lutheran schools represented a "nobler and sounder culture," for they developed all the capacities of the young person's mind in a more well-rounded manner and gave it a more elevated tendency and a longer lasting goal both for society and for the individual.

The second major obstacle facing the Norwegian Lutheran schools came, according to Ristad, from certain characteristics of the Norwegian immigrants themselves. He called attention to the Norwegian "capacity to imitate" — the rapidity with which Norwegians became Americanized and a part of the new nation. One result was that they tended to regard institutions such as the Norwegian Lutheran schools with some suspicion. Furthermore, Ristad observed, most of the emigrant class, precisely the people who constituted the Norwegian Lutheran Church in America, were "simple" folk. As such they felt they did not compare favorably with the "refined" (*dannede*) people in Norway or the "fine" Americans. As a result, said Ristad, in the realm of cultural life these people have regarded themselves as weak and insecure and "they have not had confidence in the ability of their own schools to fulfill their task."

But Ristad felt that the accomplishments of the Norwegian Lutheran church people in the field of education in less than half a century testified to the fact that they strove for higher things than material comfort. He saw them as a people who, impelled by their Christian faith, "have become not only a community of believers but also a cultural community" (*ikke blot trossamfund, men ogsaa kultursamfund*). He thought that Norwegian Lutheran academies could make a valuable contribution to the development of American society, because the Christian principles on which they stood could build sound, strong, and noble characters.

Ristad closed his article with these words: "The Norwegian people are in many respects a richly gifted people. This is evident also from their history in America. They owe it to themselves, to their adopted land, and to the giver of these gifts to develop their natural endowments. The Norwegian Lutheran institutions of higher education will help our people meet this triple obligation."

Olaf M. Norlie (1876–1962), the son of immigrant parents, had an active academic and professional career. He received a Ph.D. degree from the University of Minnesota and was also awarded several honorary degrees. He served as pastor, book editor, college professor, archivist, and statistician, and as "pres., sec., or treas., of many religious, historical, educational, and statistical societies."[11] He has been described as a "tireless collector and compiler of statistical and historical matters in various areas."[12]

Norlie was also a prolific writer of books, pamphlets, and articles. Among his best known works are *Norsk Lutherske Menigheter i Amerika, 1843–1916* (2 volumes), *Norsk Lutherske Prester i Amerika* (the first issue covering the years 1843–1913, the second, 1843–1915), *Who's Who Among Pastors in All the Norwegian*

Lutheran Synods of America, 1843–1927 (jointly edited), and *History of the Norwegian People in America*. The last-named work, published in 1925, was intended to be "a scholarly, comprehensive, and authoritative history of the Norwegian people in America" to mark the centennial of Norwegian-American immigration.

Two of Norlie's works will be utilized as a basis for this discussion. The main one is *The Academy for Princes*, published in 1917. The other is a short section of the above-noted *History of the Norwegian People in America*. Written at a time when the academies were declining in enrollment, these works were a strong plea for support of and participation in these institutions. They also reflected Norlie's sense of frustration as he observed the Norwegian immigrants and their descendants increasingly giving their support to the ever more numerous public high schools.[13]

The Academy for Princes is a work of over 200 pages. It is written in a manner that seems designed to capture and hold the attention of young people and their parents. The entire book consists of conversations and discussions created by Norlie as having taken place among various people, mostly Norwegian Americans, in an unnamed rural community. These people are given names and the reader is able to associate certain viewpoints with certain individuals. In this manner Norlie provides a picture of the debate on education among Norwegian Americans in the second decade of the twentieth century. The book is illustrated with a number of pictures and graphs.

The thesis of the book is that we are "princes and princesses, real children of God," and that "as royal persons we ought to receive a royal training." To illustrate this point Norlie had one of the conversations center on a picture of the royal family of Norway hanging on a wall in a home. The young boy in the picture was Prince Olav. All who were present agreed that he would have the best training possible, including private teachers. That enabled one person to make the point that our children too are royalty who can have the best of everything, "the knowledge of the Word of God." The book sought to make the point that the Norwegian Lutheran academies can provide that knowledge while the public high schools can not.

But it is obvious from the conversations Norlie created that many Norwegian Americans of that time did not share these views. Some of the parents were pictured as maintaining that they could not afford to send their children away to school or that the academies were generally inferior to the new public high schools. Other arguments against the academies were that young people who attended them would be at a disadvantage in getting a job and that the academies were seldom accredited by the state, something that would hamper persons who wished to study at a university. Some of the young people were portrayed as reluctant to attend an academy since they did not want to be different from their friends and feared their ridicule. "I have been told," said a girl in one of the accounts, "that the boys who go to the academy nearly all become preachers, and the girls become preachers' wives or missionaries." The girl made it plain that she had no desire to do that.

Moreover, Norlie's account portrayed real differences of opinion among the clergy. One chapter consists of a conversation between a farmer — who had been an ardent supporter of the academies — and his pastor. The farmer was disturbed because he had heard that the pastor was going to send three of his children to non-Lutheran schools: a state university, a college of another denomination, and the public high school. Yet prior to that time the pastor had been an outspoken champion of the Lutheran schools and a critic of the public schools. The farmer sought to learn what had happened.

The pastor told his story. As a poor young man he had managed to work his way through a church academy and college. He then decided to teach for a time, but found that his education was not recognized as readily as was that of persons who had attended state schools. He had to accept a position at lower pay. Later he attended a state university to better his position and again encountered certain difficulties. Yet even these trying experiences did not turn him against the church schools. He emerged rather as one of their ardent defenders. "I have held," said the pastor, "that the church schools are better than the state schools, because the church schools teach Christianity. . . . On the other hand, even though the state schools have many Christian teachers, they are institutions either un-Christian or anti-Christian, and leave the mind worldly, indifferent to orthodoxy or opposed to it." That had been the uncompromising stance that he had taken in his ministry also.

Yet that position got him into trouble. At a synodical meeting the pastor was told that he was too radical, that he should hold his tongue. He was informed that "speaking against the state school was just as foolish as speaking against the secret societies. The Church in a fight with these institutions would merely make plain to the world its impotence. . . . Many of the pastors," he observed, "openly knock their own schools whenever they can" and "church people, pastors and professors included, want to be like the world." And so the clergyman who had ardently promoted the cause of the church schools was finally moved to say, "I am tired of the fight and have surrendered unconditionally." From that point on he would allow his children to choose the schools they wished to attend, for "I have dropped this academy agitation and do not want to resume hostilities." That, of course, was not what Norlie proposed to do. But the account was indicative of the struggle going on within the Norwegian-American community.

The conversations created by Norlie indicate that the Norwegian Americans of that time had a variety of attitudes toward the public schools. One was of the type attributed to the troubled pastor: they are "either un-Christian or anti-Christian." Another speaker made the related point that "the influence of the high school is tremendously secular." Repeatedly the point was stressed that the public schools do not give instruction in Christianity, although one speaker added the comment that he did not want them to do so: "It is illegal and would cause a clash between the Sects and a clamor for spoils, and a meddling into the Church's affairs by the State."

More positive attitudes were also reflected. One person spoke of the public schools as "a smelting pot, in which the raw material from Europe, Asia, Africa, and the Americas are made into good, intelligent, useful, loyal American citizens." Another man is portrayed as serving on the local school board even though he sent his own children to a Lutheran academy. He is made to say: "I think a good deal of our free public institutions, especially the public school system; and I do all in my power to improve the schools . . . by getting high-minded, moral, Christian men and women as teachers, getting textbooks that do not antagonize Christianity, keeping a check on the social and athletic life of the schools, and so on." He sent his own children to an academy so that they would get instruction in Christianity. He distinguished the two kinds of schools in this way: "The high school is a state school to train its growing generation into intelligent and moral citizenship; every one of the native-born boys at this school is in line for the presidency of the United States and is a temporal prince. The academy is a church school to train the children of God, the heavenly princes, for their work in the Church and in the State and for a successful entrance into their Father's country beyond the grave." Norlie also portrayed a professor in the service of the church as saying: "Let us quit knocking the state schools. We need them. They are really not rival schools, but allies." The professor quickly added, "they need us also," and his attitude was summed up in the words, "I believe in the public schools. They are doing good work. It is no shame to attend them. But I believe more in the church schools. They are trying to furnish the foundation and life of Christian character, and in so far, at least, far surpass the state schools."

The development of strong character was seen as one of the positive contributions of the academies. It was one person's opinion that "it takes the Word of God to make Christian character, which is the strongest and best type of manhood and womanhood." It is of interest to note that in support of that contention Norlie called attention to the high rate of crime in the United States. The question was raised as to whether the absence of Christian instruction might be the primary cause of a criminal record worse than that of Europe. Several graphs were included to depict the growth of the public schools and decay of the church schools on the one hand and the increase in crime on the other. The impression conveyed was of a relationship between the two.

Two themes noted in the views of the writers discussed earlier were also present in Norlie's book: the academies will strengthen and support the Lutheran Church; and they will foster the preservation of the Norwegian heritage and culture. Speakers in the book repeatedly made the point that it was important for young people to receive training in the Scriptural principles on which the Lutheran Church is founded. In that way they will develop a love and loyalty for their church. One example of the other motif involved a family which spoke a "cultured," that is, correct English, when English was spoken and a "cultured" Norwegian when Norwegian was used. The family made it a policy to speak Norwegian in the home, for the father believed that "it was a right and a duty and a privilege to learn about one's forefathers, their history and life, their language and religion. . . . Our roots draw nourishment from the soil of our ancestry."

Another note present in Norlie's book was that the academies provide a good setting in which to find a marriage partner. One father was described as saying to his daughter, "If you go to a church academy you may meet your partner for life there. He will probably be of your nationality and religion and standard of training and tastes." On the other hand, if she went to the public high school she would most likely meet a man of "another nationality, religion, and social set." She was told that she might get a good husband at the high school, but "the chances are better at the academy." Another father reflected a similar sentiment: "I want my children to marry Lutherans, Lutherans who have been trained to be both Christian and churchly. If I send them to a Lutheran school they may there meet their future helpmeets."

The Academy for Princes did not halt the decline of the Norwegian Lutheran academies. By 1925, when his *History of the Norwegian People in America* was published, Norlie could say, "Never before have patriotic Norwegians and consecrated Lutheran Christians pleaded so eloquently for the support of the Norwegian schools, and never have they been maintained with so much difficulty." It was his contention that the academies "prospered nicely as long as the Norwegians were Norwegian Americans, but they were starved out for want of students and other support as soon as the Norwegians became Americans." He maintained that the high-school age is a crucial period in the life of a person, a time when "moral and religious instruction of the right kind" must be provided. He regarded the "secular schools, by their very secular nature," as institutions that "are de-Christianizing the land, no matter how much some of them try not to do so." Norlie argued also that the "religious and national heritage of the Norwegians cannot be transmitted through the public schools, for the only nationalism that the public schools will tolerate is that of America, and of England as the Mother Country." It was his conviction that the public school system "tends to weaken the distinctively Lutheran and Norwegian character of the Norwegians . . . to rob them of their heritage, which should be theirs forever, and which should be their cultural contribution to America."

This study has looked at the views of three men who promoted and defended the Norwegian Lutheran academies. They wrote at different moments in the three-quarters of a century during which these schools flourished and so they spoke from and to different circumstances. H. A. Preus sought to provide a legitimation of such schools as the best means to promote "true popular enlightenment." He did so by appealing to what he regarded as certain fundamental principles in the Lutheran theological tradition. D. G. Ristad, who spoke at a time when these schools had gained acceptance, could in a sense take these principles for granted. He sought to interpret the Norwegian and Lutheran character of these schools and to show how they could assist persons of Norwegian descent in making a contribution to the American character. Olaf M. Norlie offered an apology for these principles as he sought to reverse the growing tendency of Norwegian Lutherans in

America to desert the academies in favor of the public high schools. He was convinced that the academies should be supported because they were such useful instruments in preserving the Norwegian religious and cultural heritage.

Though they wrote at different times there are certain themes that are common to all three of these men. One is that the academies would strengthen the Lutheran position in America. These men realized that they lived in a country where church and state were separate and many denominations existed. To build up the Lutheran Church in such a context called for the development of institutions that would provide for religious instruction and training. The academies, they held, could be one of those institutions.

A second theme is related to the first: the academies would also be of benefit to the state. These men believed that educated, useful, God-fearing citizens were an asset to society. They believed that the Lutheran tradition was one that sought to foster such citizens. Thus they held that the Lutheran Church could make an important contribution to American society by establishing schools that would educate its people in Christian principles.

A third common theme was that the academies were important for the preservation and transmission of the Norwegian cultural heritage. These men believed that this heritage was a valuable one and could play a useful part in the full flowering of the American character. The academies could help Norwegian Americans to understand and appreciate that heritage.

In this connection the issue of cultural pluralism versus assimilation is relevant. The historian Carl H. Chrislock has noted the existence of conflicting viewpoints within the Norwegian-American community during the early decades of the twentieth century. Some persons held that Norwegians should not strive to preserve their "Norwegianness" in America; they, like all other immigrants, should give up their Old World ways in the attempt to become fully "American." Others resisted that view, seeking to foster a genuine cultural pluralism. They held that a people did not have to abandon its heritage in order to become "American," for that which binds Americans together is not complete cultural uniformity but commitment to certain fundamental principles within a context of cultural diversity.[14]

The proponents of the academies discussed here were not primarily concerned with that issue. But their views — especially those of Norlie — can be related to that discussion. As noted, Norlie disagreed with a school system that would tolerate no "nationalism" but that of America — "and of England as the Mother Country." His *Academy for Princes* was written at a time when the issue of America's involvement in World War I was coming to the fore. And within the Norwegian-American community the controversy over language — Norwegian or English — was also becoming more intense. In his own way Norlie championed cultural pluralism, convinced that the Norwegians had a heritage "which should be theirs forever." He resisted, and perhaps resented, all the pressures that were forcing Norwegians to give up that heritage.

It may also be useful to look briefly at the Norwegian Lutheran academy movement in relation to certain developments taking place in American education. R. Freeman Butts has spoken of the "competing claims upon the American mind" in discussing the "intellectual foundations of education" in nineteenth-century America. He calls attention to the newer, more secularized and humanistic patterns of thought in such fields as religion, science, and psychology that served to challenge the traditional religious orientation of many people. Some of these thought patterns came to have a significant impact on American education. [15]

In one sense the academy movement can be seen as a defensive reaction to some of these trends. The spokesmen discussed here were committed to what they understood to be a Christian orientation and they felt that that perspective had certain implications for education. They were not prepared to surrender the field to the prophets of new and different creeds. Their goal was to establish institutions in which Christian principles could permeate and influence all areas of study. This effort was worthwhile, they were convinced, because it would have a significant impact on the individual, the church, and society at large.

Obviously, this article has told only part of the story as it relates to the academies. There were persons within the Norwegian-American community who held views that differed significantly from those discussed here. Their views too deserve to be heard. And if one thinks in terms of practical results one would have to say that the latter views prevailed: the Norwegian Lutheran academies in the United States have virtually ceased to exist. A variety of forces and attitudes contributed to the demise of one after another of these schools.

The purpose of this discussion, then, has not been to offer a defense of or apology for the academy movement. It shares instead Norlie's contention that the "history of the Norwegian Lutherans cannot be fully understood except in the light of the views these Norwegians hold with regard to education." [16] The academy movement was important to many Norwegians in America. The views of the three men discussed here can help us to understand its reason for existence.

NOTES

[1] R. Freeman Butts, A Cultural History of Western Education: Its Social and Intellectual Foundations (New York, 1955), 430–488.

[2] E. Clifford Nelson and Eugene L. Fevold, The Lutheran Church Among Norwegian-Americans, 2 vols. (Minneapolis, 1960), 2:113–119, and E. Clif-

James S. Hamre

ford Nelson, *Lutheranism in North America, 1914–1970* (Minneapolis, 1972), 52, 65, note 44.

[3] B. H. Narveson, "The Norwegian Lutheran Academies," in *Norwegian-American Studies and Records*, 14 (Northfield, Minnesota, 1944), 184–226.

[4] Rasmus Malmin, O. M. Norlie, and O. A. Tingelstad, eds., *Who's Who Among Pastors in All the Norwegian Lutheran Synods of America, 1843–1927* (Minneapolis, 1928), 463. See also the references to Preus in the chapter on the Norwegian Synod in Nelson and Fevold, *The Lutheran Church Among Norwegian-Americans*, 1:151-190.

[5] A clear statement of Preus's position in that debate is included in his *Syv foredrag over de kirkelige forholde blandt de norske i Amerika* (Christiania, 1867), 32–36. For discussions of the "common" school debate see Theodore C. Blegen, *Norwegian Migration to America: The American Transition* (Northfield, Minnesota, 1940), 241–276; Laurence M. Larson, *The Changing West and Other Essays* (Northfield, Minnesota, 1937), 116–146; Frank C. Nelsen, "The School Controversy Among Norwegian Immigrants," in *Norwegian-American Studies*, 26 (Northfield, Minnesota, 1974), 206–219; and James S. Hamre, "Norwegian Immigrants Respond to the 'Common' School: A Case Study of American Values and the Lutheran Tradition," in *Church History*, 50 (1981),302–315.

[6] See Lloyd Hustvedt, *Rasmus Bjørn Anderson: Pioneer Scholar* (Northfield, Minnesota, 1966), 67–72; Blegen, *Norwegian Migration to America*, 241–276; Larson, *The Changing West*, 116–146; and Narveson, "The Norwegian Lutheran Academies," 184–226.

[7] Hustvedt, *Rasmus Bjørn Anderson*, 72. The Preus statement, published in *Fædrelandet og Emigranten*, was entitled "Hvorledes skal sand folkeoplysning søges fremmet blandt skandinaverne her i landet?" See also *Beretning om et møde til fremmelse af folke-oplysning blandt skandinaverne i Amerika, afholdt i Madisons norsk-lutherske kirke den 5te marts 1869* (Decorah, Iowa, 1869).

[8] John Peterson, Olaf Lysnes, and Gerald Giving, eds., *A Biographical Directory of Pastors of the Evangelical Lutheran Church* (Minneapolis, 1952), 459.

[9] See Odd S. Lovoll, *A Folk Epic: The Bygdelag in America* (Boston, 1975), and Odd S. Lovoll and Kenneth O. Bjork, *The Norwegian-American Historical Association, 1925–1975* (Northfield, Minnesota, 1975).

[10] D. G. Ristad, "Om de norsk-lutherske høiskoler i Amerika," in *Symra* (Decorah, Iowa, 1906), 181–195.

[11] Peterson, Lysnes, and Giving, *Biographical Directory of Pastors*, 401.

[12] Julius Bodensieck, ed., *The Encyclopedia of the Lutheran Church*, 3 (Minneapolis, 1965), 1760.

[13] Olaf M. Norlie, *The Academy for Princes* (Minneapolis, 1917), and *History of the Norwegian People in America* (Minneapolis, 1925), 375–378.

[14] See Carl H. Chrislock, "Introduction," in Odd S. Lovoll, ed., *Cultural Pluralism versus Assimilation: The Views of Waldemar Ager* (Northfield, Minnesota, 1977), and Carl H. Chrislock, *Ethnicity Challenged: The Upper Midwest Norwegian-American Experience in World War I* (Northfield, Minnesota, 1981).

[15] Butts, *Cultural History of Western Education*, 473–511.

[16] Norlie, *Norwegian People in America*, 375.

by CLAIRE SELKURT

8   *The Domestic Architecture and Cabinetry of Luther Valley*

WHEN ONE visits Luther Valley, Wisconsin, today, it is not difficult to understand the attraction this area had for the earliest Norwegian settlers. The gently rolling hills, the clusters of woods, the dark earth, and the well-kept farm structures all reflect a successful farming community. The earliest settlers came from a dramatically different setting — the region of Numedal, which is marked by strong contrasts in topography. The Lågen River slashes deeply into that valley. Farms seem barely to cling to the sloping contours of the land. The brilliant green ground-covering is pierced by the jagged rocks that make up a good part of the barren soil. The fir trees and the wooden farm structures create striking silhouettes against the often leaden, mist-filled sky. One senses the tenacious will to survive that must have marked the day-to-day existence of these people. Emigration to the Wisconsin frontier brought with it a considerable change in their way of life. The purpose of this article is to recreate aspects of that life, based upon both extant and recorded evidence of the

247

material culture, the buildings and furniture of Luther Valley during the early period of settlement, as well as to show the persistence of certain Norwegian traditions.

By the late 1830s there were important reasons for the future founders of Luther Valley to consider leaving their homeland. The motivations were both religious and economic in nature. Gullik Gravdal, a Haugean and one of the founders of the settlement, addressed both of these issues in an interview many years later, saying that the great majority of those who emigrated from Numedal in 1839 belonged to the Haugeans. "We were not actually persecuted . . . but the 'readers' were the subject of much hostile gossip and we had to endure ridicule and scorn on the part of those who did not share our views. . . . [However] the hope of finding cheap, fertile land together with reports about good wages were definitely the determining factors for most of us."[1] For many of the famers in Numedal the effort to make a decent living had become a desperate struggle. Another early settler, Gullik Knudsen Springen, wrote: "Income from farming provided us with only the barest necessities." In return for farm labor "I could expect nothing but food and clothing. . . . When I began to think seriously of the future, the idea of emigrating occurred to me."[2] It was not surprising then that Ansten Nattestad, who returned to Numedal in the fall of 1838 from an exploratory journey that had taken him as far west as Chicago, found an eager and receptive audience. Gullik Gravdal reported that Ansten's return created about the same sensation a dead man might cause if he returned to tell of life beyond the grave.[3]

Early in June of 1839 the Nattestad party assembled in Drammen. There were approximately 140 people in the group, most of them from Rollaug and Veggli in northern Numedal. They set sail on June 12 on the *Emilie* and arrived in New York on August 26. The settlers took the usual route to the West, traveling up the Hudson River, then by way of the Erie Canal to Buffalo, and through the Great Lakes to Chicago. The majority of the group followed Ansten Nattestad to Jefferson Prairie, but two of them, Gullik Gravdal and Gisle S. Halland, were dissatisfied with the Jefferson Prairie site and settled in Rock Prairie, about seven miles west of the present city of Beloit, Wisconsin, founding the settlement of Luther Valley. In the softly rolling hills and valleys of the area they found the land they had been seeking. The settlement grew fairly rapidly. By the fall of 1840 five Norwegians had bought land in the area and the following fall another contingent of several families arrived directly from Norway. The decade of the 1840s was an active period of settlement in the area. Emigrants from other parts of Norway joined the original group which had come from Numedal, people from Hallingdal, Valdres, and Gudbrandsdalen. While most of the settlers continued to live in log houses, the first stone houses were built during this period. It was also an active period in the history of the Luther Valley congregation. In the summer of 1846 Claus L. Clausen was called to become resident pastor, and under his guidance the settlement entered a period of growth and progress. With Clausen as editor, two Norwegian language periodicals, *Norsk Luthersk Maanedstidende* and *Emigranten*, began publication in Luther Valley.[4]

While the decade of the 1850s was marked by a decrease in the influx of new settlers, it was a period of increasing stability and development for the original families. In 1854 a cholera epidemic swept through the settlement and the gravestones in the Luther Valley cemetery bear mute testimony to the degree of the devastation. In 1857 the railroad came to the neighboring village of Orfordville and in 1860 the first train of the Western Union line from Racine reached Beloit. This signified the opening of many markets previously inaccessible to the settlers. By the beginning of the Civil War Luther Valley had evolved into a thriving agricultural community.

The struggle for survival marked the earliest period of settlement in the new land. Although most of the Norwegian settlers were farmers, many aspects of life on the frontier struck them as crude and totally unlike their experience in Norway. One of the major adjustments to be faced was the need to construct log cabins hastily and the accompanying sense of insecurity and transcience. Expediency, motivated by economic constraints and the severe midwestern climate, encouraged inferior methods of construction. Every settler, however, cherished the dream of one day building a permanent dwelling. Tools were not readily available on the frontier and unfamiliar types of timber called for major technical adjustments. The tall straight trunk of the fir tree provided an excellent module for the timber structures of Norway; the often crooked trunks of American trees such as walnut, elm, and maple were more difficult to work with.

The furnishings of the earliest homes were primitive and usually built by family members. Olaus Fredrik Duus, a frontier pastor, described the furnishings of a typical home in his letters: "Along the wall on one side are some planks placed on log stumps, which serve as benches, while on the other side the bed, chests, and trunk all serve the same purpose . . . chairs are not to be found in this settlement, since the farmers have come here too recently to be able to buy things that they can do without or that they can provide in a cheaper way."[5] Many small utensils of wood and silver, as well as textiles, were brought along from Norway in large wooden trunks, but rarely any substantial pieces of furniture. Many of the farmers were skilled in various trades such as blacksmithing, cabinetry, and toolmaking. Since a great deal depended upon home industry, all members of the family were involved in producing necessary items. Virtually every woman was skilled at the spinning wheel and the loom. Timber construction and the various areas of woodworking were almost exclusively the domain of the men. As the settlements developed, local craftspeople had more time to devote to the making of furniture for themselves and their neighbors. It was not until later, when a relative degree of prosperity came to the settlers, that they could indulge in commercially-made fabrics and furnishings. Often this happened all too soon and many of the fine old handicraft traditions disappeared within decades. Factory-made products tended to be more highly regarded than handmade products; they served as symbols of the immigrant's economic progress as well as evidence of successful assimilation to the American way of life. Some of the more purely decorative areas of the craft tradition, such as *rosemaling* (rose-painting), never really gained a foothold during the early period. Necessity dictated that function be the essential criterion in the production of handmade objects.

Based upon both extant and recorded evidence gathered in Luther Valley, there were three major types of timber structures that characterized the early period of settlement. The most primitive was the log cabin, a structure built of round unhewn logs caulked with plant materials, mud, or in some cases limestone. The log cabin usually lacked windows and a chimney. A simple hole in the roof let out the smoke. Next was the log house, which was a more permanent, full two-storied structure built of hewn logs with interstices stopped with stones and plaster. The log house was much larger than the log cabin in plan and it often had plank floors, crude glass windows, and a staircase leading up into the second story. A third form found in the Luther Valley settlement was the timber storehouse or granary, which came in a variety of forms.

One might expect to find traditional details of form and construction preserved among the Norwegians not only because of the rich wood heritage of rural Norway, but also because of the tendency of the Norwegian peasants to be tradition-bound and consciously desirous of preserving their native culture in the new land. Based upon the evidence in Luther Valley, however, details and forms traditional to the Norwegian timber style were only occasionally employed. As will be shown, those forms which can be traced back to distinctly Norwegian sources are in most cases highly modified, mere shadows of the prototypes. It is understandable that during the initial period the settlers would have had to sacrifice more complex multipartite structures or details of craftsmanship such as refined joining and fitting of the logs. However, no attempt was made to develop a more refined timber style when the time and means eventually allowed it. In Luther Valley an original log building was in some cases retained and incorporated into an enlarged structure with its original identity concealed beneath siding or a limestone facing. The Norwegians in fact rejected their native tradition in favor of one brought primarily by Yankee settlers from New England, that of the stone house. It was a logical choice. The Luther Valley area abounded in rich limestone deposits and the masonry tradition was already firmly established in the area.

The first timber structure to be considered will be the log house of Knudt Crispenus Fossebrekke. Knudt Fossebrekke was a farmer, a native of Numedal. He was one of the original members of the *Emilie* expedition of

1839 and worked for two years as a farm laborer in the area around Rockford, Illinois, in order to earn sufficient funds to buy land. He purchased the land the first year, and the log house was built the second summer by a family promised shelter in exchange for their labor. According to Fossebrekke's son Nels Crispensen, the wife of the builder dug the cellar in the summer, carrying all the dirt and stones out in her apron. In the spring of the third year Fossebrekke began farming and five years after his arrival he took Gertrude Vigere from Ringerike as his bride. Three children were born to them. Nels Crispensen recalled life in the log house, "This old house used to house as many as seventeen persons in the first winters. . . . I can well remember when as kids we slept in an old homemade bed under a fur robe and in the winter mornings we often awoke under a pile of snow that had drifted through the chinks."[6]

The Fossebrekke structure is a log house constructed of oak with two full stories, planked floors both upstairs and down, three windows, one original door opening in the south, and a chimney in the west end. The house measures sixteen and one-half by seventeen feet with a ceiling height in the first story of seven feet. The logs were joined in a crude form of dovetailing, and the fitting of the logs reflects rather hasty construction. Spaces between the square-hewn logs are large, and considerable chinking has been done with mortar and limestone chips. Reflecting traditional Norwegian construction, the purlins and ridgepole project through the gable-end walls of the structure. Inside there is a steep, ladderlike, enclosed staircase which leads through a trapdoor into the second story. The second story is illuminated by one window in the east wall. An interesting detail is a hinged section of log that was used for viewing out the windowless west end of the building. Two leather

Claire Selkurt

hinges attach the section of log to the timber above and a wood peg fits into a hole in the timber below to secure it tightly. A review of some of the pieces auctioned off at the family estate sale in the late 1960s gives some indication of how the house was furnished during the early period.[7] A spinning wheel, candlemakers, two trunks — one rose-painted and one lightly ornamented on the lid with acanthus carving — punched tin lanterns, several spindle-backed chairs, three clocks, and a double-doored cupboard were all included in the estate. The cupboard, located by the author in a local collection, is a monumental piece, approximately seven and a half feet tall and crowned with a heavy cornice and distinctively Norwegian crest.

In contrast to the fully developed log house of Knudt Fossebrekke, the Gulbert Gulbertson structure is a classic example of the log cabin (Figure 1). It originally stood on land purchased from the government in January, 1848.[8] The loosely-constructed cabin has an earth floor and a loft that can be entered through a trapdoor in the ceiling. In plan it measures ten feet, six inches, by fifteen feet, eight inches, with a ceiling height close to seven feet. There were only two window openings, one centered in the north wall, the other next to the door in the south wall. Although very unrefined in construction, the joining of the logs, a rough saddle-cup with a slight overhang, reflects the Norwegian influence.[9] The spaces between the logs are filled with mortar and limestone chinking. A mere shadow of the rich timber style of Norway, this structure, more than the Fossebrekke house, is marked by the expediency of frontier life.

One of the most remarkable finds in the Luther Valley settlement is an unimposing little structure on the original Nils Olsen Weglie farmstead of 1841. Measuring only twelve feet square in plan, it has windows in the

254

Figure 1. The Gulbert Gulbertson log cabin.

east and west walls and a door in the north gable end. The logs are square-hewn with crude dovetailed joining. The interior consists of one room with a ceiling height of seven feet, five inches, featuring a distinctively Norwegian corner fireplace or *peis* in the southwest corner. The fireplace is constructed of plastered stone with a curving profile to the bottom edge of the hood, a primitive but obvious adaptation of the original Norwegian form. A quarter-turn staircase in the southeast corner leads up to a low loft. 'Spacers,' inserted into notches between the logs around the door and window openings, add resiliency to the structure by allowing for fluctuation in the size of the openings. This structure may have been the earliest dwelling on the farmstead or it may have functioned as a *bryggerhus*, a small, free-standing structure which served a number of domestic uses, such as laundry and baking.

The *stabbur*, or elevated storehouse, is traditionally the pride of the Norwegian farmstead. It is usually a

255

two-storied structure on stilt-like supports, with an overhanging second story accessible by a ladder through an opening in the outer wall or in the floor of the overhanging portion. The often lavish carving on the building reflects the importance of the structure and the relative wealth of the owner. On the Wisconsin frontier the elevated storehouse lost its more symbolic connotations and served a purely functional role. The author was able to locate evidence of two of these elevated storehouses or granaries in the Luther Valley area. The Anders Michaelson granary was located on land purchased from the government in 1843.[10] Only photographic evidence remains of this structure, which was torn down in the 1950s. It was a large bipartite log structure with an interior dividing wall that had only a window to connect the two rooms. A ramp led up to a platform that ran in front of the doors. The structure was two-storied and rested on pyramidal wooden stilts in much the same fashion as the Norwegian *stabbur*.[11]

Another local variation on the *stabbur* type is to be found on land purchased by Ole Erickson in December, 1853. The land was first owned by a Yankee settler named Jim Keep and apparently the earliest log structures were built by him.[12] The Erickson granary was obviously built of a composite of timbers from earlier dismantled structures. The laying of the logs is highly irregular, with extraneous notches throughout the structure. Joining techniques vary, with dovetailing in one corner and more of a saddle-cup form in another. While the stilts of the Michaelson granary were wood, those supporting the Erickson structure are limestone.

When time and economy allowed for the building of a more commodious and permanent dwelling in masonry or frame construction, the original log dwelling was usually relegated to the role of granary or storage shed.

Figure 2. The Paul Skavlem house, built in 1841.

In most cases it was sided over to protect the logs from the elements. In some cases, however, the original log structure was simply added onto to become part of an enlarged structure. The addition was most commonly of limestone, thereby combining the two most readily available building materials in the area. It was a logical and economical solution and an excellent example of the flexibility and organic development of a true vernacular form.

One structure will be discussed as an example of this combined form, the Paul Skavlem house erected around 1841 (Figure 2). Paul Skavlem is one of the more colorful figures in the folklore of Luther Valley. He was known for his outspoken views on community issues, his skills as a cabin builder and cabinetmaker, and his excellent home brew.[13] Skavlem left Rollaug parish in Numedal with his wife Gunhild Pedersdatter Brekke and their two children in 1841. On September 15, 1841, in partnership with Nils O. Weglie, he purchased land in Plymouth township. His earliest dwelling structure

257

was a log house solidly built of square-hewn timbers with dovetailed corners. Skavlem's legendary skill with the ax was apparent in the close fit of the timbers, contrasting strongly with other such buildings in the area.

On the interior the logs were originally exposed and whitewashed. Later the interior walls were completely paneled. The two-storied house is exceptionally large: twenty feet by twenty-four feet in plan with a ceiling height just under seven feet. These proportions give the main room the broad, low-ceilinged feeling of the traditional Norwegian *stue* or dwelling room. Continuing the Norwegian tradition, this dwelling room served various functions as a social, sleeping, and eating area. There are three windows in the main room, and in the northeast corner of the room a quarter-turn staircase leads upstairs to a large undivided room that served as a sleeping area. The only source of light or ventilation in the second story is a small window opening in the south gable end. The log portion was probably faced with fieldstone at a relatively early date. The roof was finished with a simple box cornice. The stone kitchen addition was probably built at a later date. In Paul Skavlem's home, probably more than in any other home in the area, the Norwegian traditions were kept alive. Besides building his house, he completely furnished it with beds, benches, stools, tables, built-in cupboards, and the typically Norwegian *kubbestol* or chair hewn from a single log. He also produced smaller wooden utensils: ladles, spoons, and finely turned ale bowls. To fill these fine bowls Skavlem also produced large coopered barrels for the production of his ale.[14]

As the economic situation improved, the interest of the settlers turned toward building larger, more permanent homes. Typically they drew upon the most readily available materials, and southern Wisconsin proved to be a rich repository of limestone and sandstone. A yellowish limestone was the favored building material in the Luther Valley area. Stone construction was common in the Beloit area between 1840 and 1860. In 1857 there were forty-one stonemasons reported as active in the area. Most of the masons came from the East. The masonry work typical of the Luther Valley area can be classified as regular ashlar, which is characterized by a coursing of the stone in even rows with evenly staggered vertical joints and with quoins created by laying the stones so that their faces are alternately large and small. The ashlar facing is backed by an inner structural wall of fieldstone. Most of the stone used in Luther Valley was taken from quarries on individual farms, with the work directed by the farmer himself. There is a definite similarity in style and structure among the stone buildings of Luther Valley. The prevailing Greek Revival style of the period is reflected in these structures not so much in specific detailing as in symmetry of form and careful consideration of proportion. Two classic examples of the Luther Valley stone house type will be discussed. The first has particular historical significance as the home of pastor Claus L. Clausen.

Clausen, a native of Denmark, moved to Norway when he was in his twenties. In Christiania in 1841 he was introduced to the doctrines of the pietistic reformer Hans Nielsen Hauge. After studying theology for a period in Copenhagen he left in the spring of 1843 to assist Søren Bache in the Muskego settlement. He was active in Muskego until 1845, when he was called to Luther Valley to take over the pastorate on July 31 of that year.[15] In order to build the parsonage Clausen was granted an interest-free loan of $100 from the congregation. He used this amount to buy an eighty-acre tract of land in Newark township and secure a loan for construction. By the fall of 1846 the parsonage was completed and Clausen moved into it with his wife Martha. It was the first stone parsonage built by Norwegians in Rock county and it served a variety of functions for the young congregation. The upper story served to accommodate worship services until the actual church was dedicated in the fall of 1847. The first confirmation was held in the large upper room on November 22, 1846.[16] Records of the Luther Valley congregation imply that Clausen was actively involved in the construction of the house. This may have been the case; however, since there is no indication that he had any experience as a stonemason, it can be assumed that another individual was in charge of the undertaking. Very likely this individual was Engebret Thorson, the mason who directed the construction of the first church the following year.

The Clausen parsonage is a classic example of the Luther Valley stone house type which reflects the influence of the Greek Revival style. The floor plan and placement of the windows is perfectly symmetrical, with a central hall containing a staircase and entrances at both ends of the hall. The question arises as to whether some prototype for this spatial arrangement can be found in the timber structures of Numedal. From floor plans of buildings in the parishes of Lyngdal, Veggli, and Nore the pattern of a symmetrical plan with a central hall, entrances at both ends, and a staircase within the hall appears to be quite common. The original south entrance to the Clausen parsonage is a handsome double door with a five-window transom above. Evidence indicates that there were originally three chimneys, one centrally located and one in each gable-end wall. The roof is characterized by a heavy Greek Revival molding and returning gable-end cornices. The first story of the house was originally divided into three

Figure 3. The Gullik Knudsen Springen stone house, built in 1850.

rooms. The large undivided room to the west of the hall probably always served as a kitchen. Kitchens in these houses usually functioned as multi-purpose areas for food preparation, eating, bathing, and informal socializing. The area to the east of the hallway contained two smaller rooms, probably originally a formal parlor with adjacent bedroom or study. The second story, which presumably served as a bedroom area, was divided into three rooms. In terms of interior detailing, the ceilings were originally entirely wainscoted and the walls were wainscoted up to the level of the chair-rail. The stairs leading to the second floor are extremely steep and set in against an angled backboard in a ladder-like fashion. The stair rail terminates in an elegantly turned banister post.

The finest example of the Luther Valley stone house is the Gullik Knudsen Springen house, constructed in 1850 (Figure 3). Springen had been a member of the Nattestad party of 1839. After working for a period in

261

Chicago he and his wife Margit Oldsdatter Bratt decided to buy land in Rock Prairie in 1841. Ten children were born to the Springens between the years of 1841 and 1861. The family lived in a one-room cabin with loft until 1850 when the stone house was completed.[17] A photograph presumably taken in the middle or late 1860s shows that at that time there was a long colonnaded porch projecting from the west end of the structure. The building originally had two gable-end chimneys and shutters on some of the windows. To the left of the house there was a summer kitchen constructed at a later date. Both the main house and the kitchen addition have well proportioned roofs with typical Greek Revival moldings. The main door is flanked by sidelights. Like the Clausen parsonage, the Springen house is divided by a central hallway with a staircase leading up to the second story. Recent renovations have revealed that the wood employed in the beams and studs throughout the house was oak. Originally there were four rooms on the first floor, with the summer kitchen to the northeast, and four rooms in the second story. Since the Springen family was exceptionally large, a number of the rooms were no doubt used for bedrooms. The room in the southeast corner of the first story would have logically served as a parlor while the roomy summer kitchen probably served as a family gathering place. A stone fireplace in the summer kitchen was used for heating and cooking. The ceilings of the Springen house were originally wainscoted as were the walls of the original enclosed staircase. The banisters of the staircase in the form of flat columns and the incised sunburst motif on the front door reflect the Greek Revival heritage of the building. The Springens often accommodated newcomers to the settlement, a kindness that had tragic repercussions in 1854 when they welcomed a group of immigrants fresh off shipboard who brought cholera with

them. The settlement was stricken with the worst epidemic in its history and the Springen household was
devastated. Gullik Springen later recalled, "One can
well understand the conditions when eighteen corpses
were carried from our home that summer, my parents
and one brother included."[18]

The tradition of the farmer-craftsman in Norway is as
old as the culture itself. The severe isolation of most of
Norway's valleys was not penetrated until the modern
period of mass communication and improved roadways.
Even today many of the areas remain relatively inaccessible. The farmers therefore had to be capable of producing their own farm implements as well as the furnishings for their homes. As was the case in Norway, in
the American settlements certain farmers were skilled
in a particular craft such as cabinetry or clockmaking and
would do work for other members of the community.
Numedal was a particularly remote district, and during
the period when the Luther Valley settlers still lived
there the only link to the outside was the footpath over
the high mountains that circumscribed the valley. The
stylistic traditions of the Middle Ages lingered for many
centuries in the area. During the Rococo period of the
eighteenth century, Numedal came increasingly under
the influence of the city of Kongsberg and the high Rococo style gradually filtered down to the rural level. The
Rococo led to excesses in furniture design in the area.
Structure became hidden beneath an abundance of nat-
uralistic woodcarving and applied moldings. The Empire style, a neoclassical direction which gained a strong
foothold in Scandinavia in the first decade of the nineteenth century, introduced a new clarification and simplicity of form. Since the city of Kongsberg received all
the latest emanations from the Continent, Numedal
craftwork passed quickly into the Empire style along

with the rest of Europe.[19] The Empire style was the predominant influence that the craftsmen of Luther Valley brought with them. They remained faithful to a clean-lined functionalism and in ornament restricted themselves to only the most pristine classical detailing.

The cabinetmaking of Paul Skavlem has already been mentioned. Like many Norwegian farmers of the period he was an adept craftsman, skilled as axman, carpenter, turner, and rose-painter. The only surviving evidence of his skill with the ax is the log house that has been discussed. Two examples of cabinetry that can be unquestionably attributed to Skavlem are a large cupboard with open shelves above and closed shelves below and a tall closed cupboard, both of which were found in his house. The former piece, constructed of walnut as was most of the furniture in Luther Valley, has an upper section containing open shelving and staggered tiers of small drawers, two on either side of the lower shelves (Figure 4). The piece is marked by the influence of the Empire in its simplicity of line, angularity, and refined classical details. The piece terminates in a heavy cornice ornamented with dentils. A small fluted column decorates the corners of both the upper and lower portions. The prototype for this form is the *framskap* or dish cupboard which was used by the woman of the house for the display and storage of her tableware. The other piece found in the Skavlem house is a simple, tall, double-doored cupboard with shelving. A diamond shaped opening is located in the center of both upper panels.

An additional piece which can also reasonably be attributed to Paul Skavlem is a corner cupboard that belonged to a descendant of Nils Weglie, a close friend of Skavlem. The corner cupboard or *roskap* was exclusively for the use of the man of the house. Originally it hung in the corner above the high seat, but after chairs

were introduced it evolved into a full standing structure. The Weglie cupboard is marked by clear, classical
lines. The center part of each door is beveled to form a
central ridge. An arch crowns the cornice and the piece
stands on bracket feet. The lower section is broader and
deeper than the upper section. One ale bowl has remained in the hands of a Skavlem descendant and is re-
putedly an example of Paul Skavlem's skill as a turner.
The bowl is turned in a form dating back to the Renais-
sance in Norway with a tapered rim accentuated by flut-
ing. No trace remains of any original *rosemaling*, and in
fact no pieces remain to give evidence of Skavlem's skill
as a painter. However, two firsthand sources support
the fact that the beams and ceiling of the Skavlem log
house were at one time completely rose-painted.[20]
Skavlem also made smaller objects such as wooden
spoons and kitchen utenstils for his own family and his
neighbors. A straightforward functionalism and simplicity of line typify the furniture of Paul Skavlem. His
work does not represent a unique design concept, but
rather is the work of a reasonably skilled rural craftsman
who sought to recreate a home environment reminiscent of Norway on the Wisconsin frontier. Paul Skavlem died in Luther Valley on January 10, 1866.

Gullik Olson Gravdal was one of the earliest settlers
in Luther Valley, arriving in 1839 and residing in the
area until his death in 1873. Gravdal was born in Veggli
parish, Numedal, in 1802. He had a considerable reputation in the community for his cabinetry and as a side-
line he enjoyed making toys for the children in the family. In his later years he spent many hours creating
miniature wheelbarrows, doll beds, and buggies.[21]
Five remaining pieces have been documented as his
work, including two identical walnut secretaries and
three walnut bureaus. One of the walnut secretaries,
which until recent years remained in the possession of

265

Figure 4. Cupboard made by Paul Skavlem.

Figure 5. Walnut secretary made by Gullik Olson Gravdal.

the Gravdal family, is a monumental piece standing close to eight feet in height (Figure 5). It shares certain stylistic traits with Skavlem's cupboards: a heavy cornice ornamented with dentils, an imposing massiveness and angularity of form, beveled corners suggesting the same effect as the corner columns on the Skavlem pieces, and a similar arrangement of small drawers. The upper bookcase section containing four shelves is enclosed behind glass doors. It rests on a desk section with an upper portion that is hidden behind a drop-front panel. The desk section contains pigeonholes flanked by two pairs of small drawers. Although neither of the secretaries is dated, it is reasonable to assume because of their size and complexity that they were not executed

266

until after the building of the Gravdal stone house in 1849, when Gravdal moved into a better-equipped workroom. The handsomest of the Gravdal bureaus is in the collection of Alice Thiss of Minneapolis, a great-granddaughter of Gullik Gravdal. The walnut piece measures forty-six inches in height. It rests on short turned legs, contains five drawers, and is ornamented with a scroll backboard. While the piece is less sophisticated in style than the secretary, the refinement of structural details is notable, particularly the brass keyholes and the very fine dovetailing. Like Paul Skavlem, Gravdal was a fine country craftsman. Although his work reflects the reigning Empire style of the period in its massiveness and clarity of line, there is an underlying functionalism that binds his work to the Norwegian immigrant furniture tradition.

Halvor Nilsson Aae, born September 15, 1781, in Nore parish in Numedal, came to the Luther Valley settlement in 1842 and died there in 1856. He was trained in Norway as a silversmith and clockmaker, designing not only the workings but the cabinets as well. His daughter Groe Skavlem left this account of her father shortly before his decision to leave for America: "Those never-to-be-forgotten evenings when, the day's work finished, mother and I would draw our wheels before the fireplace and by the light of the blazing logs sit spinning far into the night. At a short distance from us, surrounded by a confused assortment of tools, sat father. A host of tiny candles burned blinkingly all about him, throwing stray gleams upon the spoons with filigree handles, the quaint brooches and other articles of dainty filigree, which he fashioned with such delicate skill. As we worked he talked of America and conjectured as to the fate of our many friends who had gone to make for themselves on its vast, unsettled prairies new homes and greater fortunes."[22] Aae's silverwork is repre-

267

sented by a number of spoons in the possession of several Luther Valley families. In constructing the spoons, the silver is beaten very thin. The bowl of the typical Aae spoon is relatively shallow and tapers at the point, continuing into a narrow neck which broadens out into a flat handle that is oval in form and tapered at the end. The ornamentation on the spoons consists of delicately incised floral motifs and zig-zag borders along the edge of the handles.

Aae was also a clockmaker by trade and, according to Groe Skavlem, in 1845 he perfected the first clock made in Wisconsin. One clock cabinet attributed to Aae was found in the Beloit area. Unfortunately it no longer contains the workings. Stylistically the clock relates to the classicism typical of other early Luther Valley pieces and appears to be a somewhat naive interpretation of a Norwegian prototype. The proportions are tall and narrow and a simple profiled molding crowns the piece. While one could assume that his production of timepieces remained limited, many Luther Valley families probably acquired examples of his silverwork. There is no evidence of larger hollowware forms from Aae's hand; presumably his work was confined to smaller utensils and jewelry.

While most of the cabinetry produced in the Luther Valley settlement reflects the influence of the Empire, nowhere is this spirit more clearly expressed than in the furnishings of the West Luther Valley church. The West church, built in 1871, houses the pews, rails, altar, lectern, and pulpit designed for the first East Luther Valley church, a stone building constructed in 1847. Although there is no documentary evidence, according to church tradition the interior appointments of the first East church were designed and crafted by Claus L. Clausen himself. It does not seem likely that all the pieces are from his hand. Clausen was much too busy to have actively participated in the crafting of the furnishings. Two craftsmen who probably were involved are Peder Helgeson, who was in charge of the carpentry in the church, and the stonemason Engebret Thorson, who directed the building of the church.[23] It is very possible, however, that Clausen designed the pieces and directed their production. He had studied in both Christiania and Copenhagen in the early 1840s and would have come into direct contact with the Empire style that had reached its full fruition in the two capital cities during the first decades of the nineteenth century. Perhaps it was the glittering interior of C. F. Hansen's Christiansborg Chapel in Copenhagen that left a lasting impression on the young pastor.

The first East church was dedicated in the fall of 1847. An early photograph shows a tall narrow building with three windows on either side, two windows and a door in the front, a central steeple, and crow-step gables, very likely a tribute by Clausen to the rural churches of Denmark. Inside, a gallery in the back of the room rested upon oak pillars, painted to resemble blue-veined marble. As the furnishings exist today, dark brown railings and gold detailing accentuate the whiteness of the altar, pulpit, and columns of the altar rail and *"klokker's* pen" in a true Empire manner (Figure 6). The altar culminates in an arched top borne upon a pair of columns and segments of entablature. The arch is ornamented with three pointed finials. Two lancet arches framed in gold leaf and bearing stenciled crosses flank a high relief of the baptism of Christ surmounted by Gothic tracery. The base of the altarpiece is inscribed with the words, "Gaaer hen og lærer folk og döber dem!" (Go ye therefore and teach all nations and baptize them. Matthew 28:19). Triangular areas are set off by railings to the right and left of the altar. These areas, referred to as "pens," were used to seat the *klokker*, an unordained

269

*Figure 6. The altar and altar rail from the first
East Luther Valley church, dedicated in 1847.*

aide to the minister, and the *forsanger*, whose duty it
was to lead the congregation in singing. The baptismal
font to the left of the altar consists of a column decorated
with gold leaf rings and resting on a dark brown plinth
base. The pulpit, constructed of six molded panels, has
a dark brown railing and gold leaf borders finishing off
the panels. The pews, severe in their simplicity, complete the church furnishings. The question of Clausen's
role in the design of the East Luther Valley church furnishings will remain open for debate; however, evidence indicates that he was involved in their basic de-

sign. In any case the furnishings of the church constitute an important chapter in the history of the Luther Valley cabinetry tradition.

This study of the Luther Valley settlement demonstrates that although the settlers brought with them the skills and knowledge to continue a Norwegian tradition in building with wood they chose other alternatives. In their timber structures they retained some of the details of the Norwegian style; however, in overall form and craftsmanship the structures were influenced by the exigencies of the frontier. The eventual adoption of stone building by the Luther Valley settlers represented in most respects a rejection of their native tradition in form and material. Beginning with the more established period of the late 1840s and 1850s, the farmer-craftsmen had more time to devote to the making of furniture. From the abundant walnut in the area they created pieces of cabinetry along simple, functional lines marked by the influence of the Empire style that was predominant in Scandinavia at the time of their departure. This restrained and simplified classicism also marks the elegant furnishings of the first Luther Valley church.

NOTES

[1] C. A. Clausen, ed. and trans., A *Chronicler of Immigrant Life: Svein Nilsson's Articles in* Billed-Magazin (Northfield, Minnesota, 1982), 69.

[2] Clausen, *Chronicler of Immigrant Life*, 71.

[3] Clausen, *Chronicler of Immigrant Life*, 68.

[4] H. Fred Swanson, *The Founder of St. Ansgar, the Life Story of Claus Laurits Clausen* (Blair, Nebraska, 1949), 3.

[5] Theodore C. Blegen, ed., *Frontier Parsonage: The Letters of Olaus Fredrik Duus, Norwegian Pastor in Wisconsin, 1855–1858* (Northfield, Minnesota, 1947), 54.

[6] *Beloit Gazette*, August 19, 1939.

[7] Letter to the author from Ed Mortenson, July 24, 1973.

[8] Rock county Deed Records.

[9] The saddle-cup technique is described in detail in Kate Stafford and Harald Naess, eds., *On Both Sides of the Ocean: A Part of Per Hagen's Journey* (Northfield, Minnesota, 1984), 40–41.

Claire Selkurt

[10] Rock county Deed Records.

[11] Interview with Knut Haugen, July 15, 1973.

[12] Rock county Deed Records.

[13] Halvor L. Skavlem, *The Skavlem and Odegaarden Families* (Beloit, Wisconsin, 1915), 82.

[14] Skavlem, *Skavlem and Odegaarden Families*, 82–83.

[15] Swanson, *Founder of St. Ansgar*, 66.

[16] Swanson, *Founder of St. Ansgar*, 69.

[17] Springen family scrapbook and record.

[18] *The Luther Valley Centennial*, 44.

[19] Janice Stewart, *The Folk Arts of Norway* (Madison, 1953), 76–77.

[20] Interview with Vera Gilbertson, September 3, 1972.

[21] *The Luther Valley Centennial*, 21.

[22] Hannah Skavlem, "Account of Early Settlement Days by Groe Skavlem," in *History of Rock County* (Chicago, 1908), 442–445.

[23] Hjalmar Rued Holand, *De norske settlementers historie* (Ephraim, Wisconsin, 1908), 137.

by LARRY EMIL SCOTT

9 *The Poetry of Agnes Mathilde Wergeland*

THE CAREER of Agnes Mathilde Wergeland, doctor of philosophy, once provided the source for a small flood of assorted commentary. To some, like Maren Michelet, Wergeland was a heroine of our philistine age, her years as professor of French, Spanish, and history at the University of Wyoming finally providing adequate recompense for many years of undeserved hardship.[1] To the feminist critic Gina Krog, Agnes Wergeland was the undaunted champion of women's rights, struggling, ultimately with success, to earn her rightful place in the overwhelmingly masculine academic world.[2] Still others, Katharine Merrill[3] for instance, tend to find a strange combination of radical mind and conservative, introverted temperament in her, a combination which made it almost physically impossible for her to "sell" herself or even to present her accomplishments in the best possible light.[4]

It is not the purpose here to treat Wergeland's more public career as a champion of woman suffrage, first in her native Norway and then in America. Rather, the intent is to examine the inner life of the woman who was among the finest poets to write in Norwegian in

273

America. Her verse has a depth of feeling, range of content, and technical virtuosity that few of her fellow countrymen matched. Her two substantial volumes — *Amerika og andre digte* (America and Other Poems) in 1912[5] and the posthumously published *Efterladte digte* (Posthumous Poems)[6] — are among the gems of Scandinavian-American literature, ranking with the finest of Rølvaag's prose in skill and sophistication. Yet Wergeland the poet has attracted virtually no attention from either Norwegian scholars or American, since, as an immigrant writer who remained faithful to her native tongue for her verse, she belongs to neither literary tradition. Even more unfairly, some of Wergeland's most interesting poetry, for example "Pilgrimen" (The Pilgrim), has been cited to demonstrate her Lutheran orthodoxy as a poet, a position which this study will attempt to modify. Furthermore, Wergeland's poetry provides valuable clues to the conflicting faces she presented to the world and goes a long way toward resolving some of the thornier problems in interpretation of what it was, exactly, that she hoped to accomplish in her public life and how well she ultimately succeeded in that quest.

While she was obviously proud to be a Wergeland, the name haunted Agnes all her life, both in Norway and in America. Her father was a poor and unsuccessful cousin of the visionary poet Henrik Wergeland and his daughter, the pioneer feminist, Camilla Collett. Young Agnes knew that hers was hardly the illustrious branch of the family. Despite the great successes of her famous relatives, Agnes Wergeland felt that hers was a star-crossed family: "A Wergeland was never especially respected in Norway, and I am as 'contemptible' as all the others; . . . [I too] follow the star that characterizes them!"[7] The sense of exile weighed heavily on her; her sentimental yearnings for Norway thus take on darker dimensions. Her native land had no room for her and rejected her with finality. Her enormous capacity for love at the ideal level of patriotism was thus thwarted or, rather, unrequited. So, just as her desire for intimacy and warm human intercourse was denied her on the social level, she seemed to feel that her family name made her a kind of political pariah. The way out thus had to be an interior one. What she did realize and practiced all her life may well have been inspired by her brilliant ancestors. First of all, from Camilla Collett she got her stubborn drive to overcome any barriers that her sex might cause to be raised against her. Secondarily, from Collett also derived the corollary, almost automatic membership in the active ranks of women fighting for their rights in the larger "kvindesaken" (women's movement).

But Henrik Wergeland — mystic and poet, activist and politician, reformer and public speaker — perhaps influenced her toward the interior, the spiritual, away from the vigor and tumult of radicalism.[8] She had a visionary sense of what it meant to be a poet. With this call to poetry also came her strong tendency toward melancholia. In a notebook from the end of her stay in Munich (May and June, 1885) she sets forth a startling aesthetic credo: "Poetry is an *art*, lifted above the suffering of life and, in the truest sense, freed from it.

"The basic feature of my feeling for life and human beings is *absolute hopelessness*. There is no such thing as true happiness, only a longing for it and afterwards an utter resignation and eventual peace in death. . . . I confess to need, to stillness, to yearning, and only in poetry can I say what I feel, only in art, what I think."[9]

It is clear from her diary, self-effacingly entitled "From the Papers of a Dead Painter," that she began to write poetry seriously at this time, that is, in 1885. The problem of form plagued her from the beginning; her poetry had to be as finely crafted as her cameo-like sketches: "Consciously my ear seeks the most exquisite word, the perfect transition, the simplest and at the same time most expressive way, so that my feelings and my delicate senses can be satisfied." [10]

Poetry was, then, a deadly serious account-taking for Agnes Wergeland. The search for perfect form, for perfect beauty, was as essential as food or sleep. It was her only way of allowing her tumultuous inner self the release it so desperately needed and could not find in the daily human intercourse which she found almost impossible. Poetry became, for her, a psychological safety valve that may quite well have kept her sane, especially after her nervous breakdown in 1909. The Norwegian language was her secret ally in her poetry: ". . . a verse reproduces the inner life. I know this, I feel it, sense that it is true, that it becomes an expression of my innermost feelings; for how little would ample income, even wealth, benefit me if this language, my native tongue, could not represent for me what lives in my heart, if I could not feel myself comforted by the greeting of a fellow-countryman or by a sentence in a well-loved book? . . . I get new strength from it [Norwegian], new energy just as a plant does from the earth, while that which is foreign, alien, only touches me painfully with its noise and vain show." [11]

In an article she wrote on Henrik Wergeland (reprinted in *Leaders of Norway*), Agnes emphasized that her cousin's position as champion of an "ultra-Norwegian" culture was the correct one and that Johan S. Welhaven's pro-Danish, continental approach was quite wrong. Yet she was also aware of the danger of imprisoning poetic work in a minor language, a fate which certainly overtook Henrik Wergeland's enormous but, outside Norway, little known output of verse. Still, this was a risk she was willing to run because of the therapeutic effect poetry had for her. The other side of Henrik Wergeland, however — political activism — filled her with misgivings. She was keenly aware that he had burned himself out by the age of thirty-seven by his strenuous political efforts to establish libraries, to alleviate widespread poverty, and to rally the workers and peasants behind his Norwegian party program. Camilla Collett, too, had faced bitter denunciation over *Amtmandens døttre* (The Governor's Daughters). Many lonely years of unofficial ostracism were a price Collett paid for her outspoken denunciation of the oppressive civil-service system then in effect, especially its narrow-minded view of women.

If the sacrifices for Norwegian poetry were to be great, those required to take an active role in the liberation movements of the age would be even greater. Agnes Wergeland admitted to her diaries that hers was, and ever would remain, an extraordinarily introverted personality: "Friendship and living together with a friend are the most comprehensive of all personal relationships and carry with them the greatest pleasure and, if attained, the greatest restraint and discipline. Friendship is, according to my point of view, a cohabitation of souls — and as a result I have not a single friend, only some who seek and some who have been rejected — therefore I see that for both the present and the future this position will remain vacant." [12]

Her deep loneliness was, in fact, alleviated all her life by strong friendships, first with the Maurer family in Munich, then with Sara Bull and Katharine Merrill at Bryn Mawr and in Boston, with Dr. Benjamin Terry in Chicago, and ultimately and most intensely with Grace Raymond Hebard in Wyoming. In addition, she corresponded warmly all her life with such leaders of the Norwegian feminist movement as Camilla Collett, Fredrikke Marie Qvam, Gina Krog, and especially the

277

movement's spiritual leader, Aasta Hansteen.[13] Yet even these well-intentioned and obviously loving friends were not enough to eliminate the inner loneliness. From the moment she began to be recognized as a symbol of the women's movement because she was Norway's first woman doctor of philosophy, her life took on secondary symbolic functions which Hansteen and others were quick to exploit. Wergeland dutifully contributed various articles, for example "Hvorfor folk utvandrer" (Why People Emigrate), for Krog's *Nylænde* and "Hvad maa der gjøres for ungdommen?" (What Can be Done for Youth?) in *For Kirke og Kultur*, but, as Grace Hebard perceived, "Dr. Wergeland had never had a realistic conception of what absolute suffrage for women meant until she came to Wyoming, where women are not restricted in their right to vote in any way."[14] Wergeland felt deeply that she was not one of the soldiers at the front, like her activist friends in Norway, but she could still hope "that I have striven to break a path with my own still and quiet deeds." The answer for women, she said characteristically, was "to learn discipline, not from another person, but from an idea, and to learn to withstand longing and privation, to bear burdens for the sake of that distant future in which no one of us will ever participate . . . I demand especially much of the women. They must improve themselves, from early to late, from beginning to end, constantly. Only there lies understanding of what it is all about."[15] In a poem entitled "Ignis Fatuus," Wergeland attacks the divisive bitterness caused by politics.

> O tidens daarskap, politik
>   naar hændte det, Du træske ild,
> at Du fik makt, at Du blev til,
>   forstyrred os med luens spil,
> forbrændte vore sjæle?

O hvem kan fatte deres ve?
  De, stakkar, var kun skibbrudne
som kjendte ei dens vælde
  men drak dens vin i vildelse —
  men her ingen fælde
  og her ingen hildelse —
thi magtbegjæret brænder op,
  Dig, arme folk, til sjæl og krop![16]

Translation:

Oh politics, madness of our times,
  when did it occur, you cunning fire,
that you gained power, that you were created?
  when did it happen that you deranged us
  with your play of dancing flames,
those which burned our souls?

Oh, who can fathom your woe, oh people?
  You unfortunates were only castaways
who knew not its majesty [of politics]
  but rather drank its wine in wild abandon
but here no one conquers
  and here there is no illusion —
for the desire for power burns you up,
  Oh people, body and soul!

Political solutions thus lead to the betrayal of the people while art is, at least for the individual, a means of rising above such losses and disappointments. Moreover, art functions as a kind of irresistible energy which renews and resurrects. In "Akvareller" (Watercolors), Wergeland relates her youthful attempts at painting watercolors, which she had to give up because "Jeg havde ikke tid, og der var ingen penge: / Jeg maatte tjene først mit brød." (I had no time and there was no money: / I had first to earn my bread). This conflict, between art and need, is perhaps even more essential to an understanding of Wergeland and her work than those

279

between interior and exterior or art and politics. Feeling the mystical bent of her Wergeland blood, she was unable to indulge it; she had to shut her art and heart away to earn a living:

> Jeg elsked lys og fine farver —
> det er nok noget ifra farfars far vi arver —
> og haded støv og tøv og dovendyr og drog:
> Jeg maatte ind i møllen, blive pædagog.[17]

Translation:

> I loved light and bright colors —
> It's probably something we inherit from great-grandfather —
> and I hated dirt, and foolishness, and slothful types, and idlers:
> I had to jump on the treadmill and become a pedagogue.[18]

But "Akvareller" is more than merely clever; it is a painfully honest recognition of the cruelties and inequities of the world. Wergeland's aesthetic yearnings — her attempts "at jeg maatte faa lidt fri" (to free myself somewhat) — had to be subservient to her public figure as a scholar, one who "tog sundhedsbad i lærebøgers isblaa væld!" (took health baths in the ice-blue majesty of textbooks!)[19] In fact, she felt that even poetry was only the second of the arts, after painting:

> Det næste efter farver er da vistnok ord
> og kan man ikke male faar man skrive.

Translation:

> Second after colors are presumably words
> and if one can't paint, one then writes.

The exercise of at least one of these talents would never compensate for the sacrifice she had made — one wonders if she was ever envious of her brother, Oscar, a successful painter — but it would keep her soul alive:

> Min Gud! Man har en sjæl, man være vil ilive —
> og ord jeg drømte om, hvorend jeg fôr.
> En gylden kop jeg længted efter,
> hvori jeg kunde gyde mine tankers saft:
> Jeg skrev paa tysk, paa engelsk, øved mine
>   kræfter —
> men mest jeg kræved modersmaalets stille kraft.[20]

Translation:

> My God! One has a soul, one wants to be alive —
> and I dreamt of words, wherever I travelled.
> I yearned for a golden cup,
> into which I could pour the nectar of my
>   thoughts:
> I wrote in German, in English, exercised my
>   powers —
> but most I craved my mother tongue's quiet
>   force.

The significance that poetry had for Wergeland, then, was literally life-sustaining, one of the forces that uplifted her and helped to alleviate the sense of loss she felt after abandoning art for academics.[21] What kind of poetry did she write, then, when she was not being openly tendentious, confessional, or didactic?

The problem of poetic form seems to have been one that particularly occupied Wergeland's efforts. In "Ord" (Word), she metaphorically places form above diction and even content:

> Men ordet blir formen
> et fint krystal
> som holder i ave
> lik haardt metal
> den viltre tanke
> bak skjør pokal.[22]

Translation:

> But the word becomes the form,
> a fine crystal

which restrains
like hard metal
the boisterous thought
within a delicate goblet.

The vessel's form ("pokal") then overwhelms every other aesthetic consideration as Wergeland conjures it forth in a startling variety of manifestations:

Et gyldent støp, et meislet kar,
en Vaphiokop, en vase bar
for alt, kun linjen kysk og klar,
et prægtig fat, en jaspisskaal
som holder sikkert drømmens maal,
prismatiskt glar, muranske glas,
et 'ziergefæss' kun skabt til stas,
et bæger dypt, bredbarmet karm
hvor tanken svulmer rik og varm
en mosagat, en hul juvel
hvor tanken gløder ren og hel —

Translation:

A gilded casting, an engraved vessel,
a cup from Vaphio, a vase bare
of ornament, only its lines chaste and clear,
a splendid dish, a jasper bowl
which hold securely the goal of dreams;
prismatically clear Murano glass
an ornamental vessel made only for show;
a chalice deep, a broad-rimmed vessel
wherein the thought luxuriates, rich and warm,
a moss agate, a hollow jewel
in which the thought gleams whole and pure.

There is , in fact, no single predominant verse form in either of Wergeland's collections. Long lines, short lines, enjambed lines; end rhyme, doggerel, blank verse; *ballades*, sonnets, Persian ghasels, even two dramatic sketches, one realistic and one fantastic, all appear in *Amerika og andre digte* and *Efterladte digte*. The subject matter of her poetry ranges from philosophical ruminations on Goethe and Schiller ("Nur die Lumpen sind Bescheiden") to ringing denunciations of assimilation among Norwegian Americans ("Et Ord"), from the twin poles of her patriotism ("America magna" and "Det større Norge"), from nature lyricism ("Vaaren" and "Sommer") to intimate studies of domesticity ("Mit hjem" and "Mine blomster") that rarely descend to the sentimental.

But the poems which stand out as among her best because of their originality are poems on art, poetry, and beauty itself. If the political Wergeland felt betrayed by the world ("Ignis Fatuus"), Wergeland the aesthete did not. In poem after poem, she sings of beautiful things, objects like the vessels in "Ord," which are to be admired only for their inherent beauty. Sometimes the beauty is of a fatal or grotesque nature, reminiscent of Poe, as in her vision of the Grand Canyon in "Rosen." Wergeland saw it as an almost demonic phenomenon, the remnants of some titanic and unholy struggle of the elements:

> Lat avgrunden lyse med lyn og flammer,
> et farvevælde som spotter ord,
> med svidende pile det øiet rammer,
> det er som gjennem en sværdet fór —
> for dybet dernede minder om bølger
> av helveds størknede taareflod,
> den glimrende maske kun pine dølger,
> det tomme blik som stivner ens blod.[23]

Translation:

> Let the abyss glow with lightning and flames,
> an empire of color that mocks words,
> with scorching shafts it attacks the eye,
> it is as though a sword pierced it —
> for the distant deep below remembers the waves
> of Hell's strengthening river of tears,

the glittering mask conceals only torment,
the empty gaze which freezes one's blood.

Several exercises in pure fantasy are also among her best efforts. In "Glasspillet," the sound of the wind calls up a phantasmagoric vision of

Alfer og feer som danser i ring —
natgale gnomer,
besjælte atomer?
tussetøi, elvehøi —
støi?
ingenting?[24]

Translation:

Elves and fairies who dance in a ring —
night-mad gnomes,
animated atoms?
troll-stuff, elf-hill,
uproar?
nothing?

which quickly becomes an exquisite Japanese dream:

I foraarsfloret
smaabitte damer
med pil i haaret
og svære sløifer,
drager og sole
paa side kimoner,
papirsparasol
og elfenbensvifter —

Translation:

In springtime profusion
tiny damozels
with long pins
and black bows in their hair,
dragons and suns on
long kimonos,
paper parasols
and ivory fans.

Many of Wergeland's letters refer to her poetry as
"mystical" or "dreamlike." Much of it is unquestionably escapist in tone, for this was the therapeutic character that art retained for her after she had "betrayed"
her muse for scholarship and her daily bread. "In Memoriam" gives us a fine image of her hidden dreams and
buried thoughts; again, Poe comes to mind:

> Det er et gravrum i mit hjertes tempelhal,
> hvor jeg har skrinlagt mine bedste drømme,
> hvor jeg har jordet mine tanker ømme,
> nedsænket alt mit hjerte led av mandefald.
>
> Der er der skyggeluft! Av grønne ranker
> i sol og dag gror tætte klynger utenfor;
> men her er dæmpet lys for hjertesorg og saar,
> og vissent løv og orgelsang for mine tanker.
>
> I templet ovenfor er solens fulde glans,
> er billeder av mennskelivets store guder;
> der straaler stolte haab og seirens friske krans,
> og skinner smilende bak glade ruter.
>
> Dog, naar i andagts søte jubelstund
> mit hjerte løfter sig til pris for stridens dage,
> Du lukker graven op — med smil om bleke mund
> Du svæver mig forbi i orglets dype klage.[25]

Translation:

> There is a burial chamber in the temple of my
>   heart,
> where I have buried my best dreams,
> where I have put my tenderest thoughts in the
>   earth,
> put down everything my heart suffered.
>
> Here there are shadows! From green vines
> tightly twined lianas grow outside in sun and
>   daylight

but here is dimmed light for sorrow of the heart
and wounds,
and withered leaves and the song of the organ for
my thoughts.

In the temple up above is the sun's full radiance,
and images of the great gods of human life;
up there beams proud hope and the fresh wreath
of victory,
and it shines laughingly behind cheery window-
panes.

But when in meditation's sweet moment of
triumph
my heart lifts up in praise of the day of struggle,
You then unlock my grave — with a smile on pale
lips
You glide past me to the organ's deep lament.

Thus, the Wergeland melancholia is intimately involved with the resurrection of her buried dreams and
is therefore a necessary and fundamental element of her
poetry. Her bolder attempts to sound a strident note for
"stridens dage" have a hollower ring, a lesser imaginative breadth, than her "aesthetic" poetry. This is particularly evident if one compares Wergeland's two extant
longer works, "Fire prinsesser" (Four princesses), from
Amerika og andre digte, and "Paa ballet" (At the ball),
from *Efterladte digte*. Both pieces are cast as dramatic
sketches, with detailed descriptions of the setting and a
cast of characters.

But "Paa ballet" is conceived as a realistic and critical
dissection of petty bourgeois society in contemporary
Norway.[26] Wergeland's own social shortcomings — her
shyness, her aloofness, her inability to make small talk
— show up most glaringly when she tries to describe a
dance, one of the most social of situations. The attempts
at creating believable characters (each of whom then

speaks in an appropriate verse form) fall pitifully flat;
even the attempts to convey the different dances, such
as the polonaise and the waltz, by varying the poetic
form cannot breathe life into the stereotypical two-
dimensional characters — the Mayor, the Poet, the Au-
thoress, the Teacher, the Conservative — who stalk this
dramatic fragment. Her models were apparently Camilla Collett, Jonas Lie, and perhaps even Knut Hamsun (for example, the ball scene in *Pan*), but in this case
the inspiration proved stronger than the imitation.

"Fire prinsesser," on the other hand, is an almost
perfect gem of Norwegian aesthetic poetry.[27] Wergeland uses the homely subject matter of her immediate
environment — in this case, the rose garden at Laramie
— to fashion a melancholy fairy tale in the manner of
Oscar Wilde. The goddess of the moon turns four roses
into four human princesses in gratitude for the homage
they alone still pay her. But she warns them of the vi-
cissitudes and undeserved suffering they will en-
counter in life, a warning which, like Cassandra's, goes
unheeded. Needless to say, all the prophecy comes to
pass. Each flower sings haughtily of its own unique
beauty, a narcissism which the poet somewhat wistfully
associated with the innocence and confidence of youth.
The little play's "Ouverture" is perhaps the finest example of Wergeland's overripe style, reminiscent of the
British aesthetes of the 1890s, Ernest Dowson, Arthur
Symons, or even Algernon Swinburne, poets little
known and less imitated in Norway.

> Glimrende klarhet, smeltende skygge,
> maanelys nat!
> Spred Dine vinger, dunhvite drømmefugl!
> Ro i de brede, lysfyldte strømme!
> Bad Dig i glansens dæmpete flod!
> Skjul Dig i sløret som dækker
> stjernernes glans!

287

Skvulpende sø!
Mumlende mund som sladrer i
natten om dybets mirakler!
Dyssende søt er Din stemme!
Danser ei havfru, guldhaaret, hvitbrystet,
rækker de glitrende arme
ut mot den favnende straale,
segner med glansen
ned til Din bund?

Viftende vind!
Sagtelig vrister Du drømmen fra
træernes slumrende munde,
aander den atter med latter i
skyggernes lydhøre øre!
Nynnende følger Du nattens let
rytmiske dans ad de lysende baner,
spiller paa strengen som
dirrer i luftens guldspundne azur —
synker til jordens svagt
bankende bryst.[28]

Translation:

Brilliant clarity, melting shadows,
moonlit night!
Spread your wings, down-white dreambird!
Soar in the wide, light-filled beams!
Bathe in the subdued flood of radiance!
Hide yourself in the veil which covers
the luster of the stars!

Rippling sea!
Mumbling mouth which gossips in
the night about the miracles of the deep!
Soothingly sweet is your voice!
A mermaid dances, golden-haired,
white-breasted,
stretches her glittering arms
out toward the embracing beams,

does she descend with her gaze
down to your realm?

Fluttering wind!
Slowly you wring the dream from
the sleeping mouths of the trees,
breathe it again with laughter
into the keen ears of the shadows!
Humming, you follow the night's lightly
rhythmic dance on the radiant paths,
play on the string which
trembles in the gold-spun azure of the air,
sink back to the earth's weakly
beating breast.

One final poem proves once again how oddly Wergeland's life and even her very ideas were distorted,
especially by her few close and obviously well-intentioned friends. In "Pilgrimen," the poet-pilgrim pauses
beneath a Gothic arch in Rheims Cathedral and humbly
admires a statue of Christ. The soul of the wanderer is
now satisfied; there is no reason to go any farther. Michelet insists that "Pilgrimen" reflects only Wergeland's "dype og alvorlige sindelag og troen paa en
frelser" (deep and serious frame of mind and belief in a
personal savior).[29] The theme of a return to heaven and
its promise of rest for the weary pilgrim is certainly present, but the pilgrim here is really a seeker after beauty,
not salvation. In the glory of Rheims, this desire is satisfied: it is some mystical reflection of what heaven's
visions will resemble. Thus, it is not only the *requiem
aeternam* the pilgrim seeks but an aesthetic consolation
as well. At the very heart of Wergeland's personal credo
was her faith in the power of art to lift the soul over the
vagaries of the world; the poet-pilgrim in this late poem
confesses his similar creed with equal conviction:

O nei, hans sind vil hvile,
vil i et større syn end det

289

> som her hans øie monne se
> den dag hans sjæl skal smile,
> den dag naar han faar ile,
> hvor der er ikkun lys og fred,
> og intet savn, og ingen sorg,
> i himmelens faste kongeborg.[30]

Translation:

> Oh no, his senses want to rest,
> want to see yet a greater vision than that
> which his eye has been able to see here
> that day his soul can smile,
> that day when he makes haste,
> where there is only light and peace
> and no loss and no sorrow
> in the mighty fortress of heaven.

The aim of this study has been to show how Agnes Mathilde Wergeland's highly personal poetry helps illuminate the contradictions of character noted without much comment by her various biographers. The twin pulls of public pragmatism and mystical aestheticism emphasized here seem best to demarcate the extremes of her life and to be one of the primary sources of her all-pervasive melancholy. More than anything else, the author's intention has been to shed light on the technical skills and great artistic range of one of Norway's — and America's — unsung poets.

NOTES

[1] The main source of information on Wergeland is Maren Michelet's *Glimt fra Agnes Mathilde Wergelands liv* (Glimpses from Agnes Mathilde Wergeland's life) published as a *mindeutgave* (memorial edition) in 1916 by Folkebladet Publishing Company's Trykkeri in Minneapolis. While Michelet had unlimited access to Wergeland's correspondence and other papers, her worshipful attitude toward her subject makes *Glimt* rather shaky as an interpretive biography. A "privately printed" English edition was also issued for Wergeland's closest friends and for contributors to Michelet's efforts.

[2] Gina Krog, one of Norway's leading feminist journalists, was the editor of *Nylænde* (New Ground). The entire March, 1915, number was given over to a biography of Wergeland.

[3] Katharine Merrill edited and arranged Wergeland's best prose works, titled *Leaders in Norway and Other Essays* (Menaska, Wisconsin, 1916). In this she included a brief biographical sketch of the author as well as English versions of "Haanden" ("A Song of Thy Hand"), "Mit Hjem" ("My Home"), and "Charons komme" ("Charon Forgetful?"), three of Wergeland's most revealing autobiographical writings.

[4] Erik Aanonsen, following Michelet's biography, produced a popular illustrated article for *The Norseman*, "Pioneer Professor in Wyoming," 1974, 15–19. See also Ingrid Semmingsen, "A Pioneer: Agnes Mathilde Wergeland, 1857–1914," in Odd S. Lovoll, ed., *Makers of an American Immigrant Legacy: Essays in Honor of Kenneth O. Bjork* (Northfield, Minnesota, 1980), 111–130.

[5] *Amerika og andre digte* (Decorah, Iowa, 1912). This volume will be cited hereafter as *Amerika*.

[6] Grace Hebard saw the volume through the press and Maren Michelet was responsible for the transcribing and editing. *Efterladte digte* was published by the Free Church Book Concern of Minneapolis as a Norwegian centenary volume in July, 1914.

[7] Michelet, *Glimt*, 161. The translations from Norwegian are from this work, unless otherwise specified, and are the author's throughout.

[8] Michelet, *Glimt*, 161.

[9] Michelet, *Glimt*, 50–51.

[10] Michelet, *Glimt*, 254–255.

[11] Michelet, *Glimt*, 255.

[12] Michelet, *Glimt*, 51.

[13] Her longest friendship was with Aasta Hansteen, the doyenne of the Norwegian feminist movement and, by the turn of the century, its undisputed and venerable leader. Hansteen served as the model for the impetuous, unorthodox seeker of truth, Lona Hessel, in Ibsen's great social drama *Samfundets støtter (Pillars of Society)*. Wergeland and Hansteen had met first in Norway in 1875 and they kept up their warm but formal friendship mainly by correspondence.

[14] Michelet, *Glimt*, 203.

[15] Michelet, *Glimt*, 200, 201–202.

[16] *Efterladte digte*, 43–44. The literal translations that follow each poem are the author's.

[17] "Akvareller," *Amerika*, 28.

[18] For the record, her most important scholarly work is considered to be the rather slight *Slavery in Germanic Society During the Middle Ages* (Chicago, 1916). The original edition was published in 1896 and reprinted in September, 1916. "Loyal affection to Dr. Wergeland's memory should suggest the thought of reprinting her monograph," wrote J. Franklin Jameson of the Carnegie Institute in Washington in the preface. He also supplied the information, not found in Michelet, that most of the book had appeared as "lesser writings" in the *Journal of Political Economy*.

[19] "Akvareller," *Amerika*, 28. These desperate and bitter lines are from the period around 1890.

[20] "Akvareller," *Amerika*, 29.

[21] A clue to what she sought in poetry is given in her article on "Modern Danish Literature and its Foremost Representative," in *The Dial*, September 16, 1895, 135–137. In it she praises Holger Drachmann for the purity

of his language, his openness to fresh new ideas, and his freedom from cant. All these are qualities she most admired and envied in others.

[22] "Ord," *Efterladte digte,* 14.
[23] "Rosen," *Efterladte digte,* 140.
[24] "Glasspillet," *Efterladte digte,* 89–90.
[25] "In Memoriam," *Amerika,* 79.
[26] *Efterladte digte,* 58–85.
[27] *Amerika,* 211–243.
[28] "Fire prinsesser," *Amerika,* 211–212.
[29] Michelet, *Glimt,* 83.
[30] "Pilgrimen," *Efterladte digte, 164.*

compiled by C. A. CLAUSEN
with Norwegian listings
by JOHANNA BARSTAD

Some Recent Publications

BOOKS AND PAMPHLETS

AGER, WALDEMAR. *Sons of the Old Country.* Lincoln, Nebraska, 1983. 255 pp. Translated by Trygve M. Ager, with a foreword by Odd S. Lovoll.

"Ager gives a vivid description of the early Norwegian settlers, their struggles and triumphs, the slow and painful process of assimilation and, finally, their trials in the battlefields, hospitals, and prisons in the South during the Civil War."

AHOLA, DAVID JOHN. *Finnish-Americans and International Communism: A Study of Finnish-American Communism from Bolshevization to the Demise of the Third International.* Washington, D.C., 1981. ix, 346 pp.

ARNDT, KARL J. R. *Economy on the Ohio 1826–1834.* Worcester, Massachusetts, 1984. xxii, 1056 pp.

A documented history of the Harmony Society during its period of greatest influence.

ÅSVANG, ARNT O. *Emigranter. Vevelstad-fjerdinger som dro mot vest 1869–1930.* Forvik, Norway, 1977.

Emigration from the community of Vevelstad in northern Norway.

BERGENDOFF, CONRAD. *The Augustana Ministerium: A Study of the Careers of the 2,504 Pastors of the Augustana Evangelical Lutheran Synod/Church 1850–1962.* Rock Island, Illinois, 1980. 246 pp.

"A convenient directory of all the pastors who served the Augustana Synod through its 112 years of existence."

293

BILLINGTON, RAY ALLEN. *Land of Savagery, Land of Promise: The European Image of the American Frontier in the Nineteenth Century*. New York, 1981. xv, 364 pp.

". . . the frontier [after the Civil War] was depicted as a place of opportunity, as opposed to one of perpetual mayhem. America was glad to have the newcomers; Europeans often regarded such siphoning off as an answer to their problems of overpopulation."

BLY, CAROL. *Letters From the Country*. New York, 1981. vi, 184 pp.

A collection of thirty-one essays which deal with country life near Madison, Minnesota.

BOWEN, R. H., ed. and trans. *A Frontier Family in Minnesota: Letters of Theodore and Sophie Bost, 1851–1920*. Minneapolis, 1981. xxv, 391 pp.

BRØNNER, HEDIN. *Landkjenning: reiser i et liv*. Foreword by Johan Hambro. Oslo, 1983. 226 pp.

Reminiscences of a much-traveled Norwegian-American intellectual and diplomat.

BURAAS, ANDERS. *De reiste ut*. Oslo, 1982. 226 pp.

Essays about seven Norwegians who went to America — most of them to stay: Agnes Wergeland, Ole Evinrude, Anders Furuseth, Knute Rockne, Harry Irgens Larsen, Hans Christian Heg, and Ole Bull.

BURZLE, J. ANTHONY, ed. *Yearbook of German-American Studies*, 18. Lawrence, Kansas, 1983. 295 pp.

Nineteen articles by well-known scholars commemorating the tricentennial of German immigration to the United States; also bibliography of items published on German-Americana in 1982.

CHRISTIANSON, J. R. AND BIRGITTE, eds. and trans. *The Dream of America*. Mankato, Minnesota, 1982.

An adaptation for American readers of seven Danish studies of European emigration. Individual volumes are:

EVOLD, BENT. *They Came to America*. 96 pp.

The experiences of Axel Brandt, who immigrated at the age of seventeen and settled in a Danish community in Minnesota where he spent the rest of his life.

HVIDT, KRISTIAN. *The Westward Journey*. 91 pp.

Living conditions aboard the ships and railway cars which brought the immigrants to the American West.

KOUSTRUP, SØREN. *Ireland in Flight*. 99 pp.

A discussion of the adverse conditions in Ireland which caused the great emigration to America.

KOUSTRUP, SØREN. *Shattered Dreams: Joe Hill*. 69 pp.

The life story of the legendary Swedish-American labor agitator and writer of protest songs.

SOME RECENT PUBLICATIONS

KRUSTRUP, ERIK V. *Gateway to America: New York City.* 71 pp.
New York City as seen and experienced by the numerous immigrants who settled there.

SKOVMAND, SVEN. *America Forever.* 94 pp.
A discussion of the various forces which gave rise to the America fever.

SKOVMAND, SVEN. *Europe and the Flight to America.* 77 pp.
An analysis of the causes for the exodus to America.

DAVIS, JOHN L. *The Danish Texans.* San Antonio, 1979. 122 pp.
A volume in the series of studies concerning ethnic groups in Texas published by the University of Texas Institute of Texan Culture.

DEBLANC, SVEN. *Samuels döttrar.* Stockholm, 1982. 335 pp.
"For those particularly interested in emigration and immigration, *Samuels döttrar* is far more than an absorbing story about believable human beings. It will help explain situations at home in Sweden that led to emigration, and it presents not only what the emigrant left but what she came to, in this instance Manitoba."

DINER, HASIA R. *Erin's Daughters in America.* Baltimore, 1983. xvi, 185 pp.
A history of Irish immigrant women in the nineteenth century.

DUNAE, P. A. *Gentleman Emigrants: From the British Public Schools to the Canadian Frontier.* Vancouver, 1981. 276 pp.
"It makes a signal contribution to our knowledge of certain English influences which students of the nation have always assumed to be central to the Canadian experience."

DURIEUX, MARCEL. *Ordinary Heroes: The Journal of a French Settler in Alberta.* Edmonton, Alberta, 1980. xviii, 115 pp.
"The 'ordinary heroes' of this journal are the members of the Charles Durieux family who homesteaded near Stettler, Alberta, in 1906."

DURNBAUGH, DONALD F. *The Brethren Encyclopedia.* Philadelphia, 1983. 2 vols., 1402 pp.
Information on those religious bodies that trace their origin to the Brethren movement which began in Germany in 1708 and includes the various Brethren, Dunkard, and Old German Baptist churches in the United States.

ENGEN, ARNFINN, ed. *Utvandringa — det store oppbrotet.* Oslo, 1978. 186 pp.
Ten articles by Norwegian scholars on aspects of immigration.

ENGLEMAN, RUTH. *Leaf House: Days of Remembering.* New York, 1982. 245 pp.
"A warm yet unsentimental account of the author's childhood in a tiny Finnish settlement in Wisconsin."

ENQUIST, ANNA. *Scandia — Then and Now*. Scandia, Minnesota, 1982. 200 pp.
"The story of Scandia in Washington county, the first permanent Swedish settlement in Minnesota, founded in 1850, told by the acknowledged expert on the subject."

FOSS, H. A. *Husmannsgutten*. Afterword by Liv Kristin Asheim. Olso, 1984. 176 pp.
New edition of the popular immigrant novel.

GALLO, P. J. *Old Bread, New Wine: A Portrait of the Italian-Americans*. Chicago, 1981. xi, 365 pp.

GARCIA, MARIO J. *Desert Immigrants: The Mexicans of El Paso, 1880–1920*. New Haven, 1981, xii, 316 pp.

GIESKE, M. L. *Minnesota Farmer-Laborism: The Third-Party Alternative*. Minneapolis, 1979. ix, 389 pp.
Men like Henrik Shipstead, Floyd B. Olson, and Elmer Benson were prominent leaders in the third-party movement.

GRIFFIN, W. D. *Portrait of the Irish in America*. New York, 1981. xi, 260 pp.

Guide to Swedish-American Archival and Manuscript Sources in the United States. Chicago, 1983. xxx, 600 pp.

HALE, FREDERICK, ed. and trans. *Danes in North America*. Seattle, 1984. 256 pp.
A collection of immigrant letters written by Danes in America.

HALE, FREDERICK. *Danes in Wisconsin*. Madison, 1981. 32 pp.

HALE, N. C. *The Spirit of Man: The Sculpture of Kaare Nygaard*. Austin, Texas, 1983. 159 pp. Photographs by Amy Binder.

HARNEY, R. F. and SCARPACI, J. V., eds. *Little Italies in North America*. Toronto, 1981. 210 pp.
"There are discussions of 'Little Italies' in Montreal and Toronto, in addition to treatment of those in various parts of the United States."

HAUGE, ALFRED. *Cleng Peerson. Møte med vandringsmannen*. Stavanger, 1983. 99 pp.
English edition entitled *The True Saga of Cleng Peerson* (Dallas, Texas, 1982).

HAUGEN, EINAR. *Ole Edvart Rölvaag*. Boston, 1983. 164 pp.
Volume 455 in Twayne's United States Authors Series. "The book is a well-researched critical study of Rölvaag . . . who burst upon the American literary scene in 1927 with *Giants in the Earth*."

296

HEDBLOM, FALKE. *Svenska-Amerika Berettar*. Stockholm, 1982. 186 pp.

During the 1960s Hedblom and Torsten Ordeus visited Swedish America with the most modern recording equipment in order to study Swedish dialects which might be better preserved here than in Sweden. This book covers Swedish-American life from early pioneer days to the 1960s.

HEILBUT, ANTHONY. *Exiled in Paradise: German Refugee Artists and Intellectuals in America from the 1930s to the Present*. New York, 1983. xiv, 506 pp.

Especially about refugees from Nazi Germany and their adaptation to American life.

HERSCHER, URI D. *Jewish Agricultural Utopias in America, 1880–1910*. Detroit, 1981. 197 pp.

"Herscher draws an interesting comparison between the success of the kibbutzim of Israel and the failure of the American collectivist ideal."

HOERDER, DIRK, ed. *American Labor and Immigration History, 1877–1920s: Recent European Research*. Urbana, Illinois, 1983. ix. 286 pp.

HOVDHAUGEN, EINAR. *Utvandringa til Amerika frå Ringebu*. Ringebu, Norway, 1983. xiii, 177 pp.

Immigration from the community of Ringebu, Norway.

HOVELSEN, LEIF. *The Flying Norseman*. Ishpeming, Michigan, 1983. 132 pp.

An account by his son of the life of Carl Hovelsen, a Norwegian skier who later came to America where he promoted the skiing sport for many years.

HUNNESTAD, STEINAR. *Prærien i vest*. Oslo, 1980. 215 pp.

Account of a journey across America, including visits to areas of Norwegian settlement.

HUSEBOE, ARTHUR R., ed. *Siouxland Heritage*. Sioux Falls, South Dakota, 1982. 92 pp.

This volume contains articles by "Einar Haugen, Fredrick Manfred, and John Milton on the history and culture of South Dakota with its strong Scandinavian and largely Norwegian contributions."

HUTCHINSON, E. P. *Legislative History of American Immigration Policy, 1798–1965*. Philadelphia, 1981. xv, 685 pp.

It traces "one of America's largest and most complex bodies of legislation, perhaps exceeded only by the federal tax code."

"The Immigrant in America." Research Publications, Woodbridge, Connecticut.

C. A. Clausen

"A major microfilm collection covering the field of immigration history and ethnic studies to 1929, with the first and most complete bibliography for this period of immigration history."

JONASSEN, CHRISTEN T. *Value Systems and Personality in a Western Civilization: Norwegians in Europe and America.* Columbus, Ohio, 1983. 382 pp.

JONES, PETER D'A. and HOLLI, M. G., eds. *Ethnic Chicago.* Grand Rapids, Michigan, 1981. viii, 384 pp.

KARNI, MICHAEL G., ed. *Finnish Diaspora.* Vol. 1, Canada, South America, Africa, Australia, Sweden; Vol. 2, United States. Toronto, 1981. 305 pp.; 319 pp.

"The contributors to *Finnish Diaspora* are from Canada, Finland, and the United States and represent a wide range of disciplines. Their 36 essays reflect the lively state of Finnish migrant study in all three countries."

KEIL, HARTMUT and JENTZ, JOHN B., eds. *German Workers in Industrial Chicago, 1850–1910: A Comparative Perspective.* DeKalb, Illinois, 1983. 252 pp.

Thirteen essays focusing on how German workers shaped the American labor movement.

KOSTIAINEN, AUVO. *The Forging of Finnish-American Communism.* Turku, 1978. 225 pp.

A study in ethnic radicalism.

LANTZ, MONICA, ed. *Emigrantvisor.* Stockholm, 1981. 144 pp.

A selection of songs which "deal with the emigration to North America during the second half of the 19th century and the beginning of the 20th century."

LARSEN, ARTHUR C. *Next Year will be Better.* Sioux Falls, South Dakota, 1980. 200 pp.

Life in a Danish rural community in northeastern Montana during the years 1908–1922.

LARSEN, ULLA M. *En kvantitativ undersögelse af udvandringen fra Danmark til USA 1870–1913.* Odense, Denmark, 1979. 157 pp.

"An econometric study of emigration from Denmark to the United States."

LOFGREN, JOHN Z. *The American Swedish Institute.* Minneapolis, 1979. 48 pp.

A booklet with text and pictures about the institute and its mansion in Minneapolis.

LOKEN, GULBRAND. *From Fjord to Frontier: A History of the Norwegians in Canada.* Toronto, 1980. 264 pp.

LOVOLL, ODD S. *Det løfterike landet.* Oslo, 1983. 230 pp.
"A major contribution to the history of Norwegian emigration and of Norwegians in North America."

LOVOLL, ODD S., ed. *Norwegian-American Studies,* Vol. 29. Northfield, Minnesota, 1983. 402 pp.
Published by the Norwegian-American Historical Association. The contents are listed individually by authors in the following section on articles. "Seven of the twelve essays in the present collection are devoted to the Norwegian background, based on investigation of local communities throughout Norway."

LOVOLL, ODD S. *The Promise of America.* Minneapolis, 1984. 239 pp.
English version of *Det løfterike landet.*

LOWITT, RICHARD, ed. *Journal of a Tamed Bureaucrat: Nils A. Olsen and the B A E, 1925–1935.* Ames, Iowa, 1980. viii, 245 pp.
A native of Illinois of Norwegian ancestry, Olsen joined the Bureau of Agricultural Economics in 1923 and in 1928 became its chief.

MAC HAFFIE, INGEBORG NIELSEN. *Danish in Portland, 1882–1982.* Tigard, Oregon, 1983. 287 pp.

McCORMICK, R. ALLEN, ed. *Germans in America: Aspects of German-American Relations in the Nineteenth Century.* New York, 1983. 203 pp.

MØLLER, ARVID. *Høvding Herman. Fortellingen om Herman Smith-Johannsen.* Oslo, 1980. 150 pp.
Norwegian pioneer in skiing in the United States and Canada.

MOLTMANN, GÜNTER, ed. *Germans to America: 300 Years of Imigration, 1683–1983.* Stuttgart, 1982. 192 pp.

MOORE, DEBORAH. *B'nai B'rith and the Challenge of Ethnic Leadership.* Albany, New York, 1981. xvi, 288 pp.
"B'nai B'rith is the oldest secular Jewish organization in the United States and as such is as diverse as American Jewry itself."

MØRCK, GEORGE HJALMAR. *My American Roots.* 3rd edition. Oslo, 1983. 113 pp.

NAG, MARTIN. *Det indre lys. Strand-kvekerne — deres nærmiljø i Ryfylke og i Amerika.* Foreword by Wilhelm Aarek. Ås, Norway, 1983. 506 pp.
History of the Quakers from Strand in Ryfylke, Norway, both there and in America.

NERGÅRD, LARS. *Utvandrarhistorie frå Rindal.* Rindal, Norway, 1977. 127 pp.

History of immigration from the community of Rindal in Trøndelag, Norway.

OLSON, J. S. *The Ethnic Dimension in American History.* New York, 1979. xxv, 440 pp.

"Olson has included not only the familiar immigrant groups in his analysis, but also those — Africans, Mexicans, and native Americans — who have been incorporated into the American population by conquest and force."

OLSON, MORGAN A., trans. *Rollin Olson, Civil War Letters.* Minneapolis, 1981 (?). 161 pp.

Letters written by a member of the 15th Wisconsin Regiment, "The Norwegian Regiment," translated by his grandson.

OLSON, NELS. *Time in Many Places: Wood Has Been Kind to Me.* St. Cloud, Minnesota, 1980. 206 pp.

The autobiography of a Norwegian immigrant whose work as lumberjack, mill worker, boat builder, and general carpenter took him to many places in Wisconsin and Michigan. "Olson's story is one of regional interest, told in a comfortable style."

OLSSON, NILS WILLIAM. *Swedish Passenger Arrivals in U.S. Ports, 1820–1850 (except New York).* St. Paul, Minnesota, 1979. 139 pp.

This volume supplements the author's earlier work: *Swedish Passenger Arrivals in New York, 1820–1850.*

OUDENSTAD, HALVARD. *Utvandringen til Amerika fra Biri, Snertingdal, Vardal, Gjøvik 1846–1915.* Gjøvik, Norway, 1982. viii, 599 pp.

Immigration from communities along the western shore of Lake Mjøsa in Norway.

PAP, LEO. *The Portuguese-Americans.* Boston, 1981. 300 pp.

PINZKE, NANCY LINDBERG. *Faces of Utopia: A Bishop Hill Family Album.* Bishop Hill, Illinois, 1983 (?). 48 pp.

This album brings us face to face with members of the famous Swedish Utopian community at Bishop Hill, Illinois.

RILEY, GLENDA. *Frontierswomen, the Iowa Experience.* Ames, Iowa, 1981. 210 pp.

"Professor Riley attempts to make some sense of immigrant and black women's frontier lives."

RØLVAAG, O. E. *Peder Victorious: A Tale of the Pioneers: Twenty Years Later.* Lincoln, Nebraska, 1982. vii, 325 pp.

ROSENDAHL, PETER J. *Han Ola og han Per.* Edited by Joan N. Buckley and Einar Haugen. Oslo, 1984. 165 pp.

Distributed in the United States by the Norwegian-American Historical Association.

ROSENSTAND, HOLGER. *From the Land of the Great Lakes: Pioneer Days in Michigan.* Des Moines, Iowa, 1981. 118 pp. Translated by Rev. Willard R. Garred.
   The experiences and observations of a Danish Lutheran pastor in the Great Lakes area during the 1870s.

Scandinavia Today Minnesota. Minneapolis, 1983. 218 pp.
   This special issue of *Twin Cities* magazine (5:8, 1982/1983), published in connection with the year-long "Scandinavia Today" events of 1982–1983, contains "articles on Scandinavian cultural and intellectual life as well as historical material on the Nordic presence in the Midwest."

SELLER, MAXINE, ed. *Immigrant Women.* Philadelphia, 1981. x, 347 pp.
   "A comprehensive and wide-ranging anthology of works by and about immigrant women."

SEYERSTAD, PER E. *From Norwegian Romantic to American Realist: Studies in the Life and Writings of Hjalmar Hjorth Boyesen.* Foreword by Marc Ratner and eight essays by Boyesen. Oslo, 1984. 192 pp.

SJURSEN, JOHN ALFRED. *Utvandrerne fra Vossestrand 1843–1926. Etterkommere i U.S.A., slektninger i Norge.* Bergen, 1980. 3 vols., 54, 32, 37 pp.
   Immigrants from Vossestrand, Norway, their descendants in America, and their relatives in Norway.

SKARKERUD, OSKAR. *Amerikaminner: fra skogen, prærien og nybyggerlivet 1904–1912.* Gjøvik, Norway, 1983. 203 pp.
   Reminiscences of an immigrant who returned to Norway.

SKOUEN, ARNE. *Sigrid Undset skriver hjem. En vandring gjennom emigrantårene i Amerika.* Oslo, 1982. 149 pp.
   Letters written from America by the renowned Norwegian novelist.

SOWELL, THOMAS. *Ethnic America: A History.* New York, 1981. 353 pp.

SPEISMAN, S. A. *The Jews of Toronto.* Toronto, 1980. iv, 380 pp.
   "Between 1881 and 1931 Toronto's Jewish population increased from 534 to 45,305; even more significant was the growing religious and ethnic diversity within the Jewish community."

STAFFORD, KATE and NAESS, HARALD, trans. and eds. *On Both Sides of the Ocean: A Part of Per Hagen's Journey.* Northfield, Minnesota, 1984. 70 pp.
   Volume 10 of the Norwegian-American Historical Association's Travel and Description Series. "Though assuming the format of a

C. A. Clausen

historical novel, the narrative has an authentic quality, casting light on social conditions both in Norway and among Norwegian immigrants in America."

STRØM, ELIN and HERVIG, WENCHE. *Reisen til Amerika.* Oslo, 1984. 80 pp.
English edition is titled *Norwegians in America.*

STUHAUG, OMMUND G. M. *En nordmann blir amerikaner. Fortellingen om en norsk bondegutt som emigrerte til Amerika og fant sin livsførsel der, men som aldri kan glemme Norge.* New York, 1976. 159 pp.
Life story of a Norwegian farm boy who immigrated to the United States.

SUTHERLAND, D. E. *Americans and their Servants: Domestic Service in the United States from 1800 to 1920.* Baton Rouge, Louisiana, 1981. 229 pp.
Irish, German, and Scandinavian immigrants provided a large percentage of domestic servants during the period covered.

SYVERSEN, ODD MAGNAR. *Norge i Texas. Et bidrag til norsk emigrasjonshistorie.* Part I by Odd Magnar Syversen, part II by Derwood Johnson and Odd Magnar Syversen. Stange, Norway, 1982. 526 pp.
History of Norwegian immigration to Texas, 1835–1900, with chronological listing and biographical sketches of immigrants.

VEIRS, KRISTINA, ed. *Nordic Heritage Northwest.* Seattle, 1982. 159 pp. Photographs by Scotty Sapiro and text by Nancy Hausauer.

WHALBERG, GERON G. *Wagon Trails.* Saskatoon, Saskatchewan, 1980. 68 pp.
The author, who came to Canada from Sweden in 1905 at the age of two, seeks to give "a glimpse of pioneer life in rural Saskatchewan."

WUST, KLAUS and MOOS, HEINZ. *Three Hundred Years of German Immigrants in North America.* Baltimore, 1983. 185 pp.

ARTICLES

ALMQUIST, STEN. "Johan Frederik Tenggren: Soldier, Poet, Gold-miner." *Swedish-American Historical Quarterly,* 33:241–265 (1982). Translated by J. E. Norton and H. A. Barton.

ANDERSON, MRS. BERTHA J. "The Life Story of Mrs. Bertha Josephsen Anderson." *The Bridge,* 6, 1: 20–79 (1983).

Memories of pioneering in Montana and North Dakota, 1889–1907.

ANDERSON, ODIN W. "The Lynching of Hans Jakob Olson, 1889: The Story of a Norwegian-American Crime." *Norwegian-American Studies*, 29:159–184 (1983).

ANGIER, KATE. "Artist Floyd Johnson — A Viking's Vision." *Sons of Norway Viking*, 81:38–42 (February, 1984).

A well-known Norwegian-American artist who "expresses his Scandinavian background through painting" though legally blind.

ARESTAD, SVERRE. "Sigbjørn Obstfelder and America." *Norwegian-American Studies*, 29:253–292 (1983).

The experiences of a famous Norwegian poet in America as revealed in letters to his brother, 1890–1892.

BACKLUND, OSCAR J. "Childhood Dreams and Youthful Visions." *Swedish-American Historical Quarterly*, 34:49–69 (1983). Translated by C. George Ericson.

Reminiscences of a prominent Swedish-American pastor, poet, and journalist.

BAILY, S. L. "The Adjustment of Italian Immigrants in Buenos Aires and New York." *American Historical Review*, 88:281–305 (April, 1983).

BARSTAD, JOHANNA. "Aslak O. Lie og boken hans." *Norvegica*, January 1, 1983, 109–128.

BEATTY, WM. K. "Christian Fenger, An Embodiment of Truth." *The Bridge*, 6,1:95–123 (1983).

Christian Fenger (1840–1902) was a Danish-born and educated surgeon who came to Chicago in 1877 and made his name as a pathologist.

BEIJBOM, ULF. "Emigration Historians and Immigration Research in Sweden." *Swedish-American Historical Quarterly*, 34:130–139 (1983).

BEIJBOM, ULF. "Swedish-American Migration Research: Its Standing Today and Perspectives for Tomorrow." *Swedish-American Historical Quarterly*, 34:153–170 (1983).

BENGTSON, BENNIE. "A Giant in the Earth: Ole Rolvaag — the Outstanding Immigrant Novelist." *Sons of Norway Viking*, 81:50–52 (1984).

BLAGEN, NILS J. "A Short History of the Life of N. J. Blagen." *The Bridge*, 6, 2:46–78 (1982).

Autobiographical sketch of a prominent Danish-American architect who helped to build the cities, industries, and transportation systems of Oregon and Washington one hundred years ago.

C. A. *Clausen*

"A Brief Survey of Scandinavian Studies in the U.S." *Scandinavian Review*, 70:86–94 (September, 1982).

CHRISTIANSON, J. R. "Scandinavia and the Prairie School: Chicago Landscape Artist Jens Jensen." *The Bridge*, 5,2:5–18 (1982).

Jens Jensen (1860–1951) came from Denmark to Chicago in 1886 and soon became a leading member of the "Prairie School" as artist, architect, and city planner.

CLAUSEN, C. A. "Some Recent Publications." *Norwegian-American Studies*, 29:359–378 (1983).

A compilation of books and articles published largely during the years 1978–1982 dealing with immigration history.

DOKKEN, LARS OLSEN. "Borgerkrigen Brevene." *Hallingen*, March, 1982, 16–20.

Two Civil War letters. Other Civil War letters by Dokken appear in *Hallingen*, December, 1982, and March, 1983.

DVERGSDAL, LEIV H. "Emigration from Sunnfjord to America Prior to 1885." *Norwegian-American Studies*, 29:127–158 (1983). Translated by C. A. Clausen.

ENGEN, ARNFINN. "Emigration from Dovre, 1865–1914." *Norwegian-American Studies*, 29:210–252 (1983). Translated by C. A. Clausen.

ERICKSON, ROLF H. "Chicago for 75 år siden: Nordmennenes nest største by." *Nordmanns-Forbundet*, 131–133 (4, 1982).

A survey of the history of the Norwegian colony in Chicago, "the second largest Norwegian city."

FARR, W. E. "Germans in Montana Gold Camps: Two Views." *Montana Magazine of History*, 32:58–73 (Autumn, 1982).

FIRMAN, AXEL. "Two Swedes in the California Goldfields: Allvar Kullgren and Carl August Modh, 1850–1856." *Swedish-American Historical Quarterly*, 34:102–130 (1983).

FLATIN, KJETIL. "Det norske Amerika og norsk kulturpolitikk." *Nordmanns-Forbundet*, 73–77 (3, 1984).

A historical survey of Norwegian official interest — or lack of it — in Norwegian-American matters.

FRIIS, ERIK J. "The Scandinavian of the Month." *Scandinavian-American Bulletin*, 28:10–11 (February–March, 1983).

Martin Allwood, who through his many writings and translations has done much to further cultural communications between the English-speaking and the Scandinavian-speaking worlds.

FRIIS, ERIK J. "The Scandinavian of the Month." *Scandinavian-American Bulletin*, 28:10–12 (May, 1983).

304

Donald V. Mehus, a well-known Norwegian-American educator, author, and journalist.

GARNAAS, TOLLOF B. "Reminiscences of Early Pioneer Days." *Hallingen*, June, 1983, 8–10.

GIBSON, LOIS L. "Sanderson-Mehus: Unto a New Land." *Hallingen*, December, 1983, 21–27.
History of two Halling families in America.

GILMAN, RHODA R. "A Land of Migrants." *Roots*, 12:3–19 (Fall, 1983).
A survey of immigration to Minnesota.

HALE, FREDERICK. "The Americanization of a Danish Immigrant in Wisconsin, 1847–1872." *Wisconsin Magazine of History*, 64:202–215 (Spring, 1981).
The experiences of Andreas Frederiksen Herslev as revealed in his correspondence.

HALLDIN, DAVID. "Pioneering in Alberta's Peace River Country." *Swedish-American Historical Quarterly*, 33:43–61 (1982).

HAMRE, JAMES S. "Norwegian Immigrants Respond to the 'Common' School: A Case Study of American Values and the Lutheran Tradition." *Church History*, 50:302–315 (September, 1981).

HIGHAM, JOHN. "Integrating America: The Problem of Assimilation in the Nineteenth Century." *Journal of American Ethnic History*, 1:7–25 (Fall, 1981).

"Home of the Pioneers." *The Norseman*, 40–41 (2, 1982).
The parsonage at Snåsa in North Trøndelag was the childhood home of two prominent Norwegian-American immigrants: Ole Rynning, author of the influential book, *True Account of America*, and Bernt Julius Muus, founder of St. Olaf College in Northfield, Minnesota.

"I Skied Better 100 Years Ago." *The Norseman*, 54 (2, 1983).
A biographical sketch of Herman Smith-Johannsen, age 108, who helped popularize skiing in Canada.

JACOBSON, CHARLOTTE. "Index to Volumes 1–29 of *Norwegian-American Studies*." *Norwegian-American Studies*, 29:380–401 (1983).

JANSSEN, VIVEKA K. "Swedish Settlement in Alberta, 1890–1930." *Swedish-American Historical Quarterly*, 33:111–123 (1982).

JØRGENSEN, OLE. "Adolf Gundersen og hans sønner." *Nordmanns-Forbundet*, 90–93 (3, 1982).

C. A. Clausen

The founders of the famous Gundersen Clinic in LaCrosse, Wisconsin.

KÄVLEMARK, ANNA-SOFIE. "Utvandring och självständighet: några synpunkter på den kvinnliga emigrasjonen från Sverige." *Historisk tidskrift*, 140–174 (2, 1983).
"Emigration and emancipation. Some views on the emigration of women from Sweden."

KEILLOR, S. J. "A Country Editor in Politics: Hjalmar Petersen, Minnesota Governor." *Minnesota History*, 48:283–294 (Fall, 1983).

KJAR, IVER and LARSEN, MOGENS B. "Danish in Dakota." *The Bridge*, 6,1:5–19 (1983).
"Analysis of specific Danish-American communities as part of a general description of the linguistic development of Danish immigrants in the United States."

KJARTANSSON, H. S. "Emigration Fares and Emigration from Iceland to North America, 1874–1893." *Scandinavian Economic History Review*, 28:55–71 (1980).

KLEIN, HERBERT S. "The Integration of Italian Immigrants into the United States and Argentina: A Comparative Analysis." *American Historical Review*, 88:306–346 (April, 1983).
These pages also contain comments by Jorge Balan, J. D. Gould, and Tulio Halperin-Donghi.

LARSEN, ULLA M. "A Quantitative Study of Emigration from Denmark to the United States, 1870–1913." *Scandinavian Economic History Review*, 30:101–128 (1982).

LARSSON, EVERT A. "Lidköping to Lindsborg: Reminiscences, 1924–1929." *Swedish-American Historical Quarterly*, 33:84–110 (1982).
These reminiscences of a young Swedish immigrant are continued in the following issue of the *Swedish-American Historical Quarterly*, pp. 183–206.

LJUNGMARK, LARS. "Canada's Campaign for Scandinavian Immigration 1873–1876." *Swedish-American Historical Quarterly*, 33:21–42 (1982).

MAMEN, H. CHR. "Misjon og emigrasjon. Tema belyst ved historien om norsk utvandring til Amerika," in *Misjonskall og forskerglede* (Oslo, 1975), 138–152.
A study of the Norwegian Missionary Society's influence in motivating Norwegian pastors to minister to Norwegian immigrants in America.

MAWE, CARL-ERIK. "Svenskkolonier i Alaska." *Bryggan*, 13,2:51–56 (1981).

This article concerning Swedish settlements in Alaska is continued in the following issue of *Bryggan*, 13,3:73–80 (1981).

NELSON, PEDER H. "Hans Andersen Foss." *Ringerike*, 54:41–43 (1982).

Biographical sketch of the popular Norwegian-American author of *Husmandsgutten* and other novels.

NELSON, PEDER H. "Sagaskriveren O. S. Johnson." *Western Viking*, March 6, 1981.

Johnson wrote extensively about immigration, especially from Ringerike, Norway.

NELSON, SIDSEL THORMODSGAARD. "The History of the Thormodsgaard Family." *Hallingen*, June, 1983, 27–31.

The history of a Halling family in Norway and the United States. The story is continued in subsequent issues of *Hallingen*.

"Nils Brandt Served for Seven Decades in Midwest." *Budstikken*, 12:20–21 (December, 1981).

Biographical sketch of a noted pastor and professor.

"Norskedalen: 'Wisconsins svar på Maihaugen?'" *Nordmanns-Forbundet*, 14–15 (1, 1983). Photographs by Per Krussand.

An outdoor museum near Coon Valley, Wisconsin, which aims to recreate a Norwegian pioneer homestead.

OLDEN, ANNA-MARGARETE. "Religiøs forfølgelse bak utvandrings-starten." *Nordmanns-Forbundet*, 138–140 (4, 1982).

Religious persecution as a motive force behind the first Norwegian emigration to America, on the ship *Restauration* in 1825.

ORDAHL, SVERRE. "Emigration from Agder to America, 1890–1915." *Norwegian-American Studies*, 29:313–338 (1983). Translated by C. A. Clausen.

ORR, WILLIAM J. "Rasmus Sørensen and the Beginnings of Danish Settlement in Wisconsin." *Wisconsin Magazine of History*, 65:195–210 (Spring, 1982).

"Rasmus Sørensen is generally acknowledged to be the first and perhaps most influential promoter of Danish settlement in the United States."

PATRIAS, CARMELLA. "Hungarian Immigration to Canada before the Second World War." *Polyphony*, 2:17–44 (1979–1980).

"Preserving a Musical Heritage: The Hardanger Fiddle Association of America." *The Norseman*, 163–165 (5/6, 1983).

The Association was launched at a meeting June 18, 1983, at Mount Horeb, Wisconsin. The Hardanger fiddle is often referred to as "the national folk instrument of Norway."

QUACKENBUSH, MICHELLE and SYLVESTER, LORNA, eds. "Letter of Jacob Schramm in Indiana to Karl Zimmermann in Germany, 1842." *Indiana Magazine of History*, 77:268–287 (September, 1981). Translated by Julie Simonton.

A letter discouraging emigration to America.

REITZ, J. and ASHTON, MARGARET. "Ukranian Language and Identity in Urban Canada." *Canadian Ethnic Studies*, 12,2:33–54 (1980).

RUNDBLOM, HARALD. "The Swedes in Canada: A Study of Low Ethnic Consciousness." *Swedish-American Historical Quarterly*, 33:4–20 (1982).

SANDELL, STEPHEN. "Digging deeper, branching out." *Roots*, 12:33–39 (Fall, 1983).

A guide to primary and secondary sources for the study of immigration to Minnesota.

SANNER, EGIL KR. "Utvandringen til Canada." *Nordmanns-Forbundet*, 102–104 (3, 1982).

The article is largely based on Gulbrand Loken's book, *From Fjord to Frontier: A History of the Norwegians in Canada.*

SEIDEL, JOAN. "Minnesota's Newest Immigrants." *Roots*, 12:20–29 (Fall, 1983).

Immigrants from Southeast Asia and their life in Minnesota.

SEMMINGSEN, INGRID. "Haugeans, Rappites, and the Emigration of 1825." *Norwegian-American Studies*, 29:3–42 (1983). Translated by C. A. Clausen.

Religious aspects of the earliest Norwegian emigration to America.

SEMMINGSEN, INGRID. "A Unique Collection of America Letters in Norway." *Swedish-American Historical Quarterly*, 35:316–321 (July, 1984).

SEMMINGSEN, INGRID. "Unique Letter Collection." *Sons of Norway Viking*, 81:59–61 (1984).

An analysis of sixty-seven America letters written in the New York area in 1896 but not discovered in Norway until 1981.

STRICKON, ARNOLD and IBARRA, ROBERT A. "The Changing

Dynamics of Ethnicity: Norwegians and Tobacco in Wisconsin." *Ethnic and Racial Studies*, 6:174–195 (April, 1983).

SIMONSON, HAROLD F. "*Angst* on the Prairie: Reflections on Immigrants, Rølvaag, and Beret." *Norwegian-American Studies*, 29:89–110 (1983).

> Beret is the principal female character in Rølvaag's pioneer novel.

SJÖBERG, LEIF. "The Early Years of Albin Widén — Ordinary or Extraordinary?" *Swedish-American Historical Quarterly*, 34:142–152 (1983).

> Widén is a prominent author and historian who has written numerous works dealing with Swedish-American life.

SKAAREN, KJELL ERIK. "Emigration from Brønnøy and Vik in Helgeland." *Norwegian-American Studies*, 29:293–312 (1983). Translated by C. A. Clausen.

"Snowshoe Thompson baner vei for Auburn Skiclub!" *Nordmanns-Forbundet*, 41–42 (2, 1984).

> An imposing monument of the famed mail carrier stands near the museum of the Auburn, California, Ski Club.

STANDAL, RAGNAR. "Emigration from a Fjord District on Norway's West Coast, 1852–1915." *Norwegian-American Studies*, 29:185–209 (1983). Translated by C. A. Clausen.

STEEN, ROALD. "Han leder verdens største varehus." *Nordmanns-Forbundet*, 10–11 (1, 1984).

> Archibald Boe, the son of Norwegian immigrants, is president of the Sears-Roebuck Company, "the world's largest department store."

STEEN, ROALD. "Hjalmar Olsen og hans sønner." *Nordmanns-Forbundet*, 96–99 (3, 1982).

> Hjalmar Olsen and his five sons served with distinction in the United States Navy.

STEEN, ROALD. "Ivar Giaever og 'tunnel-effekten'." *Nordmanns-Forbundet*, 151–153 (5/6, 1983).

> Ivar Giaever emigrated from Norway in 1954 and eventually became connected with General Electric laboratories. In 1973 he shared the Nobel prize for physics.

STEEN, ROALD. "They Came from Norway: Immigrant Senators and Governors." *The Norseman*, 8–12 (1, 1982).

SUNDE, RASMUS. "Emigration from the District of Sogn, 1839–1915." *Norwegian American Studies*, 29:111–126 (1983). Translated by C. A. Clausen.

C. A. Clausen

SVALESTUEN, ANDRES A. "Emigration from the Community of
Tinn, 1837–1907: Demographic, Economic, and Social
Background." *Norwegian-American Studies,* 29:43–88
(1983). Translated by C. A. Clausen.

SVALESTUEN, ANDRES A. "Reiseruter og reisevilkår for Tele-
marks-emigrantene i seilskutetida." *Telemark Historie,*
23–53 (3, 1983).
Emigration from Telemark, Norway, during the age of the sailing ships.

SVANOE, HAROLD. "An Old Friend Remembered on his 90th
Birthday." *Western Viking,* May 18, 1984.
A biographical sketch of O. Myking Mehus, educator, author,
civil servant, and Norwegian-American cultural leader.

TEDEBRAND, LARS-GÖRAN, "Strikes and Political Radicalism in
Sweden and Emigration to the United States." *Swedish-
American Historical Quarterly,* 34:194–210 (1983).
The author's aim here is to consider connections between labor
unrest in Sweden and emigration to the United States.

THELANDER, HULDA E. "The Immigrants' Children." *Swedish-
American Historical Quarterly,* 34:211–222 (1983).
The experiences of a second-generation Swedish-American
girl.

UHL, ROBERT. "A Painter of Floating Property." *American
Heritage,* 34:78–85 (April, May, 1983).
The Danish-born painter Antonio Jacobsen was "the most pro-
lific of all American marine artists."

WEINSTOCK, JOHN. "Sondre Norheim: Folk Hero to Immigrant."
Norwegian-American Studies, 29:339–358 (1983).

WHAL, PALMA. "The Bizarre Voyage of Niels Haagenson Rud
and Family from Ness, Hallingdal, to Rock Prairie, Wisconsin, 1846." *Hallingen,* June, 1982, 30–32.

WILSON, ELMER. "A Swede's First Logging Camp." *Swedish-
American Historical Quarterly,* 34:257–280 (1983). Trans-
lated by Henry Axel Persson.
This article describes life in a logging camp in the state of
Washington in the early part of this century.

by CHARLOTTE JACOBSON

From the Archives

ALFARNES, ARNE

De Haarde Aar i Vesten, the recollections of an emigrant who came to the United States in 1909, but after a few years of wandering in the West returned to his home in Norway. The material was originally published in *Aandalsnes Avis.*

BERGMANN, LEOLA NELSON

An issue of the State Historical Society of Iowa *Palimpsest,* March, 1956, entitled "Scandinavian Settlement in Iowa." Mrs. Bergmann is the author of *Americans from Norway* (New York, 1950) and *Music Master of the Middle West* (Minneapolis, 1954).

BERVEN, JACOB AMUNDSON

An account of an emigrant journey in 1872 from Bergen to Lee county, Illinois, and clippings of memorial tributes to friends. Part of his written work is compiled in *Reisebreve og digte* (Radcliffe, Iowa, 1916).

BONDEUNGDOMSLAGET OF NEW YORK

Papers of a society organized in Brooklyn in 1925. In 1930 the group built a cabin at Lake Telemark, Rockaway, New Jersey, to serve as a social center and a vacation place. Their folk dancers became a popular entertainment group in the area.

BORDEWICK, HENRY

Papers of an emigrant from the Lofoten Islands who came to Chicago in 1864. He enlisted in the Navy and served on a

311

Mississippi River gunboat during the Civil War. After sailing on the Great Lakes for three years he came to Granite Falls, Minnesota, in 1872, where he held various offices. In 1897 he was appointed to a consular post in Christiania, Norway, in which capacity he served until his death.

CHICAGO HISTORY COMMITTEE OF THE NORWEGIAN-AMERICAN HISTORICAL ASSOCIATION

Papers presented at a 1982 symposium, "Norwegians in Chicago: Their History," which was designed to present an overview of the colony in what was at one time the Norwegian capital of America. Topics presented were medical care; the landscape artist, Jens Jensen; Norwegian artists; the Danish editor and poet, Anton Kvist; Knut Hamsun; the artist and feminist, Aasta Hansteen; the sculptor, Kristian Schneider; Kristofer Janson's novel *Sara*; and a general history.

DYRESEN, DYRE

Several papers covering the history of the Seventh-Day Adventist Church among Danish and Norwegian immigrants.

EVANS, CHRISTOPHER

The translated diary of an Iowa farmer who came from Vang, Valdres, in 1850, to Winneshiek county, Iowa.

EVANS, EYVIND

Clippings from Norwegian newspapers about a Kasson, Minnesota, farmer and writer who came to the United States in 1920. The clippings cover his visit to Norway in August, 1979.

FLETRE, LARS

Papers of an artist from Voss who came to Chicago in 1923. In 1933 he returned to Norway and was in charge of Vossevangen Steinhoggeri. His sculptures include a war memorial in Bømoen, a memorial to Lars Osa in Ulvik cemetery, and an altarpiece in the Mjølfjell mountain chapel. He returned to Chicago in 1954, where, in addition to his work as sculptor and wood-carver, he was active in Norwegian cultural circles.

GRAFF, OLGA

Papers of a Norwegian-American journalist, much of whose work appeared in a Norwegian women's magazine *Urd*. Also included are articles by her husband, Harald Graff, a physician in Eau Claire, Wisconsin, and drawings by her daughter, Gerda, an artist in Oslo.

HAFSTAD, LAWRENCE RANDOLPH

Papers of a Norwegian-American physicist who was a research scientist at the Carnegie Institution of Washington, 1928–1941. During World War II he was part of a scientific team at the Applied Physics Laboratory of the Johns Hopkins University, which developed the proximity fuse for use in anti-aircraft weaponry. This development was hailed as a significant improvement in ordnance for the Army and the Navy. For his part in the achievement Hafstad was awarded the Medal of Merit of the United States Navy and the King's Medal in Defense of Freedom of the British Government in 1946.

HAGEN, CARL

Memoirs of a Norwegian American covering farm and village life in the Halloway, Minnesota, area from the 1890s to 1908. Hagen was later on the staff of the National City Bank of New York and spent part of his career in Latin America.

HANSEN, KNUTE

Papers of a Norwegian-born musician who, during his 48-year career in Chicago, was conductor of many choral groups there. On several occasions he was chief conductor of the Norwegian Singers' Association and of the American Union of Swedish Singers.

HANSON, JOHN F.

An autobiographical sketch of an immigrant from Stavanger whose life was largely spent in Quaker ministry. Also included is a diary kept by his daughter, Estella Hanson Watland, which adds to her father's story and gives a graphic description of her childhood, youth, and early married life.

HAWAII

An early labor contract, newspaper clippings, and other data regarding Norwegian immigration to Hawaii in 1881. Some of the material was collected for the centennial celebration of this event.

HJELM-HANSEN, PAUL

Om Amerika, a book by the Norwegian journalist who came to the United States in 1867 and whose writings influenced a great number of Norwegians to come to the Red River Valley. Also included is a paper by Tor Henning Ormseth about Paul Hjelm-Hansen.

JACOBSON, J. RODE

Miscellaneous papers of a composer, teacher, and organist who came to Chicago in 1898 and was influential in the musical life of the city.

JEVNE and ALMINI, CHICAGO

Information about a decorating firm in Chicago whose publication *Chicago Illustrated* has been called "the best source for the physical appearance of the city that the Great Fire destroyed."

JORGENSON, OLOF MEYER

Papers of a Baptist minister who came in 1903 from Fiskenes on the island of Andøy. After his ordination in 1911 he served parishes of the Norwegian Baptist Conference in Minnesota, North Dakota, and Washington.

LARSON, JULIUS ANSGAR

Autobiography and other papers of a Norwegian-born forester who received a master's degree in forestry from Yale University in 1910. After working with the United States Forest Service he joined the faculty of the forestry department at Iowa State University, Ames, Iowa, in 1924.

LEVORSEN, BARBARA

An unpublished manuscript "The Quiet Conquest," by a native of Pelican Rapids, Minnesota, describing frontier life in central North Dakota as she remembered it fifty years later. Two chapters of the manuscript have been published in *Norwegian-American Studies*: "Early Years in Dakota," in volume 21, and "Our Bread and Meat," in volume 22.

LUNDE, JOHAN P.

Diaries and other papers of an immigrant who came to Chicago in 1880. They reveal the introspective nature of a devout Quaker struggling with problems related to education, military service, and employment in Norway and in the United States.

LUNDE, THEODORE H.

Papers of an emigrant from Hamar who established the American Industrial Company for the manufacture of piano hardware. Because of his refusal to make war materials during World War I, he lost his factory. A son, Erling N. Lunde, was court-martialed for being a conscientious objector in 1918. A pamphlet covering his defense is included.

NELSON, CARL

Memoirs, poems, humorous anecdotes, and biographical data of a Norwegian-American editor and poet who lived at Cando, North Dakota.

NELSON, THEODORE G.

"Scrapbook Memories," covering the experiences of a political activitist in North Dakota, who was secretary of the Independent Voters' Association. Later, when he lived in Oregon, he was active in cooperative marketing, real estate, and retirement home movements.

NIELSEN, FREDRIKKE

Data concerning an evangelist of the Methodist Church, who before her conversion had been a leading actress for twenty-five years in the theaters of Bergen and Trondheim. She traveled widely in the United States, visiting some 300 cities, and received a great deal of acclaim as a powerful preacher.

NINETY-NINTH INFANTRY BATTALION, UNITED STATES ARMY

A newsletter of the Viking Battalion, which was composed of "men of Norwegian extraction, Norwegian nationals, and Americanized Norwegians," organized for particular missions during World War II.

NORWEGIAN IMMIGRATION

Promotional booklets written in Norwegian by railways and immigration bureaus, designed to give favorable and practical information for immigrants into Wisconsin, Minnesota, and the Dakotas.

NORWEGIAN IMMIGRATION SESQUICENTENNIAL

Papers of the six different commissions organized to arrange for the celebration in 1975 of the 150th anniversary of the arrival of the ship *Restauration* in New York. Major publications of the commissions are in the St. Olaf College Library.

NYHAMMER, LOUIS

Diaries of a Norwegian-born riverboat captain who held master pilot licenses on the Ohio, Missouri, and Mississippi rivers.

RACHIE, AMANDA LIEN

An account written by the granddaughter of Nils Gunnarson

315

Lien, who emigrated from Vang, Valdres, in 1852 and came to Goodhue county, Minnesota, in 1857.

REINDAL, KNUTE

A pamphlet about the making of violins by a Chicago craftsman who won recognition at the Paris Exposition, 1900, and at the Columbian Exposition in Chicago, 1893, for the violins he had made.

REINERTSEN, PEDER INGBART REINERT

Autobiographical account of an immigrant from Sandviken, near Bergen, in 1875, who was educated in the schools of the Norwegian Augustana Synod. Among the parishes he served was Elk Point, South Dakota, from which he recommended Ole Rølvaag for admission to St. Olaf College.

ROSDAIL, J. HART

A collection of the papers used in compiling *The Sloopers; Their Ancestry and Posterity*. Rosdail was a descendant of a "Slooper" family.

ROSENDAHL, PETER JULIUS

Bound copies of the first and second compilations of "Han Ola og han Per," the only continuing Norwegian cartoon published in America.

SATRANG (SAETRANG), ANTON OLSEN

Scrapbooks, albums, and unidentified photographs which belonged to an immigrant from Satrang, Haug parish, Ringerike, Norway, who came to Chicago in 1892. He was active in Normennenes Singing Society and was national treasurer of the Norwegian Singers Association.

SELJAAS, HELGE

Translation of Julie Ingeröd, *Et aar i Utah, eller mormonismens hemmeligheder*, which was originally published in Chicago in 1867.

STAGEBERG, OLAF

"The Poems of Olaf Stageberg," compiled by his son Rolf Stageberg with translations by Clarence Clausen and Rosanna Gutterud Johnsrud. Stageberg taught at Jewell Lutheran College, Waldorf College, and Red Wing Seminary.

STAGEBERG, SUSIE WILLIAMSON

Papers of the daughter of Norwegian immigrants who was active in education, politics, and journalism in Iowa and Minnesota. Among the papers is a diary kept when she was a "validated member of the press at the Congress for Disarmament and International Cooperation in Stockholm, July, 1958." She was influential in the Farmer-Labor party in Minnesota and ran for office on that ticket; in 1950 she ran for lieutenant governor on the Minnesota Progressive party ticket.

STRAND, THEODOR ELLINGSON

"The Norwegian Fox Lake Settlement," the memoirs of a Rice county, Minnesota, pioneer about the church life in the community and the building of the church.

SVENDSEN, JULIE

"Dagbog over Atlanterhav" kept by a passenger on the ship *Thingvalla* during the journey of July 27 to August 14, 1882. Included is a translation by Serena Bjornstad.

THESEN, OLAF

"Trekk ved Utvandringa fra Ringsaker 1839–95," an academic thesis for the University of Oslo. The thesis deals with conditions in Ringsaker which created and encouraged emigration.

TOLLEFSRUDE, HANS C.

Diary of a journey to California from Rock county, Wisconsin, via New York and Panama, in search of gold, ending with disillusionment.

TORRISON, MARTHA

Papers concerning a prominent family who were descendants of Osul Torrison, pioneer merchant and ship owner in Manitowoc, Wisconsin.

TOSTENSON, OLE

Biographical notes of a Wisconsin resident, telling of his father's problems in selling his farm and of his own military service in the 15th Wisconsin Regiment from 1861–1865.

TUSKIND, OLE

Biographical sketch of Ole and Karen Tuskind, who emigrated from Solør in 1871 and settled in Dakota Territory in 1872.

VERKEFINGEREN

An issue of a Norwegian humor magazine, November, 1925, published by Eivind Rudie, Minot, North Dakota.

317

Charlotte Jacobson

VETLESEN, TORBION

An "America letter" about 1850 from "Havre Dalen i Amerika." The writer describes the journey from Norway to Koshkonong, Wisconsin, in 1842, via New York, Albany, Buffalo, and Milwaukee, and tells of his satisfaction with the move to America.

WESTNES, P. ROLF

A collection of the works of a Chicago writer active in the Norwegian literary circles of that city. His poems, stories, and articles have been published in Norwegian-American newspapers and in Norway.

Contributors

Lloyd Hustvedt, the Association's executive secretary, holds the King Olav V Professorship in Norwegian Studies at St. Olaf College. He is currently writing a history of Norwegian-American literature.

Patsy Adams Hegstad is a political scientist with special interest in western Europe. She is continuing her studies in the field of Nordic immigration.

Terje I. Leiren, a member of the Association's Board of Publications, serves on the Scandinavian faculty at the University of Washington. He is preparing a manuscript on the Norwegian labor leader Marcus Thrane's years in America.

Sverre Arestad is professor emeritus of Scandinavian languages and literature and of comparative literature at the University of Washington. He is a frequent contributor to the series.

Kenneth O. Bjork, the Association's editor from 1960 to 1980, continues research and writing on the Norwegians on the Pacific Coast, a field in which he has pioneered.

Rangvald Kvelstad is a retired high school teacher in Poulsbo, Washington, and an expert on the area's history. He is presently writing a book for the Poulsbo centennial observance in 1986.

James S. Hamre teaches in the department of religion at Waldorf College, Forest City, Iowa. His study of Georg Sverdrup, a prominent Norwegian-American theologian, will introduce a new series in the Association's publication program.

Claire Selkurt is on the faculty of Mankato State University, Mankato, Minnesota, where she teaches art history. As a descendant of one of the earliest settlers in Luther Valley, she has a personal interest in this pioneer Norwegian settlement.

Larry Emil Scott is chairman of the department of Scandinavian studies at Augustana College, Rock Island, Illinois. He has published works on Swedish poetry as well as on Swedish settlement in the state of Texas.

C. A. Clausen is a member of the Association's Board of Publications. He is one of the most faithful contributors to the series and has since volume 19 in 1956 prepared lists of recent publications of interest to the Association's readers.

Charlotte Jacobson is the Association's archivist. Her report indicates the significant historical documents that continue to arrive at the Association's archives.

320

NORWEGIAN-AMERICAN HISTORICAL ASSOCIATION

Officers

Publications

Forties and Fifties, by Albert O. Barton; Emigration As Viewed by a Norwegian Student of Agriculture in 1850: A. Budde's "From a Letter about America," translated by A. Sophie Bøe, with an introduction by Theodore C. Blegen; An Immigration Journey to America in 1854, a letter translated and edited by Henrietta Larson; Chicago As Viewed by a Norwegian Immigrant in 1864, a letter translated and edited by Brynjolf J. Hovde; The Historical Value of Church Records, by J. Magnus Rohne; A Norwegian-American Landnamsman: Ole S. Gjerset, by Knut Gjerset; The Icelandic Communities in America: Cultural Backgrounds and Early Settlements, by Thorstina Jackson.   Out of print

VOLUME IV. Northfield, 1929. 159 pp. A Contribution to the Study of the Adjustment of a Pioneer Pastor to American Conditions: Laur. Larsen, 1857–1880, by Karen Larsen; Report of the Annual Meeting of the Haugean Churches Held at Lisbon, Illinois, in June, 1854, translated and edited by J. Magnus Rohne; The Attitude of the United States toward Norway in the Crisis of 1905, by H. Fred Swansen; Immigration and Social Amelioration, by Joseph Schafer; The Mind of the Scandinavian Immigrant, by George M. Stephenson; Three Civil War Letters from 1862, translated and edited by Brynjolf J. Hovde; The Sinking of the "Atlantic" on Lake Erie, a letter translated and edited by Henrietta Larson; An Account of a Journey to California in 1852, by Tosten Kittelsen Stabæk, translated by Einar Haugen.   Price $8.00

VOLUME V. Northfield, 1930. 152 pp. An Early Norwegian Fur Trader of the Canadian Northwest, by Hjalmar R. Holand; Immigrant Women and the American Frontier, Three Early "America Letters," translated and edited by Theodore C. Blegen; From New York to Wisconsin in 1844, by Johan Gasmann, translated and edited by Carlton C. Qualey; Social and Economic Aspects of Pioneering As Illustrated in Goodhue County, Minnesota, by Theodore Nydahl; Norwegian-American Fiction, 1880–1928, by Aagot D. Hoidahl; Bjørnson and the Norwegian-Americans, 1880–81, by Arthur C. Paulson; The Beginnings of St. Olaf College, by I. F. Grose; Some Recent Publications Relating to Norwegian-American History, compiled by Jacob Hodnefield.   Price $8.00

VOLUME VI. Northfield, 1931. 191 pp. Illustrations, map. Norwegians in the Selkirk Settlement, by Paul Knaplund; Claus L. Clausen, Pioneer Pastor and Settlement Promoter: Illustrative Documents, translated and edited by Carlton C. Qualey; Lars Davidson Reque: Pioneer, by Sophie A. Bøe; A Pioneer Pastor's Journey to Dakota in 1861, by Abraham Jacobson, translated by J. N. Jacobson; The Campaign of the Illinois Central Railroad for Norwegian and Swedish Immigrants, by Paul W. Gates; Norwegians at the Indian Forts on the Missouri River during the Seventies, by Einar Haugen; The Convention Riot at Benson Grove, Iowa, in 1876, by Laurence M. Larson; Bjørnson's Reaction to Emigration, by Arne Odd Johnsen; Alexander Corstvet and Anthony M. Rud, Norwegian-American Novelists, by Albert O. Barton; The Norwegian-American Historical Museum, by Knut Gjerset; Norwegian Migration to America before the Civil War, by Brynjolf J. Hovde; Some Recent Publications Relating to Norwegian-American History, II, compiled by Jacob Hodnefield.   Price $8.00

VOLUME VII. Northfield, 1933. 139 pp. Illustrations. Social Aspects of Prairie Pioneering: The Reminiscences of a Pioneer Pastor's Wife, by Mrs. R. O. Brandt; The Fraser River Gold Rush: An Immigrant Letter of 1858, translated and edited by C. A. Clausen; O. E. Rølvaag: Norwegian-American, by Einar I. Haugen; Some Recent Publications Relating to Norwegian-American History, III, compiled by Jacob Hodnefield; A Hunt for Norwegian-American Records, by Carlton C. Qualey; Ole Edvart Rølvaag, 1876–1931: In Memoriam, by Julius E. Olson.   Out of print

VOLUME VIII. Northfield, 1934. 176 pp. Tellef Grundysen and the Beginnings of Norwegian-American Fiction, by Laurence M. Larson; The Seventeenth of May in Mid-Atlantic: Ole Rynning's Emigrant Song, translated and edited by Theodore C. Blegen and Martin B. Ruud; Johannes Nordboe and Norwegian Immigration: An "America Letter" of 1837, edited by Arne Odd Johnsen; The First Norwegian Migration into Texas: Four "America Letters," translated and edited by Lyder L. Unstad; Norwegian-Americans and Wisconsin Politics in the Forties, by Bayrd Still; The Emigrant Journey in

the Fifties, by Karl E. Erickson, edited by Albert O. Barton;
The Political Position of *Emigranten* in the Election of 1852:
A Documentary Article, by Harold M. Tolo; The Editorial
Policy of *Skandinaven*, 1900–1903, by Agnes M. Larson;
Some Recent Publications Relating to Norwegian-American
History, IV, compiled by Jacob Hodnefield; Fort Thompson
in the Eighties: A Communication.   Price $8.00

VOLUME IX. Northfield, 1936. 131 pp. Immigration and Puritanism, by Marcus L. Hansen; Svein Nilsson, Pioneer Norwegian-American Historian, by D. G. Ristad; The Sugar
Creek Settlement in Iowa, by H. F. Swansen; Pioneer Town
Building in the West: An America Letter Written by Frithjof
Meidell at Springfield, Illinois, in 1855, translated with a
foreword by Clarence A. Clausen; A Typical Norwegian Settlement: Spring Grove, Minnesota, by Carlton C. Qualey;
Marcus Thrane in America: Some Unpublished Letters from
1880–1884, translated and edited by Waldemar Westergaard;
The Missouri Flood of 1881, by Halvor B. Hustvedt, translated by Katherine Hustvedt; The Collection and Preservation of Sources, by Laurence M. Larson; Some Recent
Publications Relating to Norwegian-American History, V,
compiled by Jacob Hodnefield.   Price $8.00

VOLUME X. Northfield, 1938. 202 pp. Language and Immigration, by Einar I. Haugen; Two Early Norwegian Dramatic Societies in Chicago, by Napier Wilt and Henriette C. Koren
Naeseth; A School and Language Controversy in 1858: A
Documentary Study, translated and edited by Arthur C. Paulson and Kenneth Bjørk; A Newcomer Looks at American Colleges, translated and edited by Karen Larsen; The Norwegian
Quakers of Marshall County, Iowa, by H. F. Swansen; The
Main Factors in Rølvaag's Authorship, by Theodore Jorgenson; Magnus Swenson, Inventor and Engineer, by Olaf Hou-
gen; Some Recent Publications Relating to Norwegian-
American History, VI, compiled by Jacob Hodnefield.
                                                Price $8.00

VOLUME XI. Northfield, 1940. 183 pp. *A Doll's House* on the
Prairie: The First Ibsen Controversy in America, by Arthur C.
Paulson and Kenneth Bjørk; Scandinavian Students at Illinois

State University, by Henry O. Evjen; Stephen O. Himoe, Civil War Physician, by E. Biddle Heg; A Pioneer Church Library, by H. F. Swansen; Norwegian Emigration to America during the Nineteenth Century, by Ingrid Gaustad Semmingsen; Jørgen Gjerdrum's Letters from America, 1874–75, by Carlton C. Qualey; The Introduction of Domesticated Reindeer into Alaska, by Arthur S. Peterson; The Unknown Rølvaag: Secretary in the Norwegian-American Historical Association, by Kenneth Bjørk; The Sources of the Rølvaag Biography, by Nora O. Solum; Some Recent Publications Relating to Norwegian-American History, VII, compiled by Jacob Hodnefield. Price $10.00

VOLUME XII. Northfield, 1941. 203 pp. Norwegian-American Surnames, by Marjorie M. Kimmerle; Norwegian Folk Narrative in America, by Ella Valborg Rølvaag; A Journey to America in the Fifties, by Clara Jacobson; James Denoon Reymert and the Norwegian Press, by Martin L. Reymert; Recollections of a Norwegian Pioneer in Texas, by Knudt Olson Hastvedt, translated and edited by C. A. Clausen; Norwegian Clubs in Chicago, by Birger Osland; Buslett's Editorship of *Normannen* from 1894 to 1896, by Evelyn Nilsen; Ole Edvart Rølvaag, by John Heitmann; Ole Evinrude and the Outboard Motor, by Kenneth Bjørk; Some Recent Publications Relating to Norwegian-American History, VIII, compiled by Jacob Hodnefield. Out of print

VOLUME XIII. Northfield, 1943. 203 pp. Pioneers in Dakota Territory, 1879–89, edited by Henry H. Bakken; An Official Report on Norwegian and Swedish Immigration, 1870, by A. Lewenhaupt, with a foreword by Theodore C. Blegen; Memories from Little Iowa Parsonage, by Caroline Mathilde Koren Naeseth, translated and edited by Henriette C. K. Naeseth; A Norwegian Schoolmaster Looks at America, an America letter translated and edited by C. A. Clausen; A Singing Church, by Paul Maurice Glasoe; A Norwegian Settlement in Missouri, by A. N. Rygg; Carl G. Barth, 1860–1939: A Sketch, by Florence M. Manning; Pioneering on the Pacific Coast, by John Storseth, with a foreword by Einar Haugen; Materials in the National Archives Relating to the Scandinavian Countries; The Norwegians in America, by Halvdan Koht; Some Recent Publications Relating to Norwegian-American History, IX, compiled by Jacob Hodnefield; Notes and Documents: Norway, Maine, by Halvdan Koht. Out of print

VOLUME XIV. Northfield, 1944. 264 pp. A Migration of Skills, by Kenneth Bjørk; An Immigrant Exploration of the Middle West in 1839, a letter by Johannes Johansen and Søren Bache, translated by the Verdandi Study Club; An Immigrant Shipload of 1840, by C. A. Clausen; Behind the Scenes of Emigration: A Series of Letters from the 1840's, by Johan R. Reiersen, translated by Carl O. Paulson and the Verdandi Study Club, edited by Theodore C. Blegen; The Ballad of Oleana: A Verse Translation, by Theodore C. Blegen; Knud Langeland: Pioneer Editor, by Arlow W. Andersen; Memories from Perry Parsonage, by Clara Jacobson; When America Called for Immigrants, by Halvdan Koht; The Norwegian Lutheran Academies, by B. H. Narveson; Pioneering on the Technical Front: A Story Told in America Letters, by Kenneth Bjørk; Some Recent Publications Relating to Norwegian-American History, X, by Jacob Hodnefield; Notes and Documents: Karel Hansen Toll, by A. N. Rygg.

Price $10.00

VOLUME XV. Northfield, 1949. 238 pp. A Norwegian-American Pioneer Ballad, by Einar Haugen; Our Vanguard: A Pioneer Play in Three Acts, with Prologue and Epilogue, by Aileen Berger Buetow; An Immigrant's Advice on America: Some Letters of Søren Bache, translated and edited by C. A. Clausen; Lincoln and the Union: A Study of the Editorials of *Emigranten* and *Fædrelandet*, by Arlow W. Andersen; Thorstein Veblen and St. Olaf College: A Group of Letters by Thorbjørn N. Mohn, edited by Kenneth Bjork; Kristian Prestgard: An Appreciation, by Henriette C. K. Naeseth; Julius B. Baumann: A Biographical Sketch, by John Heitmann; Erik L. Petersen, by Jacob Hodnefield; Scandinavia, Wisconsin, by Alfred O. Erickson; Some Recent Publications Relating to Norwegian-American History, XI, by Jacob Hodnefield; Notes and Documents: Norway, Maine, by Walter W. Wright.

Price $10.00

VOLUME XVI. Northfield, 1950. 218 pp. Hvistendahl's Mission to San Francisco, 1870–75, by Kenneth Bjork; Oregon and Washington Territory in the 1870's as Seen through the Eyes of a Pioneer Pastor, by Nora O. Solum; From the Prairie to Puget Sound, by O. B. Iverson, edited by Sverre Arestad; Life in the Klondike and Alaska Gold Fields, letters translated and edited by C. A. Clausen; From the Klondike to the Kougarok, by Carl L. Lokke; Some Recent Publications Relating to Norwegian-American History, XII, compiled by Jacob Hodnefield.   Price $10.00

VOLUME XVII. Northfield, 1952. 185 pp. The Struggle over Norwegian, by Einar Haugen; Brother Ebben in His Native Country, by Oystein Ore; Norwegian Gold Seekers in the Rockies, by Kenneth Bjork; Søren Jaabæk, Americanizer in Norway: A Study in Cultural Exchange, by Franklin D. Scott; First Sagas in a New World: A Study of the Beginnings of Norwegian-American Literature, by Gerald H. Thorson; Controlled Scholarship and Productive Nationalism, by Franklin D. Scott; The Second Twenty-five Years, by Theodore C. Blegen; Some Recent Publications Relating to Norwegian-American History, XIII, by Jacob Hodnefield.
Price $10.00

VOLUME XVIII. Northfield, 1954. 252 pp. Maps. Norwegian Migration to America, by Einar Haugen; Rasmus B. Anderson, Pioneer and Crusader, by Paul Knaplund; Early Norwegian Settlement in the Rockies, by Kenneth Bjork; A Little More Light on the Kendall Colony, by Richard Canuteson; Segregation and Assimilation of Norwegian Settlements in Wisconsin, by Peter A. Munch; The Novels of Peer Strømme, by Gerald Thorson; Norwegian-American *Bygdelags* and Their Publications, by Jacob Hodnefield; Some Recent Publications Relating to Norwegian-American History, XIV, by Jacob Hodnefield.   Price $10.00

VOLUME XIX. Northfield, 1956. 218 pp. The Immigrant Image of America, by Theodore C. Blegen; Boyesen and the Norwegian Immigration, by Clarence A. Glasrud; Norwegian Forerunners among the Early Mormons, by William Mulder;

329

Publications

"Snowshoe" Thompson: Fact and Legend, by Kenneth Bjork; Norwegian-Danish Methodism on the Pacific Coast, by Arlow William Andersen; A Quest for Norwegian Folk Art in America, by Tora Bøhn; The Trials of an Immigrant: The Journal of Ole K. Trovatten, translated and edited by Clarence A. Clausen; Norwegian Emigrants with University Training, 1830–1880, by Oystein Ore; Some Recent Publications Relating to Norwegian-American History, XV, compiled by Clarence A. Clausen. Price $10.00

VOLUME XX. Northfield, 1959. 246 pp. Ibsen in America, by Einar Haugen; Still More Light on the Kendall Colony: A Unique Slooper Letter, by Mario S. De Pillis; A Texas Manifesto: A Letter from Mrs. Elise Wærenskjold, translated and edited by Clarence A. Clausen; History and Sociology, by Peter A. Munch; Beating to Windward, by Otto M. Bratrud, edited by Sverre Arestad; Pioneering in Alaska, by Knute L. Gravem; Marcus Thrane in Christiania: Some Unpublished Letters from 1850–51, translated and edited by Waldemar Westergaard; A Centenary of Norwegian Studies in American Institutions of Learning, by Hedin Bronner; Elizabeth Fedde's Diary, 1883–88, translated and edited by Beulah Folkedahl; The Content of Studies and Records, Volumes 1–20, compiled by Helen Thane Katz; "With Great Price," by John M. Gaus; Some Recent Publications Relating to Norwegian-American History, XVI, compiled by Clarence A. Clausen. Price $10.00

VOLUME XXI (*Norwegian-American Studies*). Northfield, 1962. 311 pp. Theodore C. Blegen, by Carlton C. Qualey; The Scandinavian Immigrant Writer in America, by Dorothy Burton Skårdal; Questing for Gold and Furs in Alaska, edited by Sverre Arestad; Norwegians Become Americans, translated and edited by Beulah Folkedahl; Cleng Peerson and the Communitarian Background of Norwegian Immigration, by Mario S. De Pillis; Early Years in Dakota, by Barbara Levorsen; A Pioneer Diary from Wisconsin, by Malcolm Rosholt; A Covenant Folk, with Scandinavian Colorings, by Kenneth O. Bjork; Reiersen's Texas, translated and edited by Derwood Johnson; J. R. Reiersen's "Indiscretions," by Einar Haugen;

Some Recent Publications, compiled by Beulah Folkedahl; From the Archives, by Beulah Folkedahl.   Price $10.00

VOLUME XXII. Northfield, 1965. 264 pp. Illustrations. A Pioneer Artist and His Masterpiece, by Marion John Nelson; Kristofer Janson's Lecture Tour, 1879–80, by Nina Draxten; Two Men of Old Waupaca, by Malcom Rosholt; Pioneering in Montana, edited by Sverre Arestad; Seven America Letters to Valdres, translated and edited by Carlton C. Qualey; Music for Youth in an Emerging Church, by Gerhard M. Cartford; Our Bread and Meat, by Barbara Levorsen; The Independent Historical Society, by Walter Muir Whitehill; Some Recent Publications, compiled by Beulah Folkedahl; From the Archives, by Beulah Folkedahl.   Price $10.00

VOLUME XXIII. Northfield, 1967. 256 pp. The Norwegian Immigrant and His Church, by Eugene L. Fevold; Some Civil War Letters of Knute Nelson, edited by Millard L. Gieske; An Immigrant Boy on the Frontier, by Simon Johnson, translated with an introduction by Nora O. Solum; The Gasmann Brothers Write Home, translated and edited by C. A. Clausen; Knud Knudsen and His America Book, by Beulah Folkedahl; Kristofer Janson's Beginning Ministry, by Nina Draxten; Knut Hamsun's America, by Arlow W. Andersen; The Romantic Spencerian, by Marc L. Ratner; Some Recent Publications, compiled by Beulah Folkedahl; From the Archives, by Beulah Folkedahl.   Price $10.00

VOLUME XXIV. Northfield, 1970. 301 pp. Thor Helgeson: Schoolmaster and Raconteur, by Einar Haugen; The Letters of Mons H. Grinager: Pioneer and Soldier, collected by Per Hvamstad, translated by C. A. Clausen; The Norwegian Press in North Dakota, by Odd Sverre Løvoll; H. Tambs Lyche: Propagandist for America, by Paul Knaplund; The Social Criticism of Ole Edvart Rølvaag, by Neil T. Eckstein; A Thanksgiving Day Address by Georg Sverdrup, by James S. Hamre; Hamsun and America, by Sverre Arestad; Gold, Salt Air, and Callouses, by Thomas L. Benson; Norwegians in New York, by Knight Hoover; Some Recent Publications, compiled by Beulah Folkedahl; From the Archives, by Beulah Folkedahl.   Price $10.00

Publications

VOLUME XXV. Northfield, 1972. 293 pp. The *Bygdelag* Movement, by Odd Sverre Løvoll; Knut Gjerset, by David T. Nelson; Norway's Organized Response to Emigration, by Arne Hassing; The Founding of Quatsino Colony, by Kenneth O. Bjork; Norwegian Soldiers in the Confederate Forces, by C. A. Clausen and Derwood Johnson; Lars and Martha Larson: "We Do What We Can for Them," by Richard L. Canuteson; Ibsen in Seattle, by Sverre Arestad; From Norwegian State Church to American Free Church, by J. C. K. Preus; The 1842 Immigrants from Norway, by Gerhard B. Naeseth; Some Recent Publications, compiled by Beulah Folkedahl and C. A. Clausen; From the Archives, by Beulah Folkedahl and C. A. Clausen.   Price $10.00

VOLUME XXVI. Northfield, 1974. 271 pp. Scandinavian Migration to the Canadian Prairie Provinces, 1893–1914, by Kenneth O. Bjork; The Story of Peder Anderson, translated and edited by Eva L. Haugen; Emigration from Land Parish to America, 1866–1875, by Arvid Sandaker, translated by C. A. Clausen; The Brothers Week, by Malcolm Rosholt; Rølvaag's Search for Soria Moria, by Raychel A. Haugrud; Notes of a Civil War Soldier, by Bersven Nelson, translated and edited by C. A. Clausen; Farewell to an Old Homestead, by Ethel J. Odegard; Georg Sverdrup and the Augsburg Plan of Education, by James S. Hamre; Factors in Assimilation: A Comparative Study, by Torben Krontoft; The School Controversy among Norwegian Immigrants, by Frank C. Nelsen; Norwegians in "Zion" Teach Themselves English, by Helge Seljaas; Breidablik, by Rodney Nelson; Some Recent Publications, compiled by C. A. Clausen.   Price $10.00

VOLUME XXVII. Northfield, 1977. 323 pp. Hegra before and after the Emigration Era, by Jon Leirfall, translated and edited by C. A. Clausen; Marcus Hansen, Puritanism and Scandinavian Immigrant Temperance Movements, by Frederick Hale; Three America Letters to Lesja, translated and edited by Carlton C. Qualey; Berdahl Family History and Rølvaag's Immigrant Trilogy, by Kristoffer F. Paulson; *Decorah-Posten*: The Story of an Immigrant Newspaper, by Odd S. Lovoll; *Symra*: A Memoir, by Einar Haugen; Erik Morstad's Missionary Work among Wisconsin Indians, by A. E. Morstad; Polygamy among the Norwegian Mormons, by Helge Seljaas; Wisconsin Scandinavians and Progressivism, 1900–1950, by David L. Brye; Name Change and the Church, 1918–1920, by Carl H. Chrislock; American Press Opinion and Norwegian Independence, 1905, by Terje I. Leiren; The Kendall Settlement Survived, by Richard L. Canuteson; The Popcorn Man, by Rodney Nelson; An Outsider's View of the Association, by Rudolph J. Vecoli; Some Recent Publications, compiled by C. A. Clausen; From the Archives, by Charlotte Jacobson.   Price $10.00

VOLUME XXVIII. Northfield, 1979. 367 pp. Authority and Freedom: Controversy in Norwegian-American Congregations, by Peter A. Munch; *Skandinaven* and the John Anderson Publishing Company, by Jean Skogerboe Hansen; Martha Ostenso: A Norwegian-American Immigrant Novelist, by Joan N. Buckley; Norwegians, Danes, and the Origins of the Evangelical Free Tradition, by Frederick Hale; Two Immigrants for the Union: Their Civil War Letters, by Lars and Knud Olsen Dokken, translated by Della Kittleson Catuna, edited by Carol Lynn H. Knight and Gerald S. Cowden; Oslo on the Texas High Plains, by Peter L. Petersen; Dark Decade: The Declining Years of Waldemar Ager, by Clarence Kilde; Methodism from America to Norway, by Arne Hassing; Beret and the Prairie in *Giants in the Earth*, by Curtis D. Ruud; The Vossing Correspondence Society and the Report of Adam Løvenskjold, translated and edited by Lars Fletre; The Danish-Language Press in America, by Marion Marzolf; Norwegian-American Pastors in Immigrant Fiction, 1870–1920, by Duane R. Lindberg; Carl L. Boeckmann: Norwegian Artist in the New World, by Marilyn Boeckmann Anderson; Some Recent Publications, compiled by C. A. Clausen; From the Archives, by Charlotte Jacobson.   Price $10.00

VOLUME XXIX. Northfield, 1983. 402 pp. Haugeans, Rappites, and the Emigration of 1825, by Ingrid Semmingsen, translated by C. A. Clausen; Emigration from the Community of Tinn, 1837–1907: Demographic, Economic, and Social Background, by Andres A. Svalestuen, translated by C. A. Clausen;

Publications

Angst on the Prairie: Reflections on Immigrants, Rølvaag, and Beret, by Harold P. Simonson; Emigration from the District of Sogn, 1839–1915, by Rasmus Sunde, translated by C. A. Clausen; Emigration from Sunnfjord to America Prior to 1885, by Leiv H. Dvergsdal, translated by C. A. Clausen; The Lynching of Hans Jakob Olson, 1889: The Story of a Norwegian-American Crime, by Odin W. Anderson; Emigration from a Fjord District on Norway's West Coast, 1852–1915, by Ragnar Standal, translated by C. A. Clausen; Emigration from Dovre, 1865–1914, by Arnfinn Engen, translated by C. A. Clausen; Sigbjørn Obstfelder and America, by Sverre Arestad; Emigration from Brønnøy and Vik in Helgeland, by Kjell Erik Skaaren, translated by C. A. Clausen; Emigration from Agder to America, 1890–1915, by Sverre Ordahl, translated by C. A. Clausen; Sondre Norheim: Folk Hero to Immigrant, by John Weinstock; Some Recent Publications, compiled by C. A. Clausen; Index to Volumes 1–29 of *Norwegian-American Studies*, compiled by Charlotte Jacobson.   Price $10.00

VOLUME XXX. Northfield, 1985. 340 pp. O. A. Tveitmoe: Labor Leader, by Lloyd Hustvedt; Scandinavian Settlement in Seattle, "Queen City of the Puget Sound," by Patsy Adams Hegstad; Ole and the Reds: The "Americanism" of Seattle Mayor Ole Hanson, by Terje I. Leiren; Norwegians in the Pacific Coast Fisheries, by Sverre Arestad; Reindeer, Gold, and Scandal, by Kenneth O. Bjork; The Pioneers of Dog Fish Bay, by Rangvald Kvelstad; Three Spokesmen for Norwegian Lutheran Academies: Schools for Church, Heritage, Society, by James S. Hamre; The Domestic Architecture and Cabinetry of Luther Valley, by Claire Selkurt; The Poetry of Agnes Mathilde Wergeland, by Larry Emil Scott; Some Recent Publications, by C. A. Clausen; From the Archives, by Charlotte Jacobson.   Price $10.00

TRAVEL AND DESCRIPTION SERIES

VOLUME I. *Ole Rynning's True Account of America.* Translated and edited by Theodore C. Blegen. Minneapolis, 1926. 100 pp. Historical introduction; original text of Rynning's book about America as published in Norway in 1838; and a complete English translation.   Out of print

VOLUME II. *Peter Testman's Account of His Experiences in North America.* Translated and edited by Theodore C. Blegen. Northfield, 1927. 60 pp. Historical introduction; facsimile of Testman's account of America as published in Norway in 1839; and a complete English translation.   Price $3.00

VOLUME III. *America in the Forties: The Letters of Ole Munch Ræder.* Translated and edited by Gunnar J. Malmin. Published for the Norwegian-American Historical Association by the University of Minnesota Press, Minneapolis, 1929. 244 pp. Historical introduction, frontispiece, index. A series of informal travel letters written 1847–48 by a Norwegian scholar who was sent by his government to America to make a study of the jury system.   Out of print

VOLUME IV. *Frontier Parsonage: The Letters of Olaus Fredrik Duus, Norwegian Pastor in Wisconsin, 1855–1858.* Translated by the Verdandi Study Club of Minneapolis and edited by Theodore C. Blegen. Northfield, 1947. 120 pp. Historical introduction, index.   Out of print

VOLUME V. *Frontier Mother: The Letters of Gro Svendsen.* Translated and edited by Pauline Farseth and Theodore C. Blegen. Northfield, 1950. 153 pp. Historical introduction, frontispiece, index.   Out of print

VOLUME VI. *The Lady with the Pen: Elise Wærenskjold in Texas.* Translated by the Verdandi Study Club of Minneapolis and edited by C. A. Clausen; foreword by Theodore C. Blegen. Northfield, 1961. 183 pp. Historical introduction, illustrations, index.   Out of print

VOLUME VII. *Klondike Saga: The Chronicle of a Minnesota Gold Mining Company.* By Carl L. Lokke. Preface by Kenneth O. Bjork; foreword by Senator Ernest Gruening. Published for the Norwegian-American Historical Association by the University of Minnesota Press, Minneapolis, 1965. 211 pp. Illustrations, maps, appendices, index.   Out of print

VOLUME VIII. *A Pioneer Churchman: J. W. C. Dietrichson in Wisconsin, 1844–1850.* Includes Dietrichson's Travel Narrative and Koshkonong Parish Journal. Edited and with an Introduction by E. Clifford Nelson. Translated by Malcolm

Publications

Rosholt and Harris E. Kaasa. Published for the Norwegian-American Historical Association by Twayne Publishers, Inc., New York. 1973. 265 pp. Introduction, appendices, index, illustrations, maps. Price $9.00

VOLUME IX. *Pathfinder for Norwegian Emigrants.* By Johan Reinert Reiersen. Translated by Frank G. Nelson. Edited by Kenneth O. Bjork. Northfield, 1981. 239 pp. Historical introduction, frontispieces, appendices, index. Price $12.00

VOLUME X. *On Both Sides of the Ocean: A Part of Per Hagen's Journey.* Translated, with Introduction and Notes, by Kate Stafford and Harald Naess. Northfield, 1984. 70 pp.
Price $8.00

SPECIAL PUBLICATIONS

Norwegian Sailors on the Great Lakes: A Study in the History of American Inland Transportation. By Knut Gjerset. Northfield, 1928. 211 pp. Illustrations, index. Out of print

Norwegian Migration to America, 1825–1860. By Theodore C. Blegen. Northfield, 1931. 412 pp. Illustrations, maps, appendix, index. Out of print

Norwegian Sailors in American Waters: A Study in the History of Maritime Activity on the Eastern Seaboard. By Knut Gjerset. Northfield, 1933. 271 pp. Illustrations, index.
Out of print

The Civil War Letters of Colonel Hans Christian Heg. Edited by Theodore C. Blegen. Northfield, 1936. 260 pp. Historical introduction, illustrations, index. Price $10.00

Laur. Larsen: Pioneer College President. By Karen Larsen. Northfield, 1936. 358 pp. Illustrations, bibliographical note, index. Out of print

The Changing West and Other Essays. By Laurence M. Larson. Northfield, 1937. 180 pp. Illustrations, index. Price $8.00

Norwegian Settlement in the United States. By Carlton C. Qualey. Northfield, 1939. 285 pp. Illustrations, maps, appendix, bibliography, index. Out of print

336

The Log Book of a Young Immigrant. By Laurence M. Larson. Northfield, 1939. 318 pp. Illustrations, selected list of Larson's writings, index.   Price $9.00

Norwegian Migration to America: The American Transition. By Theodore C. Blegen. Northfield, 1940. 655 pp. Illustrations, appendix, index.   Out of print

A Long Pull from Stavanger: The Reminiscences of a Norwegian Immigrant. By Birger Osland. Northfield, 1945. 263 pp. Portrait, index.   Price $8.00

Saga in Steel and Concrete: Norwegian Engineers in America. By Kenneth Bjork. Northfield, 1947. 504 pp. Illustrations, index.   Price $10.00

Grass of the Earth: Immigrant Life in the Dakota Country. By Aagot Raaen. Northfield, 1950. 238 pp. Index. Out of print

A Chronicle of Old Muskego: The Diary of Søren Bache, 1839–1847. Translated and edited by Clarence A. Clausen and Andreas Elviken. Northfield, 1951. 237 pp. Historical introduction, portrait, appendix, index.   Price $10.00

The Immigrant Takes His Stand: The Norwegian-American Press and Public Affairs, 1847–1872. By Arlow William Andersen. Northfield, 1953. 176 pp. Bibliography, index.
                    Out of print

The Diary of Elisabeth Koren, 1853–1855. Translated and edited by David T. Nelson. Northfield, 1955. 381 pp. Historical introduction, illustrations, index. Available through Vesterheim, the Norwegian-American Museum, Decorah, Iowa.

West of the Great Divide: Norwegian Migration to the Pacific Coast, 1847–1893. By Kenneth O. Bjork. Northfield, 1958. 671 pp. Illustrations, maps, index   Out of print

John A. Johnson: An Uncommon American. By Agnes M. Larson, Northfield, 1969. 312 pp. Illustrations, appendixes, index.   Price $8.00

A Folk Epic: The Bygdelag *in America.* By Odd Sverre Lovoll. Northfield, 1975. Illustrations, bibliography, index.
                    Price $15.00

Publications

The Norwegian-American Historical Association, 1825– 1975. By Odd Sverre Lovoll and Kenneth O. Bjork. Northfield, 1975. 72 pp. Appendix. Price $3.00

Guide to Manuscripts Collections of the Norwegian-American Historical Association. Compiled and edited by Lloyd Hustvedt. Northfield, 1979. 158 pp. Price $7.50

Makers of an American Immigrant Legacy: Essays in Honor of Kenneth O. Bjork. Edited by Odd S. Lovoll. Northfield, 1980. 223 pp. Frontispiece. Tabula Gratulatoria. Out of print

The Promise of America: A History of the Norwegian-American People. By Odd S. Lovoll. Published in cooperation with the University of Minnesota Press, Minneapolis, 1984. 239 pp. Illustrations, bibliography, index. Price $35.00

Han Ola og han Per: A Norwegian-American Comic Strip. By Peter J. Rosendahl. Introduced and edited by Joan N. Buckley and Einar Haugen. Published in cooperation with Universitetsforlaget, Oslo, 1984. 262 pp. Price $30.00

AUTHORS SERIES

VOLUME I. *Hjalmar Hjorth Boyesen.* By Clarence A. Glasrud. Northfield, 1963. 245 pp. Illustrations, bibliography, index. Price $8.00

VOLUME II. *Rasmus Bjørn Anderson: Pioneer Scholar.* By Lloyd Hustvedt. Northfield, 1966. 381 pp. Illustrations, bibliography, index. Out of print

VOLUME III. *Kristofer Janson in America.* By Nina Draxten. Published for the Norwegian-American Historical Association by Twayne Publishers, Inc., Boston, 1976. 401 pp. Illustrations, bibliography, index.
Price $12.00

VOLUME IV. *Theodore C. Blegen: A Memoir.* By John T. Flanagan. Northfield, 1977. 181 pp. Bibliography, index.
Price $8.00

VOLUME V. *Land of the Free: Bjørnstjerne Bjørnson's America*

Letters. Edited and translated by Eva Lund Haugen and Einar Haugen. Northfield, 1978. 311 pp. Illustrations, bibliography, index. Price $15.00

VOLUME VI. *A Chronicler of Immigrant Life: Svein Nilsson's Articles in* Billed-Magazin, *1868–1870.* Translated and introduced by C. A. Clausen. Northfield, 1982. 171 pp. Illustrations, index. Price $12.00

TOPICAL STUDIES

VOLUME I. *A Voice of Protest: Norwegians in American Politics, 1890–1917.* By Jon Wefald. Northfield, 1971. 94 pp. Bibliography, index. Out of print

VOLUME II. *Cultural Pluralism versus Assimilation: The Views of Waldemar Ager.* Edited by Odd S. Lovoll. Northfield, 1977. 136 pp. Frontispiece. Price $6.00

VOLUME III. *Ethnicity Challenged: The Upper Midwest Norwegian-American Experience in World War I.* By Carl H. Chrislock. Northfield, 1981. 174 pp. Illustrations, index. Price $10.00